S0-CBW-898

# NEW MEXICO IN 1850
## A MILITARY VIEW

# NEW MEXICO IN 1850: A MILITARY VIEW

COLONEL GEORGE ARCHIBALD McCALL

EDITED AND WITH AN INTRODUCTION BY

ROBERT W. FRAZER

UNIVERSITY OF OKLAHOMA PRESS : NORMAN

*By Robert W. Frazer*

*Mansfield on the Condition of the Western Forts, 1853–54* (editor) (Norman, 1963)
*Forts of the West* (Norman, 1965)
*New Mexico in 1850: A Military View*, by Colonel George Archibald McCall (editor) (Norman, 1968)



*Library of Congress Catalog Card Number: 68-15682*

 Manufactured in the U.S.A. First edition.

*For Luke and Fern Lyon*

# PREFACE

MAJOR GEORGE ARCHIBALD MCCALL, Third United States Infantry, arrived in Santa Fe in March, 1850, to rejoin his regiment from which he had been absent for almost three years. In addition to resuming his military duties, he carried instructions from the Secretary of War to urge the people of New Mexico to seek to erect their territory into a state. In this connection, McCall was to provide the War Department with the information about New Mexico which would be needed when statehood was sought. In August, 1850, McCall received his commission as colonel, Inspector General's Department, and instructions to inspect the Department of New Mexico. He completed the inspection in October and left immediately for Washington, D.C. Although McCall's tour of duty in New Mexico covered a period of less than eight months, it involved him in many facets of the New Mexican scene. In addition to his examination of the military establishment, McCall played some part in political developments and was called upon to analyze certain aspects of the social and economic conditions of the area.

McCall's inspection reports and the letter from Surgeon General Thomas Lawson, which appears as Appendix B to this volume, have not been published previously. His reports to Secretary of War George W. Crawford and Adjutant General Roger Jones were published as *Report of the Secretary of War, Communicating, in Com-*

*pliance with a Resolution of the Senate, Colonel McCall's Reports in Relation to New Mexico*, 31 Congress, 2 session, *Senate Executive Document 26*. The reports, as presented herein, are derived from McCall's original reports rather than from the published document. In editing the reports, I have retained the original spelling and made additions and deletions in punctuation only when necessary for clarity. I have, however, spelled out McCall's numerous and inconsistent abbreviations.

I wish to acknowledge my indebtedness to Miss Myra Ellen Jenkins, state of New Mexico, Records Center and Archives, and Mrs. Kitty Shishkin and Miss Ruth E. Rambo, library of the Museum of New Mexico, for their assistance. I wish also to express my appreciation to my colleagues, Professors Marvin A. Harder and George A. Schultz and Dean Emeritus John Rydjord, who read portions of the manuscript.

ROBERT W. FRAZER

*San Pedro, California*
*March 20, 1968*

# CONTENTS

| | | |
|---|---|---|
| | Preface | *page vii* |
| | List of Illustrations | *xi* |
| I. | New Mexicana | 3 |
| II. | The New Mexican Scene | 17 |
| III. | McCall and New Mexico | 59 |
| IV. | McCall's Report on Conditions in New Mexico | 79 |
| V. | McCall's Inspection Reports | 111 |
| VI. | McCall's Report on the Defensive Needs of New Mexico | 177 |
| | Appendix A: Military Personnel Mentioned in the McCall Reports | 190 |
| | Appendix B: Letter from Surgeon General Thomas Lawson to Adjutant General Roger Jones | 198 |
| | Bibliography | 201 |
| | Index | 211 |

# ILLUSTRATIONS

Old Santa Fe *facing page* 20
The Palace of Governors, Santa Fe, in 1900 and today 21
Exterior of a grist mill near Taos 36
Interior of the grist mill 37
The Santa Fe *New Mexican*, November 28, 1849 68
Sena Plaza, Santa Fe 69
A Plains Indian raid 84
Acoma Pueblo and Taos Pueblo 85

MAP: New Mexico in 1850 *page* 112

# NEW MEXICO IN 1850
## A MILITARY VIEW

# I. NEW MEXICANA

NEW MEXICO in 1850 was not exactly terra incognita, but official Washington, including the Office of Indian Affairs and the War Department, knew remarkably little about it. The population, in its size, composition, customs, and attitudes, was largely a matter of conjecture. The economic resources, particularly the mineral wealth, were more a subject for speculation than of accurate knowledge. Even the geography of what would soon become the Territory of New Mexico was imperfectly understood. From some miles below San Elizario in the south to a little above Taos in the north, the Río Grande Valley and some of the adjacent country was reasonably well known, though much remained to be learned of the people who inhabited it. The Santa Fe Trail, the north-south route along the Río Grande, the Gila River route as followed by Brigadier General Stephen Watts Kearny,[1] and the wagon route laid out by Captain

[1] Kearny was given command of the expeditionary force charged with the occupation of New Mexico and California. His commission as brigadier general carried the date of his departure from Fort Leavenworth at the start of the campaign—June 30, 1846. From Fort Leavenworth to Santa Fe his route followed the mountain branch of the Santa Fe Trail, by way of Bent's Fort and Raton Pass. After spending slightly more than a month in Santa Fe, Kearny proceeded to California. His route was south along the Río Grande to about the site of the present town of Truth

Philip St. George Cooke[2] had been mapped and official reports, in greater or less detail, published about them. Yet what remained to be learned constituted a sizable body of information, and part of the problem involved was to dispel existing misinformation. In December, 1853, William Carr Lane, former territorial governor of New Mexico, wrote of the level of knowledge in the nation's capital, "I find a deplorable state of ignorance to exist, among the officials here, on the subject of New Mex[ica]n affairs."[3]

---

or Consequences, then west to the Gila River, down the Gila to the Yuma crossing of the Colorado, and on to San Diego. The expedition is described in Dwight L. Clarke, *Stephen Watts Kearny, Soldier of the West*, 116–232.

[2] Cooke held the regular rank of captain, First Dragoons, when he went with Kearny to New Mexico. When Kearny placed him in command of the Mormon Battalion in October, 1846, he made Cooke a lieutenant colonel, Volunteers, for the duration of the assignment. Cooke was instructed to lay out a route over which wagons could travel. Cooke's route left the Río Grande at the San Diego crossing, about fifteen miles above Doña Ana, ran west through Cooks Range, then dipped south to pass through territory which remained Mexican until the time of the Gadsden Purchase. It rejoined the route taken by Kearny down the Gila, northwest of Tucson. See "Report of Lieutenant Colonel P. St. George Cooke," in 30 Cong., 1 sess., *House Exec. Doc. 41*, 552–62; and *The Official Journal of Lieutenant Colonel Philip St. George Cooke, from Santa Fé to San Diego &c.*, 31 Cong., Special sess., *Sen. Doc. 2*.

[3] Lane to Manuel Alvarez, December 20, 1853, *Read Collection*, State of New Mexico, Records Center and Archives (hereafter cited as New Mexico Archives), Santa Fe. William Carr Lane, a resident of St. Louis, Missouri, was New Mexico's second territorial governor, serving in 1852 and 1853. In the summer of 1853 he resigned to seek election as New Mexico's territorial delegate to the national Congress. Defeated in a reasonably close vote, he contested the election unsuccessfully. Shortly thereafter he left New Mexico. Ralph Emerson Twitchell, *The Leading Facts of New Mexican History*, II, 259; and Calvin Horn, *New Mexico's Troubled Years*, 48.

The paucity of information on New Mexico is both surprising and understandable. Before the nineteenth century little material specifically about New Mexico had been published, and only a portion of that published had been translated into English. Accounts of the period of exploration and early settlement, the reconquest following the Pueblo Revolt of 1680, and the work of the Franciscans constituted the bulk of the published material. The earliest published writings touching on the New Mexican area dealt with the expeditions of Fray Marcos de Niza and Francisco de Coronado. These appeared in the third volume of Gian Battista Ramusio, *Delle Navigationi et Viaggi*, in 1556, no prior Spanish edition being known. Some of this same material, in English translation, was printed in Volume III of Richard Hakluyt's *The Principall Navigations* in 1600. Undoubtedly the first New Mexican item published separately in English was Antonio de Espejo, *New Mexico. Otherwise, the Voiage of Anthony of Espeio . . .* (London, 1587), first published in Spain the previous year. It was Espejo who was responsible for the name New Mexico, which he applied to the area following his expedition of 1582–83. The only known copy of the English edition is in the Henry E. Huntington Library.

Among the other more important works of the Spanish period are Juan Martínez de Montoya, *Relación del Descubrimiento del Nuevo México* (Rome, 1602), and Gaspar de Villagrá, *Historia de la Nueva México* (Alcalá, 1610), both of which include the beginning of permanent settlement in New Mexico. Carlos Sigüenza y Góngora's *Mercurio Volante* traces the early history of New Mexico but deals chiefly with Diego de Vargas and the reconquest. Many of the Franciscan writings contain significant historical material, notably Alonso de Benavides' *Memorial* (Madrid, 1630); Estevan de Perea's brief *Verdadera Relación* and *Segunda Relación* (Sevilla, 1632 and 1633); and Agustín de Vetancurt's *Crónica de la Provincia del Santo Evangelio de México* (Mexico, 1697). Over the years some of the writings about New Mexico were translated and published in various European countries. Much better known in the United States, however, were the works which dealt with New Spain as a whole, a number of which had been translated into English.[4]

Early in the nineteenth century two works were published which began to make some knowledge of New Mexico more readily available in the United States. In 1810 the account of Zebulon Montgomery Pike's expedition was published in Philadelphia.[5] The following year, publication of Alexander von Humboldt's *Political Essay on the Kingdom of New Spain* commenced in London.[6] Humboldt had not visited New Mexico, and, even though he devoted comparatively little space to the province, his information about it was not free from error. His reputation, however, was sufficient to attract the attention of the scholarly world at least. Actually, a more valuable description of New Mexico was Pedro Bautista Pino's *Exposición sucinta y sencilla de la provincia de Nuevo México*, published in Cádiz in 1812,[7] but apparently not known in the United States for some time thereafter.

[4] The publication of Henri Ternaux-Compans, *Voyages, relations et mémoires originaux, pour servir a l'histoire de la découverte de l'Amérique* (20 vols., Paris, 1837–41), made some of the early Spanish accounts more readily available. Albert Gallatin was familiar with Ternaux when he wrote *Ancient Semi-civilization of New Mexico, Rio Gila, and Its Vicinity* (New York, 1848), as probably, was Ephraim G. Squier, "New Mexico and California," *The American Review*, Vol. VIII (November, 1848), 503–28. For a discussion of the publications of the Spanish period see Henry Raup Wagner, *The Spanish Southwest, 1542–1794*.

[5] *An Account of an Expedition to the Sources of the Mississippi, and Through the Western Parts of Louisiana, to the Sources of the Arkansaw, Kans, La Platte, and Pierre Jaun, Rivers . . . And a Tour Through the Interior Parts of New Spain, When Conducted Through These Provinces by Order of the Captain-General, in the Year 1807.*

[6] The first edition was published in Paris in five volumes in 1811. Translated into English, it was published in four volumes in London, 1811–22.

[7] Pedro Bautista Pino was elected August 11, 1810, as the first and only deputy from New Mexico to the Spanish Cortes. His *Exposición* was prepared to inform the Cortes about New Mexico. He returned to New

Following the achievement of Mexican independence in 1821 and the opening of the Santa Fe trade, the publication of material about New Mexico gradually increased. First in date of appearance was R. W. H. Hardy's *Travels in the Interior of Mexico in 1825–28*, published in London in 1829. Hardy, a British naval officer, visited parts of the present New Mexico and Arizona, although the chief object of his tour was to investigate the pearl fisheries of the Gulf of California. In 1831, James Ohio Pattie's remarkable *Personal Narrative* was published. Students have attempted ever since to determine what was fact and what was fiction in Pattie's colorful tale.[8] Only one important piece of writing by a New Mexican author appeared during the Mexican period—the *Ojeada sobre Nuevo Méjico*, published in Puebla, Mexico, in 1832. The author, Antonio Barreiro, was a lawyer and official adviser to the New Mexican government. His descriptive sketch was written at the request of the authorities in Mexico City.[9] Three pamphlets were published in 1838–39, all purporting to be accounts written by women from an emigrant party who were captured by Comanche Indians. The pamphlets describe the period of captivity, part of which was spent in eastern New Mexico, and the eventual release of the women. The authenticity of at least one of the accounts has been questioned.

Josiah Gregg's *Commerce of the Prairies*, the classic account of the Santa Fe trade, was published in New York in 1844. Before

Mexico in 1814, was again elected to the Cortes in 1820, but got only as far as Veracruz before lack of funds forced him to turn back. Angélico Chávez, *Origins of New Mexico Families*, 260; Ralph Emerson Twitchell, *Old Santa Fe*, 178, n. 341. Pino was well liked by Americans who engaged in the Santa Fe trade, and did many favors for them. James Josiah Webb, *Adventures in the Santa Fé Trade, 1844–1847*, 99.

[8] See William H. Goetzmann's introduction to Pattie, *Personal Narrative.*

[9] Antonio Barreiro was elected in 1833 and again in 1834 as New Mexico's deputy to the Mexican Congress. He was a lawyer who also briefly published a newspaper in Santa Fe. Twitchell, *Old Santa Fe*, 192, n. 372; 196, ns. 386–87.

Gregg's accidental death in 1850, the book had gone through seven editions, including publication both in England and in the Germanies.[10] Thomas James, *Three Years Among the Mexicans and Indians*, was published in 1846. The portion of James's book which deals with New Mexico recounts his experience as a pioneer in the Santa Fe trade in 1821–22. James's life seems to have been a succession of frustrations and financial failures, which undoubtedly colored his outlook. Certainly he had much to say of an uncomplimentary nature about both New Mexico and the New Mexicans.[11]

The year 1847 saw the appearance of three books which touched on New Mexico: Rufus B. Sage, *Scenes in the Rocky Mountains*; Benjamin F. Taylor, *Short Ravelings from a Long Yarn, or Camp and March Sketches of the Santa Fe Trail*; and George F. A. Ruxton, *Adventures in Mexico and the Rocky Mountains*. Sage, as a trapper, visited Taos briefly in 1842, and devoted only a few pages to his experiences in New Mexico. Taylor's anecdotal account of his trip, probably made in 1841, added little to knowledge of the area. Ruxton's work, then and since, received the greatest acclaim. A former British army officer, he was also a careful observer and a pleasing writer. His initial work was followed in 1848 by the semifictional *Life in the Far West*, a group of stories describing the fur trade. In 1849 an emigrant guide was published, compiled by Robert Creuzbaur and based largely on official government reports, entitled *Route from the Gulf of Mexico and the Lower Mississippi Valley to California and the Pacific Ocean*. The guide contained several maps and covered the route from El Paso across southern New Mexico to the Colorado River. It is of interest as the first commercial guide to include a New Mexican route. Finally, 1850 brought the publication of Hector Lewis Garrard's delightful *Wah-to-yah and the Taos Trail*. Garrard made the trip to New Mexico in 1846–47, arriving in Taos

[10] For a printing history of the book see Max L. Moorhead (ed.), in Gregg, *Commerce of the Prairies*, xxxii, n. 18. See also his reconstruction of Gregg's bibliography in *ibid.*, 445–47.

[11] See A. P. Nasatir's introduction to James, *Three Years Among the Mexicans and Indians*.

about a month after the Taos uprising. His account is fresh and entertaining, as well as historically valuable.

Newspapers added to the knowledge of New Mexico available in the United States during the Mexican period. Much that appeared in the press had to do with the Santa Fe trade. Missouri newspapers, as would be expected, took particular interest in the trade and the persons connected with it. Also notable was the New Orleans *Daily Picayune*. In 1839, an assistant editor of the *Picayune*, Matthew C. Field, accompanied the trading caravan to Santa Fe in an effort to regain his health. He prepared a series of sketches which were published in the *Picayune*, providing amusing glimpses of the trade and of New Mexico.[12] New Mexico itself acquired a newspaper when the *Santa Fe Republican* began its irregular publication on September 10, 1847.[13] Among the newspapers of the Atlantic seaboard, *Niles' Weekly Register* published more New Mexican items than any of the others, often reprinting material from western papers. Mexican newspapers undoubtedly carried occasional information about New Mexico, but it is impossible to say how much of it, if any, reached the United States. Certainly the *Registro Oficial del Gobierno de los Estados-Unidos Mexicanos*, which did from time to time print material about New Mexico that is now of great historic interest, was available to United States diplomatic agents in Mexico City.

The ill-fated Texan–Santa Fe expedition of 1841 led to a flurry of publication which tended more to inflame United States opinion against Mexico than to provide much knowledge of New Mexico. Best known and most useful of these writings is George Wilkins

[12] Field's sketches have been collected and published, together with his journal, under the title *Matt Field on the Santa Fe Trail.*

[13] Padre Antonio José Martínez is usually credited with publishing New Mexico's first newspaper, *El Crepúsculo*, at Taos for four weeks in 1834. However, see n. 9, above. In 1850, New Mexico had two newspapers, both published in Santa Fe—the *New Mexican* and the *Gazette.* According to the United States census of 1850, one was published weekly and the other tri-monthly. Together, they had a circulation of 900 copies. *The Seventh Census of the United States: 1850*, 1011.

Kendall's two-volume work, *Narrative of the Texan Santa Fé Expedition*, published in 1844. Kendall, one of the owners of the *Picayune*, accompanied the expedition as an observer. He was captured by Governor Manuel Armijo with the rest of the members of the party and underwent the subsequent imprisonment and indignities to which most of them were subjected.[14] It was the Mexican War, however, that produced the first real outpouring of published material, as many accounts by participants, observers, and secondary writers appeared in newspapers and magazines and as books. While these dealt principally with the various campaigns, they contained some descriptive passages and comments on the people, as often as not reflecting the heat engendered by the conflict. The "image" of New Mexico, as it appeared to the eyes of the United States public, was beginning to come into focus. Best known of the contemporary accounts of the occupation of New Mexico is *Doniphan's Expedition*, written by John T. Hughes and first published in 1847. Hughes, a member of one of the Missouri volunteer companies, was critical of many things, especially of military discipline, but his book contains some useful description as well. Frederick Adolphus Wislizenus, *Memoir of a Tour to Northern Mexico, Connected with Col. Doniphan's Expedition, in 1846 and 1847*, was a more important work so far as it pertained to New Mexico. Wislizenus was a medical doctor by profession, an amateur scientist, and a keen observer. His account was published by the United States government in 1848.[15]

[14] For a biography of Kendall, see Fayette Copeland, *Kendall of the Picayune.*

[15] Dr. Wislizenus, a native of Germany, came to the United States in 1835, eventually settling in St. Louis, where he practiced medicine. He had made one previous trip to the Rocky Mountains, going as far west as Fort Hall, in present Idaho, with a party of fur men. His trip to Mexico was intended for scientific investigation. Wislizenus was interested particularly in geology, botany, and meteorology. He went to Santa Fe with the trading caravan of 1846, continuing south to Chihuahua, where he later joined Colonel Alexander Doniphan's invading force, serving as a physician. Although his *Memoir* was published as a government docu-

Government documents form an important part of the New Mexican literature. Prior to 1846 their content was centered on the Santa Fe trade and its protection. Some mention of New Mexico is found in the *American State Papers*, the *Congressional Debates*, the *Congressional Globe*, and various executive documents. The first document devoted exclusively to New Mexico was *Answers of Augustus Storrs, of Missouri, to Certain Queries upon the Origin, Present State, and Future Prospects, of Trade and Intercourse between Missouri and the Internal Provinces of Mexico, Propounded by the Hon. Mr. Benton, Jan. 5, 1825.*[16] The Mexican War and the United States' occupation of New Mexico led to a more extensive examination of the area. In addition to material contained in the annual reports of the Secretary of War, there were published reports of explorations carried out in connection with the conduct of the war.[17] More important for its description of the settled portion of New Mexico was Second Lieutenant James W. Abert's report of his observations in New Mexico in 1846–47,[18] the first comprehensive official examination following the occupation.

ment, 30 Cong., 1 sess., *Sen. Misc. Pub. 26*, it was Wislizenus' personal narrative of experiences and observations.

[16] Published as 18 Cong., 2 sess., *Sen. Doc. 7*. Storrs had accompanied a trading expedition to Santa Fe in 1824. He was appointed United States consul at Santa Fe in 1825, but apparently did not function in that capacity.

[17] These include the reports of First Lieutenant William H. Emory and Lieutenant Colonel Philip St. George Cooke, and the journal of Captain Abraham R. Johnston, all published in 30 Cong., 1 sess., *House Exec. Doc. 41*. See n. 2, above.

[18] Abert, Topographical Engineers, of which corps his father, Colonel John J. Abert, was commander, started from Fort Leavenworth with General Kearny's expeditionary force, but was delayed for a time at Bent's Fort by illness. He arrived in Santa Fe on September 27, 1846, a few days after Kearny had departed for California. Abert was instructed to make a survey of New Mexico, with the assistance of Brevet Second Lieutenant William G. Peck, Topographical Engineers. The report which resulted was published as 30 Cong., 1 sess., *Sen. Exec. Doc. 23*, and also

In the years 1848–50 the number of government documents dealing in whole or in part with New Mexico increased greatly. Most of the documents fall into readily definable categories. Several were reports of the exploration of routes to New Mexico or exploration conducted within New Mexico. These added to the knowledge of the geography of the region, the Indians, and the problems of communication and defense. Especially informative are the reports on the routes from San Antonio to El Paso del Norte,[19] the reports of First Lieutenant James H. Simpson[20] and Captain Randolph B. Marcy[21] on the route from Fort Smith to Santa Fe, and Lieutenant Simpson's report on Major (Brevet Lieutenant Colonel) John Macrae Washington's[22] Navaho expedition of 1849. A second group of documents dealt with the Texas–New Mexico boundary and the Texan claims to New Mexico east of the Río Grande. Many of these contain more material on military activity and Indian depredations than they do on

as part of *House Exec. Doc. 41*. It has recently been made available in facsimile edition as *Abert's New Mexico Report.*

[19] These were published as *Reports of the Secretary of War with Reconnaissances of Routes from San Antonio to El Paso*, 31 Cong., 1 sess., *Sen. Exec. Doc. 64*.

[20] Simpson, Topographical Engineers, accompanied Captain Randolph B. Marcy from Fort Smith to Santa Fe in the spring of 1849. He remained in Santa Fe, by order of Colonel John J. Abert, to serve under Major Washington, commanding the department. Simpson's report of the Fort Smith–Santa Fe route was published in 31 Cong., 1 sess., *Sen. Exec. Doc. 12*; and *House Exec. Doc. 45*.

[21] Marcy, Fifth Infantry, in the spring of 1849 laid out a route from Fort Smith to Santa Fe along the south side of the Canadian River. He had the dual task of escorting an emigrant train and determining a usable route to New Mexico. His report was published in 31 Cong., 1 sess., *House Exec. Doc. 45*.

[22] Washington, Third Artillery, became military and civil governor of New Mexico, by virtue of his position as commander of the department, on October 11, 1848. He held the position until October 23, 1849. Simpson's report of the Navaho expedition was published in 31 Cong., 1 sess., *Sen. Exec. Doc. 64*.

the question of the boundary. A third group consists of documents relating to New Mexico's efforts to achieve a regular form of government. Included are various memorials, correspondence, and other materials which provide useful information on conditions within New Mexico, particularly as they were cause for grievance.[23] There were still other documents, many of which opposed or advocated slavery for the newly acquired territories, but added little if anything to knowledge about them. Viewed collectively, the documents published during these years added much to what was known of New Mexico. Some of the information presented was biased and some was inexact, and the picture remained incomplete. Although a distinct advance in official knowledge had been made, it was now apparent that still more information was needed before reasonable policies could be established for the area.

One final body of information on New Mexico consisted of the maps that were often prepared to accompany reports. During almost three centuries of Spanish exploration and occupation various maps of New Mexico and adjacent areas had been drawn.[24] These maps were highly inaccurate by modern standards and contained many inconsistencies in nomenclature; moreover, they apparently were not avail-

[23] Of particular interest are *New Mexico and California*, 30 Cong., 1 sess., *House Exec. Doc. 70*; *California and New Mexico*, 31 Cong., 1 sess., *House Exec. Doc. 17*, and *Sen. Exec. Doc. 18*; *New Mexico—Convention of Delegates*, 31 Cong., 1 sess., *House Misc. Doc. 39*; *Message . . . in Relation to the Formation of a State Government in New Mexico*, 31 Cong., 1 sess., *Sen. Exec. Doc. 60*; *Message . . . transmitting a Copy of the Constitution Adopted by the Inhabitants of New Mexico*, 31 Cong., 1 sess., *Sen. Exec. Doc. 74*; and *Communication of R. H. Weightman and Accompanying Memorial of the Legislature of New Mexico*, 31 Cong., 1 sess., *Sen. Exec. Doc. 76*.

[24] See, for example, the eighteenth-century maps which include the Juan Miguel Menchero map, probably of 1744, the Alzate y Ramírez map of 1768, the Miera y Pacheco maps of 1778 and 1779, and the Juan Bautista de Anza campaign map of 1779. Photostatic copies of these maps and many others are in the library of the Museum of New Mexico, Santa Fe.

able in the United States. In 1848, Secretary of State James Buchanan reported to President James K. Polk:

> The only separate map of New Mexico, of which I am aware, is that contained in the Atlas to Thompson's edition of the "Geographical and Historical Dictionary of America and the West Indies, by Colonel Don Antonio de Alcedo," published at London in 1812, a work of the highest authority.[25] The department has a copy of this work and the accompanying Atlas, with the exception of the map of New Mexico, which was taken from it by your direction, for Mr. Slidell's[26] use, and transmitted to him with his instructions. This map, it is presumed, is now with the archives of the United States legation at the city of Mexico. There is also a copy of Thompson's Alcedo belonging to the library of Congress, but I am informed that it is without the Atlas.[27]

In other words, the only map of New Mexico known to the State Department, and belonging to the government, was not even in the country.

The maps accompanying Humboldt's work on New Spain are inaccurate in the delineation of the area comprising New Mexico. The most recent map which included New Mexico, which was also "the only map referred to in the treaty between the United States and Mexico, and was the one used in negotiating that treaty," was the revised edition of the Disturnell map, published in New York in 1847.[28] Its inaccuracies, notably in the location of El Paso del Norte,

[25] Originally published as Antonio de Alcedo, *Diccionario Geográfico: Histórico de las Indias Occidentales ó América*. 5 vols., Madrid, 1786–89.

[26] John Slidell was sent to Mexico in 1845 on a special mission by President Polk. The object of the mission was to secure a permanent and satisfactory boundary with Mexico, and involved an attempt to purchase New Mexico and Upper California. Slidell was not officially received by the Mexican government, and his mission ended in failure. James M. Callahan, *American Foreign Policy in Mexican Relations*, 148–57.

[27] July 17, 1848, 30 Cong., 1 sess., *House Exec. Doc. 70*, 7.

[28] *Ibid.*; see also William H. Goetzmann, *Army Exploration in the American West, 1803–1863*, 155–56.

led to much confusion and opened a dispute which might have become serious had it not been eliminated by the Gadsden Purchase in 1853.[29] United States mapping of New Mexico began with the occupation, as routes followed through the area were mapped and the maps were published with various reports. The map prepared by Lieutenants Abert and William G. Peck to accompany Abert's report is reasonably accurate for the Río Grande Valley and some of the near-by country. These early maps, none of which covered all of New Mexico, were superseded by the "Map of the Territory of New Mexico," compiled by Brevet Second Lieutenant John G. Parke in 1851. Parke's map represented the then available knowledge of the geography of New Mexico. It labeled the northern portion of the territory, most of the western portion, and a sizable part of the eastern portion "unexplored."[30] Much of the area so described had, in fact, been explored during the Spanish period and later had been traversed by the moun-

[29] Work on the boundary survey did not commence until December, 1850. A controversy arose immediately when it was determined that El Paso del Norte was actually some distance south of the position indicated on the Disturnell map. A compromise was arranged between the United States and Mexican commissioners, but it proved unsatisfactory to the United States and even more so to the Americans in New Mexico. Territorial Governor William Carr Lane, on March 13, 1853, issued a proclamation in which he retook "possession of the said disputed Territory," to be held until the boundary could be settled by the United States and Mexico, and required "all Civil and Military Officers of the U.S. and of the Territory of New Mexico" to enforce the laws of the United States and New Mexico in the area involved. In *Read Collection*, New Mexico Archives. The military refused to comply. See Robert W. Frazer (ed.), *Mansfield on the Condition of the Western Forts, 1853–54*, 57, 76–77. A "Sketch of Disputed Territory Claimed by Both the United States and Mexico" is in *ibid.*, illustration 15, following page 112.

[30] John G. Parke was, at the time, brevet second lieutenant, Topographical Engineers. The map has been published in several places, including Annie Heloise Abel (ed.), *The Official Correspondence of James S. Calhoun while Indian Agent at Santa Fé and Superintendent of Indian Affairs in New Mexico*, rear pocket. See also Goetzmann, *Army Exploration*, 248–49.

tain men in their search for the ubiquitous beaver, but it had not as yet been officially explored under the auspices of the United States government.

In addition to the published maps, various departments of the government, notably the War Department and the Department of the Interior, had, by 1850, been provided with manuscript maps by their agents. Some of these were fairly detailed maps of particular areas; others were rough sketches. Of considerable interest is the crude map prepared in 1849 by James S. Calhoun, constituting the first American attempt to depict the location of the wild Indian tribes and the Pueblos of New Mexico.[31]

[31] Some of these maps have been published subsequently. The Calhoun map is in Abel (ed.), *Official Correspondence*, rear pocket. James S. Calhoun, of Georgia, was appointed as the first Indian agent for New Mexico in 1849, arriving in Santa Fe on July 22, 1849. Calhoun, who had served as lieutenant colonel, Georgia Mounted Volunteers, in the Mexican War, frequently found himself at odds with the military commanders in New Mexico. He felt that the co-operation which he received left much to be desired. Early in 1850 he wrote:

"If I can not be made a General or at least, succeed to the command of this Department . . . then, if it is not too late, I should like to go to Liverpool, as Consul, or to Havre.

"If none of these things can be accomplished for me, *quietly* inform me, and quickly too, that I may decently retire, for I cannot play second fiddle to any one *now* in this territory. I should be willing to serve as a Senior Colonel of Dragoons, under any one of the present Generals in the U.S. Service.

"I am content to be Superintendent of Indian Affairs in this territory but not an Agent, to be subjected to the control of a Territorial Governor."

Calhoun to Senator W. C. Dawson, February 5, 1850, *Governors' Papers*, New Mexico Archives.

On March 3, 1851, Calhoun assumed office as the first territorial governor of New Mexico, which, it must be assumed, gave him the authority he desired. He was soon in ill health, suffering from scurvy. He died in June, 1852, while en route from Santa Fe to Missouri. See Horn, *New Mexico's Troubled Years*, 21–33.

# II. THE NEW MEXICAN SCENE

By 1850 a considerable body of information, some of which was inaccurate and some of which was mere surmise, had been accumulated about New Mexico. As yet many blanks existed. The limits of New Mexico had not been fixed, nor did the Spanish and Mexican periods provide much explicit information about them. In the 1780's, New Mexico had been described as bounded on the south by the provinces of Sinaloa, Nueva Vizcaya, and Nuevo León; on the south and southeast by Florida; on the west, northwest, and southwest by the Californias; and on the north by Canada.[1] As late as 1824, El Paso del Norte district was included in New Mexico, but when Valverde was abandoned as a result of Apache raids, Socorro became the southernmost outpost of New Mexico, and El Paso district was transferred to Chihuahua.[2] Not until Doña Ana was established, probably in

[1] Frederick Webb Hodge, George P. Hammond, and Agapito Rey (trans. and eds.), *Fray Alonso de Benavides' Revised Memorial of 1634*, 229, n. 13, citing Alcedo, *Diccionario Geográfico-Histórico*, III, 183. See also Fray Juan Agustín de Morfi's more detailed description in Alfred B. Thomas (trans. and ed.), *Forgotten Frontiers: A Study of the Spanish Indian Policy of Don Juan Bautista de Anza, Governor of New Mexico, 1777–1787*, 87.

[2] Lansing B. Bloom, "New Mexico under Mexican Administration," *Old Santa Fe*, Vol. I (July, 1913), 13.

1842, was there again a settlement between Socorro and El Paso. The United States–Mexican boundary had not been surveyed along New Mexico's southern border. Indeed, John Russell Bartlett,[3] the United States commissioner, did not arrive at El Paso until November, 1850, and the work of the commission did not commence until the following month. The northern boundary of New Mexico remained unfixed apparently extending as far as Spain's claims, until the Adams-Onís Treaty of 1819 defined it for the first time. East and west of the settled portion of New Mexico were broad, unoccupied areas in which precise boundaries were lacking. In 1850 the limits were still given loosely as follows: on the north the Indian Territory, on the west California, on the south Mexico, and on the east Texas.[4]

Specific boundaries were provided in the act of September 9, 1850, which established the Territory of New Mexico,[5] but some time was to elapse before the boundaries were surveyed. The Republic of Texas had claimed all Mexican territory east of the Río Grande, and even though nothing had been accomplished to implement the claims, Texas, as a state, continued to insist upon them.[6] In the Compromise

[3] Bartlett was appointed United States–Mexican boundary commissioner in June, 1850. He replaced John C. Frémont, who had resigned. Some work had been done on the boundary from the Pacific Ocean to the Colorado River, but nothing between the Colorado and the Río Grande. The problem of determining a satisfactory boundary remained unsolved until the Gadsden Purchase permitted the United States to acquire additional Mexican territory. Bartlett's *Personal Narrative of Explorations and Incidents in Texas, New Mexico, California, Sonora, and Chihuahua* . . . is one of the more delightful travel accounts of the early United States Far West and makes up, to some extent, for the failure of his mission.

[4] "Circular," *Miscellaneous Territorial Records*, New Mexico Archives.

[5] "Organic Act Establishing the Territory of New Mexico," *New Mexico Statutes, 1953*, I, 390.

[6] In 1848, President James K. Polk admitted the "justly asserted" right of Texas "to the whole territory on this side of the Rio Grande." But he also pointed out: "Though the republic of Texas . . . had estab-

of 1850, the United States tacitly acknowledged the Texas position, and the issue was settled by the enactment of the Texas Boundary Act by the United States Congress and its acceptance by the state of Texas.[7] The actual survey of the boundary, east from the Río Grande along 32° north latitude, then north along the meridian of 103°, was not undertaken for some years because Congress failed to appropriate the necessary funds. Not until 1911 was the last dispute arising from the faulty survey of the boundary settled.[8] In the west, California gave itself an eastern boundary when it drew up a state constitution in 1849, but it was not admitted to statehood until September, 1850.

Shortly before he embarked upon his campaign in 1846, General Stephen Watts Kearny was instructed to provide California and New Mexico with "temporary civil governments," and to "assure the people of those provinces, that it is the wish and design of the United States to provide for them a free government with the least possible delay, similar to that which exists in our Territories."[9] Immediately

lished her clear title to the country west of the Nueces, and bordering upon that part of the Rio Grande which lies below the province of New Mexico, she had never conquered or reduced to actual possession, and brought under her government and laws, that part of New Mexico lying east of the Rio Grande, which she claimed to be within her limits. On the breaking out of the war we found Mexico in possession of this disputed territory."—30 Cong., 1 sess., *House Exec. Doc. 70*, 3, 5. The United States later paid Texas $10,000,000 to relinquish its claims.

[7] On November 25, 1850, the Texas State Legislature agreed to relinquish its claims to New Mexico and accept the delimitation of its northern and western boundaries as proposed by an act of the United States Congress, passed on September 9, 1850. Message of President Fillmore, 31 Cong., 2 sess., *House Exec. Doc. 8*, 1. In 1854 the Texas State Legislature appropriated $10,000 for the survey of the boundary between Texas and New Mexico, contingent upon the enactment of suitable legislation by the United States Congress. *Boundary Between Texas and the Territories*, 33 Cong., 2 sess., *House Exec. Doc. 89*, 2–3.

[8] Warren A. Beck, *New Mexico: A History of Four Centuries*, 144.

[9] William L. Marcy to Kearny, June 3, 1846, 31 Cong., 1 sess., *House Exec. Doc. 17*, 238.

after his occupation of Santa Fe, Kearny established a temporary government, appointing civilians to the principal offices.[10] Charles Bent,[11] long and intimately acquainted with New Mexico, became the first governor. At the same time, the Kearny Code,[12] a document of considerable merit but never intended to be more than a stopgap measure, was placed in effect. At the close of the Mexican War the Treaty of Guadalupe Hidalgo provided that the territory ceded by Mexico to the United States would be eligible for admission to statehood and that citizens of Mexico residing therein might, if they chose, become citizens of the United States.[13]

Because of its involvement in the slavery controversy, the territory thus annexed remained under temporary governments, even though President James K. Polk had declared that such governments "necessarily ceased to exist" when the Treaty of Guadalupe Hidalgo was signed.[14] In neither California nor New Mexico was the system thus perpetuated tolerable. In New Mexico, beginning in October, 1848, the military commander of the department acted as civil governor as well. Also, in October, 1848, a convention, called earlier by Governor Donaciano Vigil,[15] met in Santa Fe and drew up a memorial to

[10] "Appointment, by General Kearny of Civil Officers," September 22, 1846, 30 Cong., 1 sess., *House Exec. Doc. 60*, 176.

[11] Charles Bent was a native of Charleston, Virginia (now West Virginia), born on November 11, 1799. He moved with his family to St. Louis in 1806 and entered the fur trade as a young man. He went to New Mexico first in 1829 and soon acquired property in Taos. He was long associated with his brothers and Ceran St. Vrain in western commerce. General Kearny appointed him governor of New Mexico on September 22, 1846. He was killed on January 19, 1847, in the Taos uprising.

[12] The Kearny Code, entitled "Organic Law of the Territory of New Mexico," is in 30 Cong., 1 sess., *House Exec. Doc. 60*, 177–229.

[13] An annotated text of the treaty is in *New Mexico Statutes, 1953*, I, 362–80.

[14] Horn, *New Mexico's Troubled Years*, 22.

[15] Donaciano Vigil, a native New Mexican, had held various political

*Courtesy Museum of New Mexico*

Old Santa Fe, from a painting by Gerald Cassidy. The Palace of the Governors (right) is the oldest building in the United States. It was built in 1606, destroyed in 1680, rebuilt in 1697, and restored in 1911–13.

*Courtesy Museum of New Mexico*

The Palace of Governors, Santa Fe, *above*, in 1900; *below*, as it looks today. The building on the right (north) is Sena Plaza. Ft. Marcy was located 650 yards northeast of the Palace.

*Courtesy New Mexico State Tourist Bureau*

Congress requesting the "speedy organization" of a territorial government.[16] No action was taken in Washington on the memorial. Again, in September, 1849, a convention—this one composed of delegates elected in conformity with a proclamation issued by Major John Macrae Washington—met in Santa Fe and prepared a plan for territorial government, which it forwarded to Congress.[17] Hugh N. Smith[18] was elected territorial delegate and instructed to

positions during the Mexican regime. He was appointed secretary of the territory by General Kearny in September, 1846. He became acting governor upon the assassination of Governor Bent on January 19, 1847, serving in that capacity until December 17, 1847, when he was appointed governor by Brigadier General, Volunteers, Sterling Price, commanding the department. He served as governor until October 11, 1848. William C. Binkley, "Reports from a Texan Agent in New Mexico, 1849," in *New Spain and the West*, Vol. II, 167, n. 21.

[16] Twitchell, *Old Santa Fe*, 313–14. The text of the memorial is given in n. 557. Shortly after the convention ended, Major Washington, then civil and military governor, informed Secretary of War Marcy: "The system of government now in force in New Mexico is that which was established in 1846, and embraces what is commonly termed Kearny's code, to which the people, through their representatives lately assembled in convention, have happily expressed their assent, as will be seen in their memorial to Congress, and is considered adequate to the wants of the country, until another can be provided. It is, however, very advisable, for many reasons, that the territorial laws which are designed to be permanent should go into effect as soon as possible."—November 8, 1848, 31 Cong., 1 sess., *Sen. Exec. Doc. 1*, 104.

[17] *New Mexico—Convention of Delegates*, 31 Cong., 1 sess., *House Misc. Doc. 39*.

[18] According to William W. H. Davis, Smith had been sent to Washington earlier in the year to look after the interests of New Mexico. His expenses were paid by an "association of private individuals." *El Gringo; or, New Mexico and Her People*, 109. Congress also rewarded Smith with $2,000 mileage and $5.00 a day from the time of his arrival until he was denied a seat in that body. William A. Keleher, *Turmoil in New Mexico, 1846–1868*, 124, n. 44.

> urge upon the supreme government a redress of our grievances, and the protection due to us as citizens of our common country, under the constitution . . . [because] for the last three years, we have suffered under the paralyzing effects of a government undefined and doubtful in its character, inefficient to protect the rights of the people, or to discharge the high and absolute duty of every government, the enforcement and regular administration of its own laws, in consequence of which, industry and enterprise are paralyzed, and discontent and confusion prevail throughout the land; the want of proper protection against the various barbarous tribes of Indians that surround us on every side, has prevented the extension of settlements upon our valuable public domain, and rendered utterly futile every attempt to explore or develop the great resources of the territory . . . and without any adequate protection against their hostile inroads; our flocks and herds are driven off by thousands; our fellow-citizens, men, women and children, are murdered or carried into captivity; many of our citizens of all ages and sexes are at this moment suffering all the horrors of barbarian bondage, and it is utterly out of our power to obtain their release from a condition to which death would be preferable; the wealth of our territory is being diminished; we have neither the means nor any adopted plan by government for the education of the rising generation; in fine, with a government temporary, doubtful, uncertain, and inefficient in character and in operation, surrounded and despoiled by barbarous foes, ruin appears inevitably before us, unless speedy and effectual protection be extended to us by the Congress of the United States.[19]

Despite the plea, Smith was not seated as a delegate nor was any action taken on New Mexico's appeal to be granted territorial status.[20]

If no immediate answer was found to New Mexico's political difficulties, neither was there an obvious solution to the problem of Indian relations. James S. Calhoun arrived in Santa Fe in July, 1849, to assume his task as the first Indian agent appointed for New Mexico. The instructions given him are revealing:

[19] "Instructions as Adopted by the Convention," 31 Cong., 1 sess., *House Exec. Doc. 17*, 103.

[20] See *Hugh N. Smith, Delegate from New Mexico*, 31 Cong., 1 sess., *House Report 220*.

> So little is known here [Washington] of the condition and situation of the Indians in that region [New Mexico] that no specific instructions, relative to them can be given at present; and the Department relies on you to furnish it with such statistical and other information as will give a just and full understanding of every particular relating to them, embracing the names of the tribes, their location, the distance between tribes, the probable extent of territory owned or claimed by each respectively, and the tenure by which they hold or claim it; their manners and habits, their disposition and feelings towards the United States, Mexico and whites generally and towards each other, whether hostile or otherwise; whether the several tribes speak different languages, and when different, the apparent analogies between them, and also what laws and regulations, for their government, are necessary, and how far the law regulating trade and intercourse with the Indian tribes . . . will, if extended over that country, properly apply to the Indians there and to the trade and intercourse with them and what modification if any, will be required to produce the greatest degree of efficiency.[21]

This was a monumental order, indicating clearly that the Office of Indian Affairs was virtually devoid of official information of any kind concerning the Indians of New Mexico.

Calhoun found the task of assembling the required data most difficult. Despite the extensive contact between the Spaniards and the Pueblo Indians and the voluminous records kept by the mission padres, Calhoun stated in October, almost three months after his arrival, "No information, of a perfectly satisfactory character, can be obtained, as to the number of Pueblos—the number of inhabitants in each—and their respective languages." If, he wrote, the information he had been able to obtain was correct, there were twenty-three pueblos east of Zuñi.[22] Actually, Joab Houghton,[23] one of the justices of the territorial court, had provided him with an accurate list of the pueblos, including the two below El Paso del Norte on the Río

[21] William Medill, commissioner of Indian affairs, to Calhoun, April 7, 1849, in Abel (ed.), *Official Correspondence*, 3.

[22] Calhoun to Medill, October 13, 1849, *ibid.*, 44.

[23] Houghton, a native of New York, entered the Santa Fe trade in

Grande but omitting the Hopi pueblos.[24] By March, 1850, Calhoun had prepared a list of twenty-two pueblos—those named by Houghton, plus Lentis, which was, in fact, a settlement of *genízaros*.[25] Of the Pueblo Indian languages he could learn little, except from the Indians themselves. He had been unable to find anyone who could translate any of the Pueblo tongues—or, for that matter, Navaho—into English. He was unable to obtain an accurate count of the number of Pueblo Indians. Houghton estimated the number, excluding the Hopis, of those above five years of age at 6,524, and Calhoun was of the opinion that in the aggregate they would exceed 10,000.[26] Less than two weeks later he revised his figure upward, having decided that the total number of Pueblo Indians was something between 12,000 and 15,000.[27]

Information about the Pueblo Indian land grants was equally unclear. Calhoun reported in 1849 that the Pueblo Indians "hold possession of the lands which they occupy, and till, by special grants, from the government of Mexico, or Spain. The extent of these grants are not well understood here."[28] A few months later he added, "The general opinion is, not one of the Pueblos have a square of less than eight miles and a half on each side."[29] The Pueblo land grants were

---

1843. Although he had no legal training, General Kearny appointed him to serve as one of the three judges of the Superior Court of New Mexico. He held the office until New Mexico became a territory and later practiced law in Santa Fe. He was justice of the Supreme Court of New Mexico from 1865 to 1869, then resumed the practice of law. He died in Las Vegas in 1876. Twitchell, *Leading Facts of New Mexican History*, II, 272, n. 197.

[24] Calhoun to Medill, October 4, 1849, in Abel (ed.), *Official Correspondence*, 39.

[25] Calhoun to Orlando Brown, commissioner of Indian affairs, March 30, 1850, *ibid.*, 177.

[26] Calhoun to Medill, October 4, 1849, *ibid.*, 39–40.

[27] Calhoun to Medill, October 14, 1849, *ibid.*, 55–56.

[28] Calhoun to Medill, October 13, 1849, *ibid.*, 46.

[29] Calhoun to Brown, March 29, 1850, *ibid.*, 173.

based upon a royal cedula of June 4, 1697, which provided in some detail for such grants. It ordered that Indian pueblos which were in need of land "to live upon and cultivate" be given it, and this applied not only to existing pueblos but to those which might be established in the future.[30] In practice, the accepted size of the land grants for the pueblos of New Mexico came to be four square leagues, with the pueblo church at the center. Although eleven pueblos claimed grants dating from 1689, it seems clear that no grants had been made that early. The pueblo grants were confirmed by Congress on December 22, 1858.[31]

Throughout the Spanish period the Pueblo Indians had been considered wards of the Crown. However, under Mexico, citizenship was conferred upon them. The Treaty of Guadalupe Hidalgo provided that all Mexican citizens residing in the territory ceded to the United States, unless they elected to remain Mexican citizens, would become citizens of the United States. The Pueblo Indians fell within this provision, and the treaty was so interpreted, for a time, by both the New Mexican courts and the United States Supreme Court.[32] Hence, the Pueblos did not come under the provisions of the Indian Intercourse Act of 1834, and were not subject to the jurisdiction of the Office of Indian Affairs. Among other things, the Pueblo Indians were denied the protection of their land rights, normally afforded Indians living on reservations.[33] It was not until 1913 that the United States Supreme Court reversed its earlier decision and gave the Pueblo Indians equal status with other reservation Indians.[34] Their land rights were further guaranteed when Congress enacted the Pueblo Lands Act in 1924.

[30] Ralph Emerson Twitchell, *The Spanish Archives of New Mexico*, II, 475–76.

[31] *Ibid.*, 477; and Herbert O. Brayer, *Pueblo Indian Land Grants of the Rio Abajo, New Mexico*, 13–16.

[32] *New Mexico Statutes, 1953*, I, 370.

[33] Edward H. Spicer, *Cycles of Conquest*, 172–73; and Brayer, *Pueblo Indian Land Grants*, 22.

[34] *New Mexico Statutes, 1953*, I, 370.

Concerning the wild Indians, Calhoun found information even harder to obtain. In 1846, Governor Charles Bent had provided the Office of Indian Affairs with data about the wild tribes of the territory, among them the Hopis. Also included were some Indian tribes whose range was wholly or partly outside the boundaries of the Territory of New Mexico as they were later established. On the other hand, many of the tribes residing in what, after 1863, became Arizona, were omitted. Bent's estimated total of the wild Indians was 36,950.[35] A copy of Bent's letter, which contained a brief discussion of each of the wild tribes, was made available to Calhoun, who did not essay a separate total. The census of 1850 did little to clarify the question. It gave the number of Pueblo Indians as 7,867, which was probably too few, and estimated the number of wild Indians as 45,000, not enumerating the separate tribes and undoubtedly including some outside the New Mexican boundaries. There was little attempt at this time to examine the culture of the wild tribes. They were labeled either hostile or friendly, and more interest was displayed in their predatory habits and warlike intentions than in other aspects of their behavior. Most of the woes of New Mexico were attributed to failure to control the hostile Indians. This had been true in the Mexican period, when New Mexico's lack of prosperity was blamed on the lack of protection afforded it. It continued to be true in the early years following the United States occupation, even though more decisive if still ineffective measures were taken to curb the Indians. In 1851, Calhoun, by this time territorial governor, found it necessary to proclaim:

> The present condition of the Territory of New Mexico, surrounded as it is by hostile Indians, whose almost daily incursions and

[35] Bent to Medill, November 10, 1846, in Abel (ed.), *Official Correspondence*, 8. That Bent's figures were probably inaccurate was recognized by William Medill, who wrote that "an almost inevitable imprecision of the boundaries of New Mexico" made the actual location of some of the tribes, especially the nomadic Apaches and Comanches, difficult to determine. Medill to Marcy, July 26, 1848, 30 Cong., 1 sess., *House Exec. Doc. 76*, 5.

depredations are the source of the greatest evils which afflict the country, has induced me to issue by virtue of my powers, as Commander-in-Chief of the Militia of the Territory, this proclamation.

I recommend to all able-bodied male citizens of the Territory, capable of bearing arms, the formation of Volunteer Corps to protect their families, property and homes.[36]

There was no simple solution to the problems imposed by the hostility of the wild Indians. In his message of 1852 to the territorial legislature, Governor Lane summed up the situation in New Mexico:

We are very distant, from the States,—difficult of access,—and surrounded by barbarians, of doubtful faith. The face of the country is mountainous, and of great elevation,—with an appearance of sterility, from a scarcity of water. . . . The population, which does not exceed 60,000 souls, is widely scattered, through distant vallies,—over an area so immense, that 20 companies of U.S. troops, are insufficient for its protection, against Indians; and your own people are so badly armed, that they cannot protect their own property from depredation. Agriculture and stock-raising, the two great interests of the Territory, are depressed,—for the want of a certain market, for the produce of the soil,—and for the want of protection, for flocks and herds. Your mines are nearly abandoned, and their products, (gold and silver excepted,) will not bear the transportation to market. Your highways are in a bad condition; and the school master, (an indispensable functionary, in a popular government,) is rarely seen amongst you.[37]

The settled portion of New Mexico, in the last half-century of the Spanish period and throughout the Mexican period, began a little below San Elizario—some twenty miles below El Paso del Norte—and extended for a distance north of Taos.[38] This area was entirely

[36] *Governors' Papers*, New Mexico Archives.

[37] *Message of William Carr Lane, Governor of the Territory of New Mexico, to the Legislative Assembly of the Territory, at Santa Fé, Dec. 7, 1852*, 3.

[38] There were some extensive gaps in the line of settlements, notably south of Socorro. Even though El Paso district was separated from New

surrounded by wild Indians.[39] The Comanches, the various Apache bands, the Navahos, and the Utes encircled that portion of New Mexico inhabited by the Mexicans and Pueblo Indians, with the Hopi and Zuñi pueblos forming further enclaves in the wild Indian country. There was never a time when the civilized New Mexicans were not plagued by conflict with one or another of the wild Indian tribes. Occasionally Spanish or Mexican arms inflicted a major defeat upon the wild Indians, but none of the tribes were conquered or brought under control. At times the New Mexicans made alliances with wild tribes, notably the Comanches, Utes, or Navahos, for campaigns against other wild tribes. There were also periods of peace. Spain and the Navahos were on friendly terms from the 1720's until 1772.[40] The Comanches declined as a threat to New Mexico after they were decisively defeated in the campaign conducted by Governor Juan Bautista de Anza[41] in 1779. In part through Comanche initiative, a

---

Mexico in 1824, it retained important economic and defensive ties with the north. Above Taos, settlement had approached close to the present Colorado line by the end of the Mexican period. Costilla, virtually on the line, was established in 1848, and the first settlement north of the line was made in 1850.

[39] An interesting variant interpretation was provided by Secretary of War Charles M. Conrad when he wrote, "Hemmed in, as they [the wild tribes] are, on all sides by the United States, by Mexico and the Rocky mountains, as our settlements advance, the scarcity of game will compel them to fall back on our weaker neighbors, whom, by the treaty of Guadalupe Hidalgo, we are bound to protect against their incursions." Conrad to Millard Fillmore, November 30, 1850, 31 Cong., 2 sess., *House Exec. Doc. 1*, part II, 5. Conrad was referring to the Plains Indians, but the same thing was rapidly becoming true of the Indians between the Rockies and the Sierra Nevadas. Both the New Mexicans and the wild Indians, in a sense, were encircled. See also Thomas L. Brent to Thomas S. Jesup, October 9, 1850, *ibid.*, 294.

[40] See Frank D. Reeve, "The Navaho-Spanish Peace: 1720's–1770's," *New Mexico Historical Review*, Vol. XXXIV (January, 1959), 9–40.

[41] Lieutenant Colonel de Anza was appointed governor of New Mexico in 1777 and assumed office late in 1778. He was one of the most ener-

peace was negotiated in 1786, essentially on Anza's terms, a peace which also constituted an alliance against the Apaches. From 1786 forward, the Comanches were at peace with the New Mexicans, scrupulously observing their treaties with them.[42] They did not, it should be noted, cease their raids into Texas and deeper into Mexico.

The New Mexicans and the Pueblo Indians suffered intensely at the hands of the wild Indians. Their crops were destroyed in the fields, their property was laid waste or stolen, tremendous numbers of livestock were killed or run off, and many persons were either killed or taken captive. The depredations of the wild Indians were a major factor in the decline of some of the pueblos and contributed to the extinction of Pecos Pueblo. For Spain and Mexico the Indians had meant shrinking frontiers and had brought about the abandonment of settlements and ranchos, some of them permanently. Under Spain adequate defenses were never provided for New Mexico. For a time a presidio was maintained at El Paso del Norte, and later, in 1773, one was established at San Elizario. These served to protect the Santa Fe–Chihuahua trade route, but they were more concerned with blocking the incursion of hostile Indians (or foreigners) to the south than with the defense of New Mexico. Occasionally proposals were made for the strengthening of New Mexico's military position,[43] but they were not carried out.

getic and effective governors of the Spanish period so far as chastising the Indians was concerned. See Thomas, *Forgotten Frontiers*.

[42] *Ibid.*, 71–83, 329–32; and H. Bailey Carroll and J. Villasana Haggard (trans. and eds.), *Three New Mexico Chronicles*, 132. Even so, in the Mexican period occasional depredations were attributed to the Comanches, such as the killing of several Mexicans near Anton Chico in 1831. See No. 1814, San Miguel del Bado, 1831, *Historical Society of New Mexico, Miscellaneous Collection*, New Mexico Archives.

[43] The recommendations of the Marqués de Rubí led to the reorganization of New Spain's northern defenses in 1773, but the *destacamento* which he proposed be established at Robledo, a little above the later Doña Ana and near the site where the United States established Fort Selden, was never built. In 1778 a council was held in Chihuahua by Teodoro de

Throughout the Spanish regime Santa Fe was the only presidial town in New Mexico. There the garrison rarely exceeded eighty men, though all able-bodied adult males might be called upon to constitute a militia force.[44] Not only did New Mexico lack manpower, but there was a chronic shortage of arms and an insufficiency of horses.[45] Small garrisons, often fewer than a dozen men, were stationed at threatened towns, such as San Miguel del Bado, Taos, Abiquiu, or Socorro. They were augmented by the local population and, sometimes, by Pueblo Indian auxiliaries. These were not enough to curb the wild Indian menace.[46] The Mexican period saw a further

---

Croix, commandant general of the Provincias Internas, which considered, among other matters, how the defenses of New Mexico could be reorganized if an additional 2,000 troops were made available (which they were not). Alfred B. Thomas, *The Plains Indians and New Mexico, 1751–1778*, 37, 41, 55–56.

[44] Prior to the Pueblo Revolt of 1680 there was neither a regular presidio nor, most of the time, a paid garrison in Santa Fe. France V. Scholes, "Civil Government and Society in New Mexico in the Seventeenth Century," *New Mexico Historical Review*, Vol. X (April, 1935), 78.

[45] In 1752 it was reported that there were 1,370 horses, 388 guns, and 53 pistols in the hands of the settlers of the province. At the same time the Pueblo Indians had 4,060 horses but no firearms, being armed chiefly with the bow and arrow. Frank D. Reeve, "Navaho-Spanish Diplomacy, 1770–1790," *New Mexico Historical Review*, Vol. XXXV (July, 1960), 211–12.

[46] In the closing years of the Spanish period the regular paid garrison in New Mexico consisted of 121 men, who received an annual salary of 240 pesos each. Twelve were stationed at Santa Fe, 39 constituted a force which could be rushed to any spot where trouble developed, and the rest were scattered in small groups at various settlements. Because the protection thus provided was considered inadequate, three militia companies of 61 men each were organized in 1808. Carroll and Haggard (eds.), *Three New Mexico Chronicles*, 69–70. On rare occasions a post was established away from the centers of population, such as Governor Pedro Fermín de Mendinueta's post on the Cerro de San Antonio in 1768,

deterioration of defense ability. Mexico itself was fraught with political unrest and economic instability, and this at a time when Navaho and Apache activities were increasing. In 1843 the Twenty-second Regiment of the Mexican Army, consisting of nine companies, a total of 979 officers and men, was stationed in Santa Fe.[47] This was a large number of troops to be located in New Mexico, but more than one visitor of the Mexican period commented on the insufficient number of uniforms and shoes and the inferior quality of the weapons with which the troops were provided.[48]

The attitude of the New Mexicans toward the Indians was colored by the long period of conflict, and that attitude was reflected, for a time, in the policy adopted by the United States. General Kearny promised the New Mexicans that the United States would protect their persons and property from the Indians.[49] This promise was later repeated and an effort was made to implement it. Secretary of War William L. Marcy issued instructions in 1848 in which he stated, "The important duty of the military force will be to protect the inhabitants of the Territory of New Mexico in the full enjoyment of life, liberty, and property."[50] In March, 1849, when additional regu-

or the post established on Oak Creek in what is now southern Colorado in 1819. See Robert W. Frazer, "Governor Mendinueta's Post on the Cerro de San Antonio," *University of Wichita Studies* (No. 49); and Chauncey Thomas, "The Spanish Fort in Colorado, 1819," *Colorado Magazine*, Vol. XIV (May, 1937), 81–95.

[47] "*Regimento Bente doz de este Departam'to*," July 9, 1843, *Read Collection*, New Mexico Archives.

[48] For example, see James, whose critical attitude is not unexpected, *Three Years Among the Indians and Mexicans*, 95–96; Gregg, *Commerce of the Prairies*, 155–56; and Matthew Field, *Matt Field on the Santa Fe Trail*, 265–67.

[49] See Kearny's address, delivered at Las Vegas, August 15, 1846, in Twitchell, *Old Santa Fe*, 259–60; and his proclamation, issued at Santa Fe, August 19, 1846, in 30 Cong., 1 sess., *House Exec. Doc. 60*, 170–71.

[50] Marcy to the Commanding Officer [John Macrae Washington], October 12, 1848, 31 Cong., 1 sess., *House Exec. Doc. 17*, 262.

lar troops assigned to New Mexico did not arrive as anticipated, Major Washington authorized the raising of five volunteer companies "for the protection of the property and lives of the inhabitants of the territory of New Mexico against the depredations of the marauding bands of Indians which infest it."[51]

In addition to protecting the inhabitants of the territory, the United States was obligated by the terms of the Treaty of Guadalupe Hidalgo:

> Considering that a great part of the territories which, by the present treaty, are to be comprehended for the future within the limits of the United States, is now occupied by savage tribes, who will hereafter be under the exclusive control of the United States, and whose incursions upon the territory of Mexico would be prejudicial in the extreme, it is solemnly agreed that all such incursions shall be forcibly restrained by the government of the United States whensoever this may be necessary; and that when they cannot be prevented, they shall be punished by the said government, and satisfaction for the same shall be exacted—all in the same way, and with equal diligence and energy, as if the same incursions were meditated or committed within its own territory, against its own citizens.[52]

This obligation, which proved impossible to fulfill, was a constant annoyance to the military. Quartermaster General Thomas S. Jesup

[51] Orders No. 2, March 20, 1849, 31 Cong., 1 sess., *Sen. Exec. Doc. 1*, 107. Actually, only four volunteer companies, two of them mounted, were called into service for six months. Later in the year, in conjunction with his campaign against the Navahos, Major Washington raised two volunteer companies, one of sixty-three New Mexicans and one of fifty-four Pueblo Indians, including representatives from at least six pueblos, for one month's service. Washington to Roger Jones, September 25, 1849, *ibid.*, 111; Jones to Crawford, November 28, 1849, *ibid.*, 184; and list of Indians accompanying the Washington expedition in 31 Cong., 1 sess., *Sen. Exec. Doc. 24*, 35–36.

[52] Article XI of the treaty, *New Mexico Statutes, 1953*, I, 372. The obligation was specifically abrogated in the Gadsden Purchase Treaty of 1853. *Ibid.*, 383.

complained that Indian depredations in Texas and New Mexico were "the natural and necessary result of our treaty for the protection of Mexico." If the Indians were permitted to carry on their predatory raids into Mexico, he held, they would not bother the United States. Otherwise, the United States either must "feed or exterminate the Indians, or prevail upon them to settle down as cultivators of the soil." There was no object in making treaties with the Indians unless their subsistence were in some way guaranteed. If it were not, it became a simple question of steal or starve.[53] One army officer in New Mexico quoted an Indian as saying, "We must steal from somebody; and if you (meaning the whites) will not permit us to rob the Mexicans, we must steal from you, or fight you."[54] Further, it was obvious that New Mexico's future economic development and its ability to attract settlers from the States depended upon the success of the government in bringing the wild Indian tribes under control.

Initially, the United States sought to protect the principal centers of population in New Mexico and to station troops where they could block the traditional routes followed by the Indians in conducting their raids. In working out a suitable military defense policy, the United States was confronted by the same manpower shortage problem that had handicapped Spain and Mexico. Kearny's occupation of New Mexico had been accomplished with a force of fewer than 1,700 men, all but 300 of them volunteers. From August, 1846, to August, 1848, there were usually between 2,000 and 3,000 troops, preponderantly volunteers, stationed in New Mexico. Beginning in August, 1848, the volunteer companies were withdrawn, leaving only three companies of dragoons and one battery of artillery in New Mexico. The number of troops in the department, as shown in the report of the Secretary of War for 1848, was 665.[55] In 1849 the number of

[53] Jesup to Osborne Cross, November 20, 1850, 31 Cong., 2 sess., *Sen. Exec. Doc. 1*, part II, 122–23.

[54] Andrew W. Bowman to Thomas L. Brent, April 21, 1850, *ibid.*, 295.

[55] The "Position and Distribution of Troops" in the annual reports of the Secretary of War were made up from the latest available post returns.

regular army officers and men increased to 885, but it is interesting to note that only 708 were actually present in the department.[56] In 1850 there was a further increase to 1,188 officers and men, of whom 1,019 were present.[57] Considering the extent of the territory to be protected and the manifold nature of the duties involved, the military force in New Mexico was in these years inadequate to achieve its purpose.

Yet small though the force was, the tendency was to spread it exceedingly thin. Military Department Number 9 was created on November 3, 1846, and was described as embracing "so much of the Mexican province of New Mexico as has been or may be subjected to the arms or the authority of the United States." By December 15, 1849, the limits of the department had been revised "to consist of New Mexico and the territory north and west of a line from a point on the Rio Grande opposite the southernmost limit of the island south of El Paso, excluding the towns of San Elizario, Socorro, and Isleta, to [the] junction of the Ensenada Choctaw (Choctaw Creek) with the Colorado or Red River, and down said river to [the] Arkansas." This description of the department is not clear, and certainly, as long as it was garrisoned, the Presidio of San Elizario was attached to the department. In 1851 the description was rectified to include that portion of Texas west of 103° longitude.[58]

Almost immediately after the occupation of Santa Fe, Fort Marcy was established on a low eminence some 650 yards northeast of the plaza.[59] It was a genuine fortification and was still in 1850 the only

The report for 1848 is dated December 2, and probably represents the returns of New Mexican posts for not later than September. 30 Cong., 2 sess., *House Exec. Doc. 1*, 184d.

[56] "Position and Distribution of Troops," 31 Cong., 1 sess., *Sen. Exec. Doc. 1*, 188d.

[57] "Position and Distribution of Troops," 31 Cong., 2 sess., *Sen. Exec. Doc. 1*, part II, 116d.

[58] Raphael P. Thian, *Notes Illustrating the Military Geography of the United States*, 49–50.

[59] The site was selected by First Lieutenant William H. Emory, Topographical Engineers. Construction of the fort commenced on August 23,

post in the department which was designated a fort. Until the close of the Mexican War the movement of troops in New Mexico remained fluid. The largest concentration was in Santa Fe, but troops were located in various towns as the need arose, particularly after the murder of Governor Bent in January, 1847, and the threatened general uprising which accompanied it. Withdrawal of the volunteer companies, the obligations resulting from the Treaty of Guadalupe Hidalgo, and permanent acquisition of the territory necessitated a re-examination of military policy. Secretary of War Marcy was of the opinion that not more than three or four posts would be required for the protection of New Mexico. The principal post would be at Santa Fe, with others located at Albuquerque and Socorro, plus a post to be established on the Río Grande, "nearly opposite to El Paso." He estimated that 1200 men would be sufficient to defend New Mexico,[60] a number still not provided in 1850. By the autumn of 1848 four military posts had been established, with detachments at two other locations. Santa Fe (Fort Marcy) was garrisoned by one company of the Second Dragoons and a battery of the Third Artillery. At each of the towns of Taos, Albuquerque, and Socorro was stationed one company of the First Dragoons. Tome was occupied by a detachment of 20 men from the company at Albuquerque, and Doña Ana by a detachment of 25 men from Socorro.[61]

The Post of El Paso, located at the ranch of Benjamin Franklin Coons,[62] across the Río Grande from El Paso del Norte, was estab-

1846. Emory, *Notes of a Military Reconnoissance, from Fort Leavenworth in Missouri, to San Diego, in California*, 30 Cong., 1 sess., *House Exec. Doc. 41*, 32.

[60] In addition, Marcy proposed that if the Gila River route proved "the most direct and practical way for transporting troops into California," one or two posts should be established on the Gila. Marcy to Polk, July 31, 1848, 30 Cong., 1 sess., *House Exec. Doc. 76*, 3–4.

[61] Washington to Marcy, November 8, 1848, 31 Cong., 1 sess., *Sen. Exec. Doc. 1*, 104.

[62] Benjamin Franklin Coons, a Missourian, acquired Ponce's Ranch, probably from Juan María Ponce de León, in June, 1849. Ponce de León

lished on September 28, 1849, with six companies of the Third Infantry, a total of 257 officers and men. For the moment, it was the strongest post in the department, but most of the troops were soon distributed among other posts.[63] The detachment had been withdrawn from Tome, but a permanent garrison had been stationed in Doña Ana. Also in 1849, the three companies of the First Dragoons and the battery of Third Artillery were replaced by four additional companies of the Third Infantry, two companies of the Second Artillery, and one company of the Second Dragoons.[64] There was a further buildup of troops in 1850. In August, the Seventh Regiment of infantry was ordered to New Mexico, but when the steamboat bringing its supplies up the Missouri from St. Louis sank, the regiment was forced to turn back and spend the winter at Jefferson Barracks.[65] Even so, by the fall of the year, there were stationed in the department five companies of the First Dragoons, four companies of the Second Dragoons, ten companies of the Third Infantry,

---

had received the property as a grant in 1827. Coons apparently called his ranch Santa Maria, but it was usually referred to as Coons' Ranch or Franklin. Coons had extensive business interests, engaging in freighting, maintaining stores in Santa Fe and at his ranch, and leasing property to the army. In 1850, an unfortunate venture in providing supplies for the Post of El Paso ruined him financially. He departed for California before the year was out. His ranch passed into the hands of William Smith, a former employee. Rex W. Strickland, "Six Who Came to El Paso, Pioneers of the 1840's," *Southwestern Studies*, Vol. I (Fall, 1963), 12–19; and Frazer (ed.), *Mansfield*, 70, n. 68.

[63] The Post of El Paso was established by Captain and Brevet Major Jefferson Van Horne. He arrived five miles below El Paso on September 8, at which time he planned to establish the post with four of his companies, stationing the other two at San Elizario. Van Horne to the Assistant Adjutant General [Santa Fe], September 10, 1849, 31 Cong., 1 sess., *Sen. Exec. Doc. 24*, 33.

[64] Jones to Crawford, November 28, 1849, 31 Cong., 1 sess., *Sen. Exec. Doc. 1*, 184.

[65] Conrad to Fillmore, November 30, 1850, 31 Cong., 2 sess., *Sen. Exec. Doc. 1*, part II, 4.

*Courtesy Museum of New Mexico*

Grist mills existed in New Mexico before 1850. This is a small mill near Taos.

*Courtesy Museum of New Mexico*

Interior of the small grist mill near Taos.

and two companies of the Second Artillery.[66] The number of posts had been increased to eleven with the addition of Abiquiu, Las Vegas, Rayado, San Elizario, and Cebolleta. With two exceptions, all of the posts were located in towns. The Post of Rayado was on Rayado Creek, on the Maxwell Land Grant, and was intended to block the movement of Plains Indians through the mountains to the Taos area. The Post of El Paso, although not in a town, was immediately across the Río Grande from the Mexican town of El Paso del Norte, in an area in which Americans were already beginning to settle.

The first policy adopted by the military was to protect New Mexico by garrisoning selected towns and blocking routes used by the Indians in their raids. The policy was intended to preserve lives and property and, in the process, to stimulate the economy and make New Mexico a more attractive area for settlement. Even as this policy was being placed in effect, the difficulty and cost of maintaining troops in New Mexico became a matter of serious concern to the War Department. It was soon to be decided that the garrisoning of towns did not provide the desired protection, but that it did increase military expenses. This opinion was expressed as early as 1850, but the original policy stayed in effect until 1851, when what was to prove a permanent policy was inaugurated.

The New Mexican economy was primitive, in most respects little above the subsistence level, and hampered by the persistence of antiquated methods and by geographic isolation. Spanish regulation of agriculture and commerce retarded economic development to some extent, but this was not the major hindrance. New Mexico produced little for which there was outside demand. Under Spain, the cost of administering the province, supporting the missionary activity, and maintaining even a small military force had exceeded the revenue which New Mexico produced. In the Spanish period the area attracted few settlers. Fernando Navarro y Noriega placed the population in 1810, more than two centuries after the first Spanish settlement had been founded, at 34,205. He broke this total down into 20 friars, 10,557 Indians, and 23,628 *castas*, giving no separate

[66] "Position and Distribution of Troops," *ibid.*, 116d.

figure for Spaniards.[67] Finally, the constant harassment by the Indians must be considered a primary cause for New Mexico's economic retardation.

The period between the outbreak of the Mexican independence movement and the occupation of New Mexico by the United States saw a distinct improvement in some aspects of the economy. For one thing, the non-Indian population apparently doubled in this third of a century.[68] The opening of commerce with the outside world had a salutary effect, involving as it did not only the Santa Fe trade per se, but also the trade through New Mexico to Chihuahua and on to the

[67] *Memoria sobre la Población del Reino de Nueva España*, table, unpaged. It must be assumed that the Indians listed were the Pueblo Indians. Alexander von Humboldt, quoting a copy of the census figures for 1793, preserved in the viceregal archives, gave New Mexico a population of 30,953. *Ensayo Político sobre el Reino de la Nueva España*, II, 14. It seems clear that neither Humboldt nor Navarro included the wild Indians. Other estimates for the closing years of the Spanish period are: 28,558 (1800); 40,000 (1803); 28,778 (1805); 40,000–50,000 (1811); 35,840 (1819); and 38,359 (1820). "Note on the Population of New Mexico, 1846–1849," *New Mexico Historical Review*, Vol. XXXIV (July, 1959), 200. Also see Hubert Howe Bancroft, *History of Arizona and New Mexico* (Vol. XVII of *Works*), 278–79, for a discussion of population trends, 1750–1800.

[68] The census of 1827, taken by order of Governor Antonio Narbona, showed a population of 43,433; that of 1840, taken by order of Governor Manuel Armijo, 55,403. Carroll and Haggard (eds.), *Three New Mexico Chronicles*, 88–89. The final census of the Mexican period—in this case, obviously, in part an estimate—was taken in 1844, by order of Governor Mariano Martínez de Lejanza, when New Mexico was divided into districts. It produced the figure 100,064. This undoubtedly included wild Indians. Twitchell, *Leading Facts of New Mexican History*, II, 15–16. The census of 1850, the first taken by the United States, and not notable for its accuracy in regard to New Mexico, gave a total of 61,525 whites and 22 free Negroes. The population was broken down as follows: born in New Mexico, 58,415; born elsewhere in the United States, 772; foreign born, 2,151; place of birth unknown, 209. *The Seventh Census of the United States: 1850*, 993, 996.

south, the trade with California, and the fur trade. There was now an increased demand for some of the products which New Mexico could supply, and Santa Fe and Taos became centers in which these were exchanged for other goods, most of which were not produced in New Mexico. Moreover, Mexican regulations were less stringent than those imposed by Spain and were less rigidly enforced. To offset these advantages, New Mexico remained a debtor province with an adverse balance of trade. A few of its people could be classified as *ricos*, but most were woefully poor and had no choice but to remain so. Helping to keep the economy backward was the increased hostility of the Indians during the Mexican period, an increase caused in part by the failure of Mexico to defend properly the province. Governor Donaciano Vigil wrote, shortly after the Treaty of Guadalupe Hidalgo brought the Mexican period to a permanent end:

> The pacification of the Indians is another necessity of the first order, for as you already know the principal wealth of this country is the breeding of livestock, and the warfare of the Indians obstructs this almost completely. These inhabitants are not miners nor agriculturalists; the first for lack of enterprise, and the second because the lands are not those which invite the laborer with the abundance of their products. He is not a manufacturer for lack of artisans and materials. There is a small number of men dedicated to commerce, a field which will in time compete with the stock raisers, but never will have all its impetus until the mines here are exploited. To improve the wools and the breed of the herds of horses and cattle will result in the stimulation of the entrepreneur.[69]

The agriculture of both the Mexicans and the Pueblo Indians was essentially for subsistence. It consisted of a few basic crops worked with crude tools and methods. The wild Indians so often stole or destroyed the crops that the Mexicans saw little reason to raise more than enough to meet their immediate needs. The Pueblo Indians, with their long experience of drought and crop destruction, sought to produce more than their immediate needs called for, storing up the

[69] Vigil to Hugh N. Smith, May 1, 1848, *Vigil Papers*, New Mexico Archives.

surplus against the lean years. Hence, when the army occupied New Mexico and attempted to buy agricultural products locally, the Mexicans had little surplus to sell and the Pueblo Indians were unwilling to sell what they had. However, the United States occupation, with its promise of protection and introduction of improved methods and implements, brought about a gradual change. Once assured of a market, the Mexicans were willing to increase their plantings of any product the army was willing to purchase. It was far more difficult to persuade the Pueblo Indians to sell their surplus crops. The United States Army provided a significant stimulus to New Mexican agriculture, but a number of years passed before supply began to equal demand. In the meantime, the New Mexicans were able to command high prices for what they had to offer.

Prior to United States occupation, agriculture was important for the very good reason that the people had to eat in order to live. The one great source of revenue—or, at least, of exchange—was the livestock industry. New Mexico had vast expanses of land suitable for grazing. True, the herds and flocks were a constant temptation to marauding Indians. The extent of the losses suffered over the period of two and a half centuries is impossible to determine, but it was unquestionably enormous. Horses and cattle were never numerous in the Spanish and Mexican periods, and, according to Antonio Barreiro, goats were not worthy of consideration, while the raising of swine was completely neglected. Sheep constituted the wealth of New Mexico. Barreiro wrote:

> The thousands of sheep raised in this territory have no parallel anywhere else in the republic. This stock increases from day to day in an incredible manner. It may be said that, if New Mexico can establish a permanent peace with the wild Indians, and if it will provide its people with knowledge of the most advantageous methods of trading in sheep, the province will prosper with the income from this branch of industry alone as much as Chihuahua has prospered from that of her mines. Happy the day when the government will extend its protecting hand to this territory; when these fields, at present

uninhabited and desolate, will be converted into rich and happy sheep ranches.[70]

The principal value of the sheep was not in their wool[71] but in their meat, and throughout the Spanish period the only significant markets were the mining districts of Chihuahua and farther to the south. The first really profitable market for sheep did not develop until after the discovery of gold in California. Once again it was the mining districts and their need for food which provided the most lucrative outlet, and they paid far more liberally than the silver mining districts of Mexico ever had. The early attempts to find a market for New Mexican sheep and wool in Missouri met with little success.[72] Although the sheep industry was the chief source of wealth in the province, it was concentrated in the hands of a few *ricos*, and the bulk of the population derived little benefit from it.

Most of New Mexico's manufacturing was limited to handcrafts produced in the home for home consumption. Much of it was crude, not through lack of skill, but because tools and equipment were crude. Wood was used extensively for household goods and furnishings, *carretas* (including the entire wheels), and such implements as hoes, spades, and plows. Yet there was not a single sawmill in New Mexico

[70] Carroll and Haggard (eds.), *Three New Mexico Chronicles*, 103. A similar thought was expressed in 1850 by the chief assistant quartermaster in New Mexico when he wrote: "In regard to the general resources of New Mexico, little can be said with certainty. The country was once celebrated for its flocks of sheep and herds of cattle. These have nearly all disappeared, from the constant forays of the Indians. Mules and horses, once a considerable production of this country, are now scarce, few or none being bred, from the same cause. Were adequate protection afforded, their production would revive."—Brent to Jesup, October 9, 1850, 31 Cong., 2 sess., *Sen. Exec. Doc. 1*, part II, 293.

[71] James W. Abert wrote in 1846, "Wool is not considered very valuable, and can be bought for 4 cents a fleece." *Abert's New Mexico Report*, 52.

[72] Max L. Moorhead, *New Mexico's Royal Road*, 191.

prior to the United States occupation.[73] Wool and, to a lesser extent, cotton were spun and woven by both the Mexicans and the Pueblo Indians, and the Navahos had already achieved a certain renown for their blankets. Coarse serapes and a rough, cheap material called *jerga*, which served both for carpeting and for clothing, were among the principal products of the Mexicans, though some finer serapes were woven also.[74] Even after the Santa Fe trade brought about a reduction in the price of imported fabrics, native weaving continued to supply the needs of the poor. The coarse woolen cloth also entered into commerce, being exported to the neighboring Mexican states and California and traded to the wild Indians. Leather and hides were put to a variety of uses, including clothing. There was little domestic manufacture of metal, a few articles being hammered out of copper. Only in work in precious metals was there anything to attract the admiration of the Americans. Josiah Gregg commented, "Gold and silversmiths are perhaps better skilled in their respective trades than any other class of artisans whatever . . . . Some mechanics of this class have produced such singular specimens of ingenious workmanship, that on examining them, we are almost unwilling to believe rude art could accomplish so much."[75] More than a decade later, William W. H. Davis[76] echoed this opinion when he wrote, "The gold and silver smiths excel all the other workmen, and some of their specimens, in point of ingenuity and skill, would do credit to the craft in any part of the world." But he also remarked of manufacturing generally, "The state of the mechanic arts among the New Mexicans is very low, and apparently without improvement since the earliest times."[77]

[73] Davis, *El Gringo*, 211.

[74] *Ibid.*, 213–14; and Gregg, *Commerce of the Prairies*, 199.

[75] *Ibid.*, 143–44.

[76] Davis, of Massachusetts, went to New Mexico in 1853 to become United States attorney for the territory. He was later secretary of the territory and was acting governor for eleven months, 1857–58. Twitchell, *Leading Facts of New Mexican History*, II, 314.

[77] *El Gringo*, 211.

Articles of baser metals were imported almost exclusively and for the poorer New Mexicans, most of these were a luxury.

Flour was milled throughout New Mexico, almost every settlement having one or more mills. Most of the mills were very small, powered by water where water was regularly available, or by horse or mule where it was not. John G. Bourke[78] described flour mills which he saw near Santa Cruz de la Cañada:

> Two of the main acequias, (ditches,) crossed the road and near the bridges we saw Mexican flour mills; these were cottonwood log edifices, about 12 ft. square and 7 ft. high, built over the ditch to allow the water to turn a small turbine wheel. I should conjecture that in an emergency, under the stimulus of a Gov't. contract, with a full complement of hands (that is to say a man smoking a cigarrito, a small boy scratching his nose, and a big dog scratching his ribs.) and running full time, one of these mills could grind a bushel of wheat in a week; the ordinary output can't be over half that quantity.[79]

A mill in the Socorro district was similarly, if less facetiously, described in 1855:

> The Mexican mill is a very primitive construction. A horizontal wheel is attached to a shaft, which extends into a little building above it, and turns one pair of small stones, which grind about *one bushel in*

[78] Bourke graduated from the United States Military Academy in 1869, ranking eleventh in a class of thirty-nine. Although he received the Congressional Medal of Honor, the highest regular rank he attained was captain, and his highest brevet rank was major. Bourke was a scholar by nature and contributed important anthropological and historical information regarding the Indians of the Southwest. See Frank Dobie's introduction to Bourke, *An Apache Campaign in the Sierra Madre*; and Francis B. Heitman, *Historical Register and Dictionary of the United States Army*, I, 232.

[79] Lansing B. Bloom (ed.), "Bourke on the Southwest," *New Mexico Historical Review*, Vol. X (January, 1935), 299. Although Bourke was describing flour mills which he saw in 1881, they had not changed since the Mexican period.

> *twenty-four hours*! The wheel is placed below the level of the stream, which through a trough is directed against it, producing the motion. The wheel is about as large as a good-sized wash-tub.[80]

Although these mills were but a step beyond the *mano* and *metate* employed by the Indians and many of the Mexicans, there were enough of them to serve the needs of the Mexican towns and settlements. A few larger mills were in existence by 1850, such as Donaciano Vigil's mill on the Pecos and Ceran St. Vrain's[81] mill on the Mora.[82] Whether any of the larger mills antedated the United States occupation is open to question.[83]

Another industry of considerable local importance was the making

[80] "Notes and Documents," *New Mexico Historical Review*, Vol. XXVII (April, 1952), 173. See also Lieutenant Abert's description of a flour mill which he observed near Manzano in 1846. *Report*, 107–108.

[81] Ceran St. Vrain was born in Missouri in 1798. He was in New Mexico at least as early as 1825. In 1830 he joined Charles Bent to form Bent and St. Vrain, predecessor of Bent, St. Vrain and Company. After the dissolution of the company in 1849 he was primarily interested in commerce and flour milling, having extensive interests in northern New Mexico and the present Colorado. His flour mill on the Mora River was one of the most important in New Mexico. St. Vrain died at Mora in 1870. Ralph P. Bieber (ed.), in James Josiah Webb, *Adventures in the Santa Fé Trade, 1844–1847*, 61, n. 78; David Lavender, *Bent's Fort*, 56–57, 312.

[82] See B. A. Reuter, "Flour Mill Erected by Gov. Vigil and Other Mills of Pecos District," 2–3, MS, dated July 28, 1939, in the library of the Museum of New Mexico, Santa Fe.

[83] Simeon Turley's mill, located at the present Arroyo Hondo, may have been an exception. Turley maintained both a mill and a distillery. George A. F. Ruxton described Turley's establishment, as it was early in 1847: "Sheep and goats, and innumerable hogs, ran about the corral; his barns were filled with grain of all kinds, his mill with flour, and his cellars with whisky 'in galore.' Everything about the place betokened prosperity." LeRoy R. Hafen (ed.), *Ruxton of the Rockies*, 194–95. Turley was killed a few days after Ruxton passed through Arroyo Hondo, at the time of the Taos uprising, and his mill was destroyed.

of wine and brandy. This activity was limited to the Río Abajo country, from above Bernalillo to El Paso district. Many visitors from the States remarked on the excellent quality of the product, particularly that of the environs of El Paso. New Mexican wines were compared favorably to those of France. In 1847, John T. Hughes reported:

> the wines of El Paso alone, yield four hundred thousand dollars per annum. The El Paso wines are superior in richness of flavor, and pleasantness of taste, to any thing of the kind I ever met with in the United States, and I doubt not that they are far superior to the best wines ever produced in the valley of the Rhine, or on the sunny hills of France.[84]

In 1849, Second Lieutenant William H. C. Whiting said of the wines of El Paso, "In skillful hands the grape here grown will produce delightful wine."[85] Writing in the same year, and at least partly dissenting, Captain Samuel G. French held, "Some of the old wine is *said* to possess a fine flavor, but the Mexicans seldom permit it to attain any age."[86] Taos lightning, a form of whisky more noted for its potency than for its appeal to the connoisseur, was produced in sufficient quantities to meet most of the local demand.

[84] *Doniphan's Expedition*, 282. See also Davis, *El Gringo*, 349–51.

[85] Whiting to Joseph G. Totten, June 10, 1849, 31 Cong., 1 sess., *Sen. Exec. Doc. 1*, 289. Whiting was a second lieutenant, Corps of Engineers. He was in command of the party which surveyed the San Antonio–El Paso route in 1849. He resigned from the army on February 10, 1861, and served with the rank of major general in the Confederate Army during the Civil War. Heitman, *Historical Register*, I, 1030; and Goetzmann, *Army Exploration*, 228–30.

[86] French to Jesup, December 26, 1849, 31 Cong., 2 sess., *Sen. Exec. Doc. 1*, part II, 312. French was a captain and acting quartermaster. He accompanied Lieutenant Colonel Joseph E. Johnston to El Paso in 1849 to reconnoiter the route to be taken by Captain Jefferson Van Horne. He resigned from the army on May 31, 1856, and served with the rank of major general in the Confederate Army during the Civil War. Heitman, *Historical Register*, I, 437.

New Mexico offered little at this time and for some time to come to fill the requirements of the Commissary and Quartermaster's Departments of the army. Enough flour was available to supply the military posts, although flour for the posts of El Paso and San Elizario came from Chihuahua rather than New Mexico.[87] A series of inspectors general pronounced the flour gritty, but there is no indication that the troops objected to it. The increased demand for flour caused the New Mexicans to plant more wheat, but, at the same time, they planted less corn. As a result, corn for use as forage for military animals was in short supply, and the price demanded for what was available increased drastically. Also, for many of the posts, the only long forage to be had was the cornstalk, which was scarce and excessively expensive.[88] Beans, onions, and salt were procured in New Mexico, and some fresh vegetables, fruits, and melons were available in season, though not in adequate amounts. Mutton was abundant and cheap. The Commissary Department purchased animals on the hoof and did its own slaughtering, estimating that one sheep would feed seven men for one day.[89] Beef was much less common, particularly in the Río Arriba country. It could usually be bought locally for the posts of Socorro and Doña Ana, and for El Paso and San Elizario it was brought on the hoof from Chihuahua or Texas.

The expenses of the department were increased and the available local supply further depleted by the demands made upon the military to provide escorts for government officials and bearers of official despatches going to the Pacific Coast. Supplies in the hands of the local inhabitants were drained away by the increasing number of emigrants hastening to California by the southern route. All produc-

[87] After Simeon Hart erected his mill opposite El Paso del Norte in 1851, he supplied flour to the southern posts. At times he found it necessary to import flour from Chihuahua to fill his orders. Frazer (ed.), *Mansfield*, 75. See also Strickland, "Six Who Came to El Paso," *Southwestern Studies*, Vol. I (Fall, 1963), 37–42.

[88] Brent to Jesup, November 20, 1850, 31 Cong., 2 sess., *Sen. Exec. Doc. 1*, part II, 291.

[89] Keleher, *Turmoil in New Mexico*, 120, n. 32.

tive parts of New Mexico were affected as the gold seekers entered the settled areas through Taos, Santa Fe, and Albuquerque, then proceeded south along the Río Grande Valley before turning west, or came across Texas and passed through the fertile district about El Paso.[90]

At this time the army rented almost all of the quarters, storehouses, and other facilities it occupied in the department. There were two partial exceptions. Fort Marcy and most of the facilities in Santa Fe belonged to the government, as did the Post of San Elizario, a former Spanish presidio. The army, when it erected its own posts, made use of local materials. Adobe, logs, and stone were the common building materials, and whichever was most readily available in the particular area dictated the type of construction. Only nails, some hardware, and window glass were imported. Firewood was to be had in the vicinity of most of the posts and was sometimes cut by the men, sometimes purchased. Other supplies and all equipment came over the Santa Fe Trail or from the Gulf Coast across Texas. The cost of transportation was a major factor in making the New Mexico posts among the most expensive in the United States to supply.[91]

One activity in which the Americans coming to New Mexico displayed much interest but little knowledge was mining. The idea was widely held that New Mexico had produced large quantities of gold and silver in the Spanish period. In fact, rumors of riches in New Mexico antedated Spanish settlement and continued, with elaboration, down through the years.[92] Very little gold or silver came out of

[90] Jesup to Cross, November 20, 1850, 31 Cong., 2 sess., *Sen. Exec. Doc. 1*, part II, 124; Brent to Jesup, October 9, 1850, *ibid.*, 292; and Joseph H. Whittlesey to Brent, April 21, 1850, *ibid.*, 300.

[91] Only Camp Independence, the future Fort Yuma, was more expensive to supply in 1850, although the short-lived Cantonment Loring in the present Idaho probably would have proved equally costly.

[92] See, for example, José Manuel Espinosa, "The Legend of Sierra Azul," *New Mexico Historical Review*, Vol. IX (April, 1934), 113–58; and Hodge, Hammond, and Rey (eds.), *Fray Alonso de Benevides' Revised Memorial*, 227–29, n. 12.

the area in either the Spanish or Mexican periods, but the excitement first aroused by the reports of the Seven Cities of Cíbola and kept alive by Antonio de Espejo's discovery of silver in 1583 in what is now western Arizona,[93] was not forgotten.

There was some mining in New Mexico in the Spanish period, but the location of the mines and the volume of production became more a matter of legend than fact. It was frequently asserted that rich mines had been worked prior to the Pueblo Revolt of 1680, but that the Indians had filled them in or otherwise concealed them before the reconquest was accomplished. Toward the close of the Spanish period Pedro Bautista Pino wrote, "There are many mineral veins in the mountains, containing silver, gold, copper, lead, etc. Assays have been made of all these metals. It is said that silver cannot be obtained except with quicksilver as a base; fire alone causes it to evaporate."[94] The most important mining activity in the late years of Spanish domination was not gold or silver but copper. The Santa Rita copper mining district, in southwestern New Mexico, was discovered in 1800. Although operations were frequently disrupted by the Apaches, the district produced large quantities of copper which were shipped by mule train to Mexico City. Isolated from the settled portions of New Mexico and oriented toward the south, the Santa Rita mines contributed little to New Mexico's economy at this time.[95]

[93] Herbert Eugene Bolton believed that Espejo reached the region of the Bill Williams Fork, west of the present Prescott, which was, presumably, where he discovered silver. *Spanish Exploration in the Southwest, 1542–1706*, 187, n. 2.

[94] Carroll and Haggard (eds.), *Three New Mexico Chronicles*, 98.

[95] The Santa Rita mines were reputed to produce as much as 4,000,000 pounds of copper a year. In the form of crude ingots, the copper was transported to the south on mule back. During the Mexican period the mine was worked much of the time by Americans, including Sylvestre Pattie, father of the amazing James Ohio Pattie, Robert McKnight, who had become a Mexican citizen, and the infamous James Kirker. Though excellent profits were made, the Apaches were a constant menace and the mines were frequently idle. See Beck, *New Mexico*, 244; and Rex Arrowsmith, *Mines of the Old Southwest*, 29–37.

Mining became more important in the Mexican period. In 1828, gold was discovered in the Ortiz Mountains, between Santa Fe and Albuquerque.[96] The district, which came to be known as the Old Placer, created considerable interest, and additional discoveries were made during the next several years. In 1839 the New Placer district was discovered in the San Pedro Mountains, across the Tuerto Valley and south of the Old Placer. Estimates of the amount of gold produced vary. Josiah Gregg wrote that the Old Placer mines yielded only $30,000 to $40,000 a year after 1835.[97] The Old and New Placer districts together produced some quarter of a million dollars' worth of gold in 1845,[98] which was probably the peak year. James W. Abert, who visited both districts in the fall of 1846, found the methods in use crude. He stated, "At present, none of the owners of these gold mines have ever become wealthy by their mining operations."[99] There was some small-scale silver mining, but the first important silver strike in New Mexico was not made until 1863.[100] The Santa Rita copper mines continued to be worked sporadically, though they were constantly menaced and periodically closed down as a result of Apache raids. There were other small producers of copper and a little lead mining.[101] One of the first important lead mines was owned by Hugh

[96] Stuart A. Northrop, *Minerals of New Mexico*, 18. Northrop states, "This is regarded as the first important discovery of gold west of the Mississippi River."

[97] *Commerce of the Prairies*, 118.

[98] Northrop, *Minerals of New Mexico*, 20. However, Governor Lane, in his message to the territorial legislature for 1852, reported, "The Placer gold mine alone, although imperfectly explored, and rudely worked, with the scanty supply of water, which was transported up the mountain on the back of asses, is said to have yielded, in the year 1845, more than half a million dollars." *Message of William Carr Lane*, 11.

[99] *Report*, 52.

[100] Northrop, *Minerals of New Mexico*, 23.

[101] See Melquiades Antonio Ortega to the Editors of the *Registro Oficial*, January 31, 1831, in "Notes and Documents," *New Mexico Historical Review*, Vol. XXIV (October, 1949), 338–39.

Stephenson[102] in the Organ Mountains of south central New Mexico, originally discovered by a Mexican in 1849.[103]

Despite the comparative unimportance of mining, Americans generally believed that New Mexico was rich in precious metals. Josiah Gregg wrote, "In truth, as some of the natives have justly remarked, New Mexico is almost one continuous *placer*; traces of gold being discovered over nearly the whole surface of the country."[104] John Greiner,[105] who was at various times Indian agent, secretary of the territory, and acting governor, stated in 1852, "The country, poor and miserable as it is in many respects, evidently abounds in mineral wealth. We hear in every direction of gold and silver being discovered."[106] The commonly voiced opinion was that the one key required to unlock the presumed treasure house was control of the Indians. James S. Calhoun expressed that idea when he wrote, "The mineral resources of New Mexico, are believed to be equal to those of any country, and yet, the most daring and enterprizing dare not

[102] Stephenson, a Kentuckian, settled in El Paso district, though at what date is uncertain. There he acquired the property known both as Stephenson's Ranch and as Concordia Ranch. His brother Archibald was a merchant in Chihuahua from at least as early as 1839 until 1847, and Hugh had been engaged in the Chihuahua trade as early as 1824. Moorhead, *New Mexico's Royal Road*, 118, n. 15; and Strickland, "Six Who Came to El Paso," *Southwestern Studies*, Vol. I (Fall, 1963), 34–37.

[103] Northrop, *Minerals of New Mexico*, 22; Arrowsmith, *Mines of the Old Southwest*, 38–43. The mine produced both lead and silver.

[104] *Commerce of the Prairies*, 123.

[105] Greiner, of Ohio, was appointed an Indian Agent for New Mexico in 1851, arriving in Santa Fe in July. He served first at Taos where the Jicarilla Apaches and some Utes were under his jurisdiction. He was appointed territorial secretary in August, 1852, holding office until May, 1853. Lansing B. Bloom (ed.), "Historical Society Minutes, 1859–1863," *New Mexico Historical Review*, Vol. XVIII (October, 1943), 421, n. 218.

[106] Greiner to ———, January 24, 1852, in Tod B. Galloway (ed.), "Private Letters of a Government Official in the Southwest," *Journal of American History*, Vol. III (No. 4, 1909), 547.

venture so far abroad as to ascertain, with any degree of certainty, the mineral wealth of the territory."[107]

The commerce of New Mexico was better known in the United States than any other aspect of the economy. Trade between the States and both Santa Fe and Taos was opened in 1821. Perhaps as early as 1822[108] United States citizens had taken the long road down the Río Grande and across the deserts of northern Mexico to Chihuahua. Later they carried their goods even deeper into Mexico. The Santa Fe trade had been examined in United States government documents and reported in the press. For the general public a more extensive treatment was provided when Josiah Gregg's *Commerce of the Prairies* was published in 1844. There can be no doubt that New Mexico benefited greatly from the Santa Fe trade. A variety of goods was made available in quantity and at a considerably lower price than Mexican products. In fact, Missouri soon replaced Chihuahua as New Mexico's principal source of imported goods. But, with a small and mostly impecunious population to serve, the New Mexican market was soon glutted. The fact was that New Mexico itself produced little to export to Missouri. Gold from the placers, some coarse woolen cloth, a few furs and hides, a small number of sheep, and a little wool made up the bulk of what it had to offer. The silver that formed such an important part of the trade came from Chihuahua or the more southern mining districts. Some buffalo robes, acquired mostly in trade with the Plains Indians, entered into the Missouri trade. Also important, particularly in the 1820's and 1830's, were mules brought into New Mexico from Chihuahua and California and traded for

[107] Calhoun to Brown, October 12, 1850, in Abel (ed.), *Official Correspondence*, 264. Adolph F. A. Bandelier, however, writing at a later date, stated, "The current notions of rich Spanish mines in New Mexico, and of great metalic wealth which the Spaniards derived from that territory, are the purest myths and fables." *Final Report of Investigations Among the Indians of the Southwestern United States, Carried on Mainly in the Years from 1880 to 1885*, I, 195.

[108] See Moorhead, *New Mexico's Royal Road*, 61–65, on the opening of the Chihuahua trade.

goods from Missouri. Barreiro described New Mexico's exports, about 1832, as

> large numbers of sheep, hides, piñones, coarse woolen cloth, tobacco [punche], and other articles which they sell at good prices. . . . Sheep trading is monopolized by a small number of men. Consequently, it must not be considered as beneficial as commerce in hides, coarse woolen cloth, etc. . . . . The eagerness displayed by New Mexicans to carry on trade with neighboring states is truly surprising. In October, especially, one may see a multitude of people going out for that purpose, scattering in all directions: some go to Chihuahua; some go to Pitic or Guaymas; some even go to the fairs of Aguascalientes or San Juan [de los Lagos]; some go to Durango; and some even go to California.[109]

Apparently the commerce with California had its beginnings in 1829 when a party of thirty-one New Mexicans, headed by Antonio Armijo, took a pack train of woolen goods over the Old Spanish Trail to San Gabriel Mission. The woolens, presumably serapes, blankets, and similar items, were traded for horses and mules. Once inaugurated, the trade was continued and grew in importance. As early as 1831, United States citizens began to participate in it.[110] By 1832 the Californians were charging that the New Mexicans were not only acquiring horses and mules in honest trade but stealing them in increasing numbers. The California authorities soon found it necessary to resort to the inspection of departing herds and the use of semi-military expeditions in an effort to recover stolen stock, but without appreciable success.[111] The last of the large pack trains carrying woolens from New Mexico to California departed in 1847 and returned in 1848. For a time the trade in mules was lucrative, but by the 1840's the supply had outstripped the demand.[112]

[109] Carroll and Haggard (eds.), *Three New Mexico Chronicles*, 109.

[110] The California trade is discussed in Leroy R. and Ann W. Hafen, *Old Spanish Trail, Santa Fé to Los Angeles*, 155–94.

[111] The attempts to deal with horse and mule stealing are discussed in *ibid.*, 227–57.

[112] Moorhead, *New Mexico's Royal Road*, 85–86.

The discovery of gold in California and the resultant influx of population greatly stimulated trade between New Mexico and California, but also changed its character. The prospectors flocking to the newly opened mining districts had to be fed, and sheep could be delivered from New Mexico on the hoof. Moreover, the sheep were sold rather than traded, and the profits increased enormously. The first big year of the sheep drives was 1850. William Z. Angney,[113] who had come to New Mexico with Kearny's expeditionary force and remained to become prominent in business and politics, arrived in California with a flock of about 5,000 sheep in the fall of 1850. He had started with 1,000 more, but they had been stolen by rascally herders near Abiquiu. He was offered $40,000 for the sheep in Los Angeles, but refused to sell because he expected to get from $12.00 to $16.00 a head at the mines. He was already planning to bring a flock of as many as 20,000 sheep to California the following year and hoped to purchase them in New Mexico at the "usual" price of $1.00 to $1.50 a head, but was willing to pay $2.00 if necessary. "Sheep are the first article of merchandize in California," he wrote, "and the market cannot be glutted."[114] Perhaps the market could not be glutted, but finding a purchaser who could pay for his sheep in cash was another matter. From San Francisco, four months later, Angney complained that no one outside the banking houses had sufficient money to buy 5,000 sheep, and he was unwilling to sell them for a bill of exchange on the East "which might never be worth a grot." His dissatisfaction was heightened because, as a result of the delay, he had lost, "at least, $50,000, not in the sheep market; but a mule speculation to the Salt Lake."[115]

[113] Angney came to New Mexico in 1846, with General Kearny's expeditionary force, as captain of a company of Missouri volunteers. A lawyer by profession, Angney became active in New Mexico politics, serving as speaker of the house in the first legislative assembly after the United States occupation. Twitchell, *Old Santa Fe*, 312, n. 554.

[114] Angney to Alvarez, December 10, 1850, *Alvarez Papers*, New Mexico Archives.

[115] Angney to Alvarez, April 1, 1851, *ibid.*

If the California sheep trade was not devoid of problems, it was profitable. Flocks were headed west from all parts of New Mexico, crossing the lower Colorado River and the Mojave Desert, then moving north through California to the mining districts. Few animals were lost, and the cost of getting them to California was negligible. The herders were paid a pittance. It cost nothing to feed the sheep, and they provided most of the subsistence for the men who drove them. There are no complete records of the number of sheep driven to California; however, by 1853 it was stated that the grazing lands of New Mexico had been depleted without meeting the demand.[116]

The most esoteric aspect of New Mexico's commerce was the Comanchero trade, which, in fact, involved other Plains tribes as well as the Comanches. Originally the trade was a reasonable development, reflecting the improved relations with the Comanche Indians. Later it degenerated into an abetment of Indian depredations. The Comanchero trade began immediately after the establishment of peace with the Comanches in 1786. One of the principal routes taken by the traders led down the Canadian River, another followed the Pecos to the Bosque Grande then turned east through the Portales Valley.[117] Josiah Gregg, in describing the trade as it was in the Mexican period, said that the Comancheros took to the Indians "trinkets and trumperies of all kinds."[118] The trade also involved iron for arrow points and files to shape the points.[119] Later firewater and firearms were pro-

[116] *Santa Fe Weekly Gazette*, March 26, 1853.

[117] Carroll and Haggard (eds.), *Three New Mexico Chronicles*, 195, n. 335. The Comanche trade was not limited to New Mexican traders. Bent, St. Vrain and Company, operating out of Bent's Fort, participated in it for years. In 1846, Ceran St. Vrain and William Bent erected Fort Adobe north of the Canadian River in the Texas Panhandle to exploit the trade. The fort was abandoned and partly destroyed, probably in 1848. Lavender, *Bent's Fort*, 405, n. 10; 412, n. 8.

[118] *Commerce of the Prairies*, 257.

[119] Ernest Wallace and E. A. Hoebel, *The Comanches*, 104.

vided to the Indians in ever larger quantities, much to the dissatisfaction of the military.[120] If the Comanches were at peace with the New Mexicans, they remained hostile to the rest of the Spanish, and later Mexican, domain. Subsequent changes in political status did not modify their attitude. From the Plains Indians the Comancheros acquired buffalo hides and robes, and, more important, they obtained horses and mules, most of them stolen in Old Mexico, as well as captive Mexicans, many of them children, who were treated as virtual slaves.[121] In the period after the Civil War stolen Texas cattle became a basic item of the trade. Many of these cattle were purchased from the Comancheros by the army to supply the posts in New Mexico.[122] The Comanchero trade continued until the buffalo disappeared from the southern plains and the Indians were forced onto reservations.

Regardless of his reason for going to New Mexico, the average visitor displayed very little tolerance for, or understanding of, the culture of the New Mexican people. Many of them praised the Pueblo Indians or wondered at them, some even found much to admire in the wild Indians, but few had more than an occasional word of compliment for the New Mexicans. In general, commentators expressed the opinion that the women of New Mexico were superior to the men.[123] The average American who bothered to set down his views was critical of the New Mexican male's lack of intelligence, his cowardice, his slothfulness, and his habits generally. The religious practices were questioned, not because they were Roman Catholic, but because they seemed to represent a different form of Roman Catholicism from that practiced in the States. New Mexican architec-

[120] See J. Evetts Haley, "The Comanchero Trade," *Southwestern Historical Quarterly*, Vol. XXXVIII (January, 1935), 157–78.

[121] Rupert N. Richardson, *The Comanche Barrier to South Plains Settlement*, 287.

[122] John McCarty, *Maverick Town, the Story of Old Tascosa*, 12–13.

[123] An interesting discussion of this subject is James M. Lacy, "New Mexican Women in Early American Writings," *New Mexico Historical Review*, Vol. XXXIV (January, 1959), 41–51.

ture drew few converts. The towns were most frequently described as resembling brick kilns. Yet most visitors admitted that the typical New Mexican home was comfortable and utilitarian.

Not all of the comments were unfavorable. The attitudes of persons from the States, both military and civilian, who visited and described New Mexico in the years following the Mexican War differed markedly. Santa Fe, as the capital and metropolis of New Mexico, received particular attention. The descriptions ran the gamut from sheer delight at the natural beauties of the country, the picturesqueness of the towns, and the friendly qualities of the people, to utter condemnation of almost everything. There can be little doubt that many who passed judgment on New Mexico adopted an attitude commonly attributed to Americans abroad. Whatever deviated from home was rejected; hence, anything new and strange was criticized adversely, regardless of its merit.

Whatever the merits of New Mexican culture may have been, there was one field in which there was adequate room for dissatisfaction, and the New Mexicans themselves had been voicing their dissatisfaction for years. This was the area of education. As early as 1825 the complaint was made that there was not a satisfactory school in Santa Fe or a properly trained teacher. What was equally disturbing, the parents of children seemed unmindful of the quality of the educational facilities.[124] Yet Antonio Barreiro recorded that no one in the province was better paid than the public school teachers. He also wrote, "The schools were in a deplorable condition. No noticeable results were achieved by primary instruction, a condition which was due both to the neglect, carelessness, and ignorance of many of the teachers and to the lack of interest shown by the authorities." At this time, about 1832, schools were located at Santa Fe, San Miguel del Bado, Santa Cruz de la Cañada, Taos, Albuquerque, and Belen. The

[124] Report of Antonio Sena, Juan Diego Sena, and Francisco Baca y Ortiz to Governor Bartolomé Baca, January 11, 1825, *Read Collection*, New Mexico Archives.

total amount paid in annual salary to the teachers was 1,850 pesos.[125]

The United States census of 1850 listed 8 school teachers in all of New Mexico and reported a total of 466 pupils attending schools, all of which were private. The number of adults who could not read and write was placed at 25,089.[126] Colonel Joseph K. F. Mansfield wrote in 1853 that there were "not more than two schools in the whole Territory" and that both were in Santa Fe. One of these had been organized by Bishop Jean B. Lamy, the other by a Baptist missionary, Hiram W. Read, who also served as chaplain at Fort Marcy. Read's school was in existence, though with a minute enrollment, in 1850, but the Roman Catholic school was not organized until 1852.[127] In addition to these schools, two others were functioning by 1853. The Academy of Our Lady of Light, the first Catholic school for girls in New Mexico, opened in Santa Fe on January 1, 1853, operated by the Sisters of Loreto. Another Baptist missionary, Samuel Gorman, had established a school for Indian children at Laguna Pueblo in 1852.[128]

An interesting document in the New Mexico Archives, unfortunately undated, is a report of the inspection of the schools of Pecos, San José, and Las Ruedas, the last of which was not examined because it was not in session. At Pecos there were eight children, five or six years of age, in "*primeras letras*." There were fifty-three children who knew how to read and write and were studying English, geography, orthography, and arithmetic. In addition, there were six young persons (*jovenes*) of ten years and up who could speak and translate

[125] Carroll and Haggard (eds.), *Three New Mexico Chronicles*, 95–96.

[126] *Seventh Census of the United States*, lx, 1002–1005. However, Lieutenant Abert observed in 1847 that "I have been much surprised by the many men and children of the lower class that I have met with who both read and write; in fact, all that we questioned seemed to be educated." *Report*, 104.

[127] Frazer (ed.), *Mansfield*, 6; and Twitchell, *Leading Facts of New Mexican History*, II, 321–23.

[128] Arnold L. Rodríguez, "New Mexico in Transition," *New Mexico Historical Review*, Vol. XXIV (October, 1949), 270, 272.

English. At San José no English was taught because the teacher himself did not know English.[129] The inspection was probably made sometime between 1854 and 1860. When the territory was created, the United States set aside certain lands for the support of schools; but, as Governor Calhoun pointed out in 1851, until they had been officially surveyed, they would be unavailable. He expressed the belief that, because of the "peculiar topography" of New Mexico and the numerous land grants in existence, much of the school land would still be unavailable, even after the surveys had been made.[130]

[129] "*El Presidente y Cuerpo de Supervisión de Escuelas*," *Vigil Papers*, New Mexico Archives.

[130] Governor's Message, December 3, 1851, *Journal of the House of Representatives*, New Mexico Archives, 12.

# III. McCALL AND NEW MEXICO

ONCE THE MEXICAN WAR had ended and the transfer of New Mexico and California to the United States was assured, the added cost of maintaining the army in the West became a matter of increasing concern. In 1850 a comparison of expenses in the area which comprised the United States prior to 1845 and the area since acquired gave a clear picture of mounting costs. Departments Numbers 1 through 7 made up the older portion of the United States. The recently added territory was divided into Departments Numbers 8 (Texas), 9 (New Mexico), 10 (California), and 11 (the Oregon Country). In the older departments the expenditures for the fiscal year 1849–50 amounted to $2,413,580.74, whereas in the newer departments they came to $7,444,261.26.[1] The expenses of the Quartermaster's Department had increased from $870,999.73 for the year ending June 30, 1844, to $4,295,298.60 for the year ending June 30, 1850. The cost of military transportation, an expense of the Quartermaster's Department, had risen for the same years from less than $120,000 to about $1,900,000.[2]

During the fiscal year 1850–51, contractors moved 422 wagon loads of supplies from Fort Leavenworth to the posts in New Mexico,

[1] "Statement of Current Expenses," 31 Cong., 2 sess., *Sen. Exec. Doc. 1*, part II, 109.

[2] Conrad to Fillmore, November 30, 1850, *ibid.*, 8–9.

a total of 2,150,414 pounds of freight. The rate per one hundred pounds to Santa Fe varied from as little as $7.87½ to as much as $14.33½. The rate to Albuquerque, based on one consignment of thirty wagons, was $9.50 per hundred pounds. For supplies sent from Fort Leavenworth to the Post of El Paso the cost ranged from $12.80 to $13.87½.[3] These charges were less than those for small private shipments sent from Independence, Missouri, which in 1850 were from 15 to 20 cents per pound.[4] Quartermaster General Thomas S. Jesup stated that the strength of the army was little more than 50 per cent greater than it had been before the Mexican War, but the transportation costs for the year 1849–50 had increased by more than 1,500 per cent. He further explained the expenses of his department thus:

> In the present condition of the newly-acquired territories, with the posts established for their defence necessarily so far from the sources of supply, and so large a portion of their garrisons mounted, more than ten thousand horses, oxen, and mules are constantly required for transportation, and for mounting guides, spies, escorts, and troops; forage is therefore a heavy item of expense. The supply of fuel is limited throughout those territories, and is obtained with difficulty at many of the present posts: it is a heavy item. So is the hire of mechanics, laborers, and other operatives; also the rent, erection and repair of quarters, barracks, storehouses, and other structures required for the service. The expense of neither can be much reduced, even with the most faithful and rigid administration, unless the circumstances of the whole country in relation to its cultivation, communications, and means of defence, be changed.[5]

[3] "Statement of Supplies Forwarded by Contractors' Trains from Fort Leavenworth, Mo.," 32 Cong., 1 sess., *House Exec. Doc.* 2, 295.

[4] Bills and receipts in *Alvarez Papers*, New Mexico Archives. However, in the case of some packages of garden seeds sent by mail carrier the shipping charge was $1.50 per pound. Waldo, Hall, and Company to Alvarez, January 31, 1851, *ibid.*

[5] Jesup to Cross, November 20, 1850, 31 Cong., 2 sess., *Sen. Exec.*

The War Department was understandably concerned at the enormous increase in the cost of maintaining a military establishment, the manpower of which had not increased proportionally. From 1842 to 1846 the legal strength of the regular army was 8,613 officers and men. Early in 1846 the regiment of mounted riflemen was added, bringing the total to 9,418. At the close of the Mexican War the legal strength was fixed at 10,120; then, by an act of Congress on June 17, 1850, it was increased on a sliding scale which provided additional strength for companies "serving on the western frontier and at remote stations."[6] The aggregate legal size of the army, as of November 30, 1850, was 12,927 officers and men, but the actual size was only 10,763, including unassigned recruits, unattached soldiers, the West Point detachment, and those absent from their posts as well as those present. The number of officers and men, including division and department staffs, at their assigned stations was 7,655, of whom 3,468 were in the four new departments. From these same four departments 470 officers and men were absent, the greatest number, 169, being absent from New Mexico.[7] It is immediately obvious that there was an incredible discrepancy between the legal strength of the army, the actual strength, and the number of officers and men present for duty at the posts. Even if all had been present, the total would have been but 4,556 in the seven old departments and 3,938 in the four new ones, or a total of 8,494.[8]

*Doc. 1*, part II, 122. The cost of transporting pork and flour, "the two most important items of supply," is revealing:

| | *For pork* | *For flour* |
|---|---|---|
| To the nearer interior posts of Texas, per barrel | $8.00 | $5.30 |
| To Santa Fe and Las Vegas | 32.00 | 21.30 |
| To Taos, Socorro, Abiquiu, and Cebolleta | 41.60 | 27.56 |
| To El Paso del Norte, San Elizario, and Doña Ana | 48.00 | 31.80 |

Conrad to Fillmore, November 30, 1850, *ibid.*, 5.

[6] Winfield Scott to Conrad, November 30, 1850, *ibid.*, 114.

[7] See tables for the "Position and Distribution of Troops," *ibid.*, following page 116.

[8] Major General Scott, in 1849, estimated that, whatever the legal

In three areas, particularly, the cost of maintaining the army in New Mexico was considered exceptionally high—transportation, purchasing supplies locally, and renting facilities. Transportation of supplies was provided under contract by private individuals or freighting companies. The only means of achieving an appreciable reduction in transportation costs would be by securing a larger portion of the supplies in the department. However, prices were generally higher for supplies purchased in New Mexico than for similar supplies in the East, though lower than on the Pacific Coast, where the gold rush had led to unchecked inflation.[9] Beginning in 1851 an effort was made to reduce expenses when all permanent posts were instructed to cultivate kitchen gardens, and all such western posts "as may be designated by department commanders" were to cultivate farms for the production of "grains for bread and forage, and long forage."[10] Both gardens and farms were planted at most of the New Mexican posts in 1852 and 1853 with an almost uniform lack of success.[11]

The other area in which costs were considered excessive was that of

---

strength of the army, only about 55 per cent of that number could be expected to be present at the posts and fit for duty. Scott to Crawford, November 23, 1849, 31 Cong., 1 sess., *Sen. Exec. Doc. 1*, 100.

[9] A sampling of bills and receipts for goods sold in Santa Fe in 1850 and 1851 gives some idea of the prices then current in New Mexico:

| | | | |
|---|---|---|---|
| tobacco (imported) | $1.75/pound | tin cups | .20 each |
| tobacco (punche) | .45/pound | calico | .25/yard |
| 1 bottle port wine | 1.20 | pant stuff | .35/yard |
| 1 bottle brandy | 2.50 | 1 dozen buttons | .25 |
| 1 box seidlitz powder | .50 | 1 under shirt | 1.50 |
| 1 ball soap | 1.00 | 1 pair gloves | 1.50 |
| candles | .25/pound | 1 handkerchief | 1.25 |
| ink | .25/bottle | sugar | .28/pound |
| 1 camp kettle | 2.50 | coffee | .34/pound |

*Alvarez Papers*, New Mexico Archives.

[10] General Orders No. 1, January 8, 1851, 32 Cong., 1 sess., *House Exec. Doc. 2*, 164.

[11] Frazer (ed.), *Mansfield*, 34, 62–64.

providing quarters and other facilities. Only at the posts of Santa Fe and San Elizario were there buildings owned by the government. At Santa Fe the Palace of the Governors was occupied by the commander of the department in his capacity as civil governor.[12] Offices and quarters for all other officers were rented. The troops were quartered in barracks erected by the Mexican government, and stables, corrals, and other structures were built by the Quartermaster's Department on land claimed by the United States. At San Elizario the old presidio had been repaired sufficiently to serve as quarters for the men and to provide all other facilities except quarters for the officers, which were rented. Because western military posts were constructed largely by the labor of troops, making use of materials available locally, the cost of building a post was soon offset by the saving in rentals. Yet the construction of posts presented a problem in some departments. In 1849, Quartermaster General Jesup made this proposal:

> It is highly important that the principal points to be occupied in all our new territories, whether as posts or depots, be determined upon with as little delay as possible; and, as the United States own no land in Texas, and probably none in New Mexico and California at the points proper to be occupied, it is necessary that the authority of Congress be obtained to purchase such sites as may be required.[13]

Beginning in 1851, a policy was inaugurated to curtail expenditures for rentals. Garrisons were removed from all towns except Santa Fe, and posts, intended to be permanent, were erected away from centers of population. Some of the posts were on land claimed by the government; others were on land leased for the purpose. By 1853 none of the posts inspected by McCall in 1850, except Santa Fe, were still in existence.[14]

[12] When James S. Calhoun received his appointment as territorial governor, Major Munroe promptly vacated the palace and turned it over to Calhoun.

[13] Jesup to Crawford, November 10, 1849, 31 Cong., 1 sess., *Sen. Exec. Doc. 1*, 194. See also Robert J. Walker to Polk, July 19, 1848, and enclosures, 30 Cong., 1 sess., *House Exec. Doc. 70*, 9–10.

[14] See Conrad to Sumner, April 1, 1851, 32 Cong., 1 sess., *Sen. Exec.*

It was into this situation of official semi-ignorance and mounting concern that George Archibald McCall moved in 1850. McCall had been born in Philadelphia, Pennsylvania, in 1802.[15] He attended the United States Military Academy, from which he graduated in 1822, ranking twenty-sixth in a class of forty. His first appointment was to the rank of second lieutenant, First United States Infantry, but he transferred to the Fourth Infantry before joining his regiment. Much of his early military career was spent in Florida, an experience which he enjoyed and which left a lasting impression on his youthful mind. Four months before he died, he wrote that Florida was a "country whose climate, in mildness and salubrity, yields to that of no other portion of our national domain; a land where the atmosphere is so pure and bright that the mere sense of existence is absolutely a physical as well as a moral pleasure, not appreciable by one who has not experienced it."[16] Perhaps he had forgotten that the first sight which greeted him upon his arrival in Florida was the corpse of a man newly dead of yellow fever.[17]

In 1831, McCall was appointed to act as aide-de-camp to Brigadier General Edmund P. Gaines.[18] Until 1836 he served at Fort Arm-

---

*Doc. 1*, 125–26. The Post of Albuquerque was abandoned in 1851 but re-established in 1852, at which time it became department headquarters. The Post of El Paso was re-established in 1854, though not in the same location, and was designated Fort Bliss that same year. The garrison at Santa Fe was drastically reduced, but the post was not abandoned. Entries for August 31, 1852, and December 23, 1852, *Executive Record, 1851–1867*, New Mexico Archives, 35, 56; and *Post Returns of Fort Marcy, New Mexico*, The National Archives.

[15] McCall to Lorenzo Thomas, August 20, 1861, Commission Branch: File M752 of 1863, Relating to George A. McCall, Records of the Adjutant General's Office, The National Archives. Much of the data for McCall's official career is taken from his service record in *ibid.*

[16] *Letters from the Frontier, Written during a Period of Thirty Years' Service in the Army of the United States*, iv.

[17] McCall to H———, November 8, 1822, *ibid.*, 12.

[18] Gaines to McCall, April 2, 1831, *ibid.*, 223–24. Brigadier General

strong, Jefferson Barracks, Memphis, and other western posts. He then spent some time in Philadelphia on recruiting service before he was transferred, once again, to the frontier, this time serving at Fort Gibson, in the present Oklahoma, where he remained until 1841. Then he returned to well-remembered Florida for a year, participating in the Seminole War, before he was sent back to the West, where he was stationed first at Jefferson Barracks, then at Fort Scott. He joined Colonel Zachary Taylor in Texas in the spring of 1845 and was involved in the Mexican War from its beginning, being twice brevetted for gallant and meritorious conduct in the early months of the war. Before the war ended, McCall was bothered by the ill health which he later attributed to the long years he had spent in malarial climates. On April 5, 1847, he was granted a four months' leave of absence.[19] Actually, almost two years were to pass before he returned to military duty, part of which time he spent in England in an effort to recuperate.[20]

Upon his return to duty in March, 1849, McCall was ordered to report to his regiment, the Third United States Infantry, stationed in New Mexico.[21] Shortly thereafter, Secretary of War George W. Crawford requested McCall to confer with him in Washington before proceeding to the West.[22] The reason for the request was simple, based on the failure of the Congress to make adequate provision for the territory annexed from Mexico at the close of the Mexican War. In view of the anomalous situation in which the territory was placed by Congressional inaction, President Zachary Taylor recommended to the people of both California and New Mexico that they "form a

and Brevet Major General Edmund P. Gaines was commander of the Western Department of the Army. Thian, *Notes Illustrating the Military Geography*, 107.

[19] General Orders No. 93, Vera Cruz, April 5, 1847, Commission Branch: File M752 of 1863.

[20] McCall, *Letters from the Frontier*, 334, 485.

[21] Special Orders No. 69, November 8, 1849, *ibid.*, 485.

[22] Crawford to McCall, November 12, 1849, 31 Cong., 1 sess., *House Exec. Doc. 17*, 280.

plan of a State constitution and submit the same to Congress, with a prayer for admission into the Union as a State."[23] James S. Calhoun, who arrived in Santa Fe on July 22, 1849, to assume his position as Indian agent, apparently declared that he had secret instructions from the government to encourage the New Mexican people to erect their territory into a state.[24] Annie Heloise Abel, editor of Calhoun's official correspondence, stated, "Calhoun was most certainly sent to Santa Fé for a purpose but what the real purpose was does not appear."[25] Certainly, when two factions developed in New Mexico, one favoring statehood and the other territorial status, Calhoun was aligned with the statehood party.

In the case of McCall there is no question. He was given specific instructions by Secretary of War Crawford to encourage the people of New Mexico to seek statehood:

> Since their annexation, these Territories [California and New Mexico], in respect to their civil governments, have in a great measure depended on the officers of the army there in command; a duty it is considered as falling beyond their appropriate spheres of action, and to be relieved from which cannot be more desired by them than by this department. This condition has arisen from the omission of Congress to provide suitable governments, and in regard to the future there is reason to believe that the difficulties of the past are still to be encountered. In every possible aspect, it is important both to New Mexico and the United States that these embarrassments should be quickly removed.
>
> It is not doubted that the people of New Mexico desire and want a government organized, with all proper functions for the protection and security of their persons and property.
>
> The question readily occurs, how that government can be supplied? I have already adverted to past and still existing difficulties, that have retarded, and may continue to retard, the action of the United States in respect to this necessary and first want. To remove it may, in some degree, be the part of the duty of officers of the army,

[23] Message of President Taylor, January 21, 1850, *ibid.*, 1–2.

[24] Davis, *El Gringo*, 111.

[25] *Official Correspondence*, xiii.

on whom, under the necessities of the case, has been devolved a partial participation in their civil affairs. It is therefore deemed proper that I should say, that it is not believed that the people of New Mexico are required to await the movements of the federal government, in relation to a plan of a government proper for the regulation of their own internal concerns.

The constitution of the United States and the late treaty with Mexico guarantee their admission into the Union of our States, subject only to the judgment of Congress. Should the people of New Mexico wish to take any steps towards this object, so important and necessary to themselves, it will be your duty, and the duty of others with whom you are associated, not to thwart but advance their wishes. It is their right to appear before Congress and ask for admission into the Union.

Other and complicated questions may arise, which are considered as merged in this essential right of these people, and for the decision of which we must look beyond the authority of the Executive.

It will be instructive, and probably necessary information, when the people of New Mexico form a constitution and seek admission into the confederacy of the States, to have your observation and views on their probable numbers, habits, customs, and pursuits of life.[26]

McCall left Philadelphia in November, 1849, and traveled overland to New Orleans, being detained some time en route by illness. From New Orleans he proceeded by steamer to Indianola, on Matagorda Bay, Texas, then overland to San Antonio, which he reached on December 31, 1849.[27] After more than a month's delay, awaiting the arrival of recruits who were to accompany him to New Mexico,[28] McCall left San Antonio on February 2, 1850. His party crossed to El Paso, then went north to Santa Fe, arriving on March 11, 1850.[29]

[26] Crawford to McCall, November 19, 1849, 31 Cong., 1 sess., *House Exec. Doc. 17*, 280–81.

[27] McCall, *Letters from the Frontier*, 486.

[28] Jefferson Van Horne to Lafayette McLaws, February 2, 1850, Abel (ed.), *Official Correspondence*, 163.

[29] McCall to M———, February 19, 1850; and March 12, 1850, *Letters from the Frontier*, 490.

"The evening of my arrival," McCall wrote, ". . . I opened to some of the leading men the object of my mission, and enlisted them in the cause I desired to advance."[30] What McCall's—or, for that matter, Calhoun's—influence upon the leading men of New Mexico may have been is difficult to determine. The very limited local press of the period casts no light on the subject, nor does the available correspondence. It must be assumed that some influence was present, and it may well have been that provided by California in its progress toward statehood, since all previous efforts in New Mexico had been directed toward the achievement of territorial status.

Whatever the impetus, the movement to secure statehood for New Mexico was stepped up. At a meeting held in Santa Fe on April 20, 1850, a resolution was prepared requesting Brevet Colonel John Munroe to call a convention.[31] Munroe complied, finding sufficient expression of opinion, "both in the form of petitions from and personal representations by the people," to justify the election of delegates to consider the formation of a state government for New Mexico.[32] Specifically, in calling for an election, he stated that "the people of New Mexico have, by public meetings held in the several counties of this Territory, expressed a desire to hold a convention for the formation of a State constitution, and to urge upon Congress the admission of this Territory into the Union as a State."[33] New Mexico was at this time divided into seven counties, embracing all of the settled portions. In how many of the counties meetings were actually held is not clear. The meeting in Santa Fe took place only three days before Munroe issued his election proclamation.

[30] McCall to M———, March 12, 1850, *ibid.*, 492.

[31] Twitchell, *Leading Facts of New Mexican History*, II, 271. Major and Brevet Colonel John Munroe, Second Artillery, assumed command of the department on October 23, 1849. He was the last military governor of New Mexico, filling the office until March 3, 1851. He remained in command of the department until July 18, 1851.

[32] Munroe to Jones, May 13, 1850, 31 Cong., 1 sess., *Sen. Exec. Doc. 60*, part II, 2.

[33] "Proclamation," April 23, 1850, *ibid.*

# NEW MEXICAN.

VOLUME I] "Magna est Veritas, es prevalebit" [NUMBER 1

DAVIS & JONES, Editors and Proprietors. | SANTA FE, N. M., NOVEMBER 24, 1849. | Published at $7.00 Per Annum, in Advance.

## PROSPECTUS

FOR A WEEKLY PUBLICATION, TO BE ENTITLED, THE NEW MEXICAN

THE subscribers propose to publish, in this city, a weekly publication, with the above title, to be devoted to the interests of the Territory of New Mexico in general.

The New Mexican, in Politics and Religion, will maintain a strict neutrality, regarding partizanship as utterly unnecessary and a barrier to the general good of our Territory.

The views entertained by the people of New Mexico, in Convention assembled, for the purpose of urging upon Congress the immediate formation of a Supreme Civil Government, will also find an able advocacy in the columns of the New Mexican. The want of more efficient means to suppress the numerous Indian tribes that surround us, will be promptly laid before our Government.

The advancement of Literature, the Arts and Sciences, and Agriculture, will meet with general attention.

The New Mexican will be published on a semi-medium sheet, and issued to subscribers at the low price of Seven Dollars per annum, or Four Dollars for six months, and Two Dollars and Fifty Cents for three months.

☞ To those of our friends residing out of the city, we would state, that Agents will be appointed in all parts of the Territory, of whom they will receive their papers regularly.

TERMS OF ADVERTISING.

Advertisements will be inserted at the rate of One Dollar per square of ten lines or less, and Seventy-five Cents for each continuance.

☞ Law or Business Cards, not exceeding five lines, inserted at the rate of Two Dollars and Fifty Cents per month.

E. T. DAVIES & W. E. JONES.

## ADVERTISEMENTS.

In the Santa Fe County Circuit Court, October Term, A. D. 1849.

John Kelly, vs John Leefe } Attachment

NOW, at this day, comes the plaintiff by his Attorney, and the said defendant not appearing to answer the action, on motion of said plaintiff, by his Attorney, it is ordered by the Court, that the said defendant John Leefe, be notified that suit has been commenced against him upon a note of hand for two hundred and eighty-four dollars and twenty-five cents, and that his property has been attached, and that unless he be and appear at the next term of the Circuit Court, to be holden in the City of Santa Fe, on the fourth Monday of February next, 1850, and plead to the action aforesaid, within two days of the commencement of said Court, judgment will be rendered against him, and his property sold to satisfy the same; and it is further ordered, that a copy of this order be published in some newspaper, published in the Territory for at least four weeks, the last insertion to be at least two weeks before the first day of the setting of said Court.

A true copy of the order.

Attest

JAMES M. GIDDINGS, Clerk.

Skinner Atty. for Plaintiff.

Santa Fe Oct 24.—No. 1.—4w

LIST OF LETTERS

RECEIVED by the Mall of the 12th of November, 1849.

A

Anderson Alex Gen — Anderson E T
Anderson James M — Ashley Philip
Anderson Jas V — Allen R L
Anderson Jos A Dr

B

Branton Thomas B — Buford James M
Blumer Charles — Bassanet Thomas
Bradley Wm L — Bohrer Alex L
Baynton Edwin N

C

Cook Morgan B — Cunliffe Henry
Coons Benj F — Cumming Jas Dr
Carson David

D

Deadarick David A — Dalton Wm T
Diffendeffer David — Deroin Emanuel
Deus Charles — Duncan John
Denny Alexander — Dickson Wm

E

Ellis Jos S — Estes Geo N
Ewing Finis Y

F

Flourney S H Dr

G

Goodfellow Wm — Graff Washington
[illegible] J P Dr

H

Harris Wm J — Honey B A
Henry W S — Hickman James P
Heslep Joseph

I J

Ingles John C & H — Jones J G 2
Iridell J B — Johnson James Lewis
Johnson Anthony D

K

Kemp Frederick — King Andrew L

L

Lucas J S, J A & W — Lee Andrew
Lee B F — Livingston Sidney S
Le Blanc F N

M

Malston Chas W — Marr John P
March Robert — Mignault Theodore
Moss Abraham — Mather Richard L
Miller David

Mc's

McNult Moses H — McShane Philip
McKnight H S — McDougal Jas A
McKinney Richard — McIntire John
McSlays Samuel — McCarty Charles

N

Newman S B

O

Owens Richard — Ogden Lewis A Dr

P

Porter John R — Pool James
Porter Wm H D — Peter Henry K

R

Rodgers Wm P — 2 Rucker Thos O
Ross James M — 2 Ramsey W H & F A
Rees E M

S

Selding de Edward — Spencer Smith Orrin
Spencer Chas B — Stone L H, M D
Senechal & Co — Smith R D
Schofield A Sprat — Stuart Jacob
Stokes Franklin E — Streck M Dr

T

Thwaits Edward — Theakston Wm
Thomas Chas Carroll — Tudor Wm

V

Venable Joseph

W

Weber John E — Williams John
White Samuel M — Williams Robt G
Wethered Geo Y — Wilbar Joseph 6
Webb John J — Ware John
Webster Christopher — Williams Henry Miller
Weyman Jane Mrs

Y

Yurley Jesse B

### Tit-For-Tat.

Some genius in the New Journal of Commerce hits off Homoeopathy in this wise:

HOMOEOPATHY

Take a little rum,
The less you take the better,
Mix it with the lakes
Of Wenner and of Wetter.

Dip a spoonful out—
Mind you don't get groggy—
Pour it in the Lake
Winnipisiogee.

Stir the mixture well,
Lest it prove inferior;
Then put half a drop
Into Lake Superior

Every other day,
Take a drop in water,
You'll be better soon;
Or, at least, you ought to. 1

1,000,000 oo

The following keen retort to the above is published in the Newark Daily Advertiser.

Allopathy.

Take some calomel,
The more you take the better,
Mix it with a drop
Or two of cistern water.

Feed some to your dog;
It will make him vomit,
And may be see stars,
And perhaps a comet.

Once in each half hour,
Take a rousing portion;
Say a tumbler full,
If that suits your notion.

Should you chance to die,
As you are not sure to,
You may safely swear
That it did not cure you. 999

1,000

## FOREIGN NEWS.

GREAT NEWS FROM CUBA!

An extra from the Delta Office, N. Orleans, placards a "Revolution in Cuba," and "Great Excitement throughout the Island." This is done on the authority of some letters from Havana, written by some one subscribing himself "The American," and who, from the tone of his correspondence is evidently himself, very much excited, and anxious that a revolution should take place whether it has or not. These letters, however, show only that there has been a movement of military from Havana to Puerto Principe, and that some militia have been ordered into service. The writer speaks too of great excitement in Havana, and it may be that he does not exaggerate it.

From his letter of the 26th ult., we take what follows:

The reports this evening are that a regiment leaves to-morrow morning for Puerto Principe, where, the BALL has opened—the troops disarmed by the people, and possession taken of the public works. Ammunition wagons, &c. have been passing all the afternoon, and the excitement is immense. All names of foreigners is being registered, particularly Americans, and it is understood they must not be found talking in parties at the corners or in their own stores or dwellings.

Monday Morning, 27th.

The reports are so varied with every newcomer from the EAST, that we hardly know what to believe—but the Government action passing under our eyes, shows that there is cause enough somewhere: a thousand men have just embarked on a steamer for Puerto Principe—a body of lancers and a battalion of artillery are on the way by land—flying artillery, guns and carriages packed on the backs of mules very neatly. The appearance of the troops is credible—they move in fatigue dress, but there is many a heart that preys for success to the cause against which they have to fight.

The reports are, that Puerto Principe, Trinidad, and St. Jago de Cuba, have pronounced for independence, and that the troops at those points have joined the people.

In a letter of the 29th, he informs us that four thousand militia are called into service, two-thirds of which are Creoles. Conde Lautevenia, Conde O'Riley, Marquis Estevan, have been appointed Commanders of Regiments.

The English Consul has written to Jamaica for all the English squadrons that can be had for the protection of British subjects and property. The American Consul does the same by this steamer—there being here will make all secure, and business will not be interrupted, at any time, twenty-four hours—six will do all needful work here. Alcoy says, if he is to be looser in the game, he will let the blacks loose upon the whites—"en junta." The General of Marines says arm old and young—Spaniards born to protect themselves in the street; which means assassinate all Creoles and foreigners. This was put down by Alcoy. To imprison all influential Creoles was negatived by the same. To levy an extraordinary voluntary forced contribution on the city, was proposed by Alcoy, and negatived by the Conde Vileo Nueve, Intendente, the only wise, good head the Government has here. This is all effervescence, and will work off without the imagined evil; for if any improper act should be proposed, Alcoy would be headless in twenty-four hours—such as the negro proposition.

### HUNGARY—ADDRESS OF M. KOSSUTH.

The following eloquent address to the nations of Europe, forms a part of a proclamation recently issued by M. Kossuth:

"The armies of the Hungarian nation have always fought out their quarrel with Austria. The liberated country need only to be made to flourish. But the House of Hapsburg Lorraine, had once more petitioned the Russian despot for aid, and he broke into Hungary at the head of 12000 Russian troops through Cronstadt, Lemberg and Vienna he broke into our country—the country of martyrs of liberty.

'We did not throw down our arms. We will fight the armies of the allied tyrants of Europe. God is just; his power is almighty; he hallows the battle field for the weak, and the strength of the mighty and wicked is broken.

'But we would speak aloud and solemn warning to the unconstitutional Governments and the nations of Europe.

'Ye Governments! ye are the official guardians of the liberty and the legitimate interests not only of your own countries, but of all Europe. A tremendous responsibility rests upon you. The punishment of every crime which you allow to be committed against liberty and the right of man will come home to you and the lands ye govern!

'Wake up, oh ye people! at the approach of this enormous danger. The tyrant's armies are banded together to tread under foot, and to silence every free word. They have begun in Germany, in Italy, and in this our land of Hungary!

'Thou haughty English nation! Hast thou forgotten that thou hast decreed this principle of non-intervention, that thou now sufferest an intervention directed against constitutional liberty, but thou lendest aid to the banner of tyranny by suffering this coalition of tyrants. The proud pennon of the British mast is threatened with disgrace God will withdraw the blessing he has lent it, if it prove untrue to the cause to which it owes its fame.

'Awake, oh people of Europe! On Hungarian grounds the battle of freedom is fighting. With this country the free world will lose a powerful member. In this nation a true and heroic champion will perish. For we shall fight until we spill the last drop of blood, that our country may either become a chosen sanctuary of freedom consecrated with our blood, or shall form a damning monument to all eternity in token of the manner in which tyrants can league to destroy free people and free nations, and of the shameful manner in which free countries abandon one another.

Signed. L. KOSSUTH, Governor.
B. SZEMERE, Pres. of Council.

Pesth, July 31.

### THE QUEEN AMONG THE IRISH.

The English papers chronicle the progress of the Queen's visit to Ireland. The royal party arrived at Cork on the 24 of August.

The reception of the Queen at Cork, Kingston, and Dublin was flattering and enthusiastic in the highest degree. The wild clamorous shout of her Majesty's Irish subjects was, it is said, a sight never to be forgotten—a sound that will be recollected for ever.

At Dublin, addresses were made to her Majesty by the Lord Mayor, and the Bishops and Arch Bishops of the Irish portion of the church of England, also by the Bishops and Arch Bishops of the Roman Catholic church, by the now subscribing Presbyterians in Ireland, and the Society of Friends, to all of which answers were given.

Of the enthusiasm of her reception on her arrival at Dublin, the European Times says:

Ladies threw away the old formula of waving of white pocket handkerchiefs, and cheered for their lives, while the men, pressing in so closely as to throng the very edge of the pavilion, waved whatever came first to hand, hand, hat, stick, wand or coat, (for the day was very hot,) and rent the air with shouts of joy, which never decreased in energy 'till their beloved sovereign was far out of sight. The Queen, turning from side to side, bowed low repeatedly. Prince Albert shared in, and acknowledged the plaudits of the people, while the royal children were objects of universal attention and admiration. Oh! Queen, dear!" screamed a stout lady, make one of them Prince Patrick, and all Ireland will die for you!" Indeed, her Majesty seemed to feel the warmth of her reception.

She paused at the end of the platform for a moment, and again making her acknowledgements, was hailed with one universal and tremendous cheer as she entered the terminus.

### ITALIAN AFFAIRS.

The London correspondent of the Philadelphia American, in a letter of the 31st August, received by the Europa, writes as follows in reference to the Pope, and the probabilities of further disturbances in Italy.

The affairs of Italy are as far from being settled as they were before a French soldier landed at Civita Vecchia. The Pope is just as far from the Eternal City, and the people are in a more disconted and revolutionary mood. Gen. Oudinot is recalled, and Gen. Rostolan is the new commander-in-chief. The conduct of the Pontificial government is displeasing to France, and to the Romans as a nation. So long as French bayonets bristle in Rome, so long all will be the peace; but the moment those 30,000 foreign troops are withdrawn, a new revolution will be commenced. Mazzini and his friends are at Geneva. Ledru Rollin and other revolutionists are also there; and they intend to hold a Congress, for the avowed purpose of organizing their respective forces, and preparing for another political campaign. If Mazzini once more reaches Italy, and Ledru Rollin reaches France at the opportune moment two Republics in Europe may yet be firmly established.

Mazzini, in a recent letter, truly says that the balance of power in Europe is destroyed. It consisted formerly in the support given to the smaller States by the great powers; now they are abandoned. France in Italy; Russia in Hungary; Prussia in Germany: these are now the masters of the continent. England is thus made a nullity.—Joseph Mazzini speaks the words of truth.

*Courtesy the* New Mexican

The *New Mexican* was one of the few sources of information about New Mexico available to the United States in 1849–50.

*Courtesy New Mexico State Tourist Bureau*

Sena Plaza, Santa Fe, the home of Juan Sena in 1850, was built in 1830. McCall lived here while writing "Report on the Conditions of New Mexico."

The delegates assembled on May 15, and ten days later concluded a state constitution. Again, Munroe was asked to issue a proclamation for an election, this time to vote on the constitution and to choose the officials for which it provided. Munroe acted promptly,[34] and the election took place on June 20. As noted by McCall, the constitution was adopted by an overwhelming majority, only thirty-nine votes being cast against it.[35] At the same time, Dr. Henry Connelly[36] was elected governor and Manuel Alvarez[37] lieutenant governor. Both houses of the state legislature were selected also. The newly elected

[34] "Proclamation," May 28, 1850, 31 Cong., 2 sess., *Sen. Exec. Doc. 1*, part II, 93–94.

[35] In the *Message from the President . . . Transmitting a Copy of the Constitution Adopted by the Inhabitants of New Mexico, Together with a Digest of the Votes for and Against It . . .*, 31 Cong., 1 sess., *Sen. Exec. Doc. 74*, the vote is given as 6,771 for the constitution and 39 against it.

[36] Dr. Connelly, a graduate of the medical school of Transylvania University, went to Chihuahua in 1828. There he engaged in business for many years, became a naturalized Mexican citizen, and married a Mexican woman. In 1848 he moved to New Mexico and was soon one of the most prominent merchants in the area. In 1849, his first wife having died, he married the widow of José Mariano Chávez, of Peralta. He was elected governor in 1850, but, because he was away in the States, he did not assume office. Connelly was appointed territorial governor of New Mexico in 1861 and reappointed in 1864. He died in Santa Fe in 1866. See Moorhead, *New Mexico's Royal Road*, 90, n.32; and Twitchell, *Leading Facts of New Mexican History*, II, 391, n. 316.

[37] Alvarez, a native of Spain, came to the United States in 1823. The following year he entered the Santa Fe trade and settled in Santa Fe, where he became a prosperous merchant, owning a large property fronting on the plaza. On March 21, 1839, he was appointed United States consul at Santa Fe, and, even though he was not granted an *exequatur* by the Mexican government, he performed the functions of consul until the United States occupied New Mexico. He became a naturalized citizen of the United States in St. Louis on April 9, 1842. He died in Santa Fe in 1856. Moorhead, *New Mexico's Royal Road*, 128, n. 16. Alvarez' naturalization papers are in the *Read Collection*, New Mexico Archives.

legislature assembled in Santa Fe on July 1 and chose two United States senators, Richard Weightman[38] and Francis A. Cunningham.[39] In the absence of Connelly, Alvarez served as acting governor of New Mexico throughout the short period the state government attempted to function.

Until the state constitution was adopted and the newly elected officials sought to conduct the duties of their offices, Major Munroe had co-operated with the New Mexicans. Now his co-operation ceased as he adopted a line of action at variance with the expressed wishes of the people and in distinct contrast to the attitude of Brevet Brigadier General Bennett Riley under similar circumstances in California. Munroe took the point of view that the political affairs of New Mexico became grave when "the new State government, organized so far only as to take the preliminary steps towards admission into the Union, has assumed to supersede the actual government, and go at once into operation." Hence, he decided that it was his duty to deny the authority of the selected state officials and continue to act as civil and military governor.[40]

Unquestionably, there was opposition to statehood in New Mexico. In a circular published prior to the convention of 1850, the merits of

[38] Weightman first came to New Mexico as a captain of one of the volunteer companies in General Kearny's expeditionary force. He remained in Santa Fe and became one of the more vocal advocates of statehood. See Twitchell, *Old Santa Fe*, 341–48; and Oliver La Farge, *Santa Fe*, 6.

[39] Cunningham began his army career as a paymaster, Volunteers, during the Mexican War, later transferring to the regular service. He was promoted to the rank of major paymaster on March 2, 1849. He was still in the army at the time he was named to be one of New Mexico's senators. Heitman, *Official Register*, I, 345.

[40] Munroe to Jones, July 16, 1850, 31 Cong., 2 sess., *Sen. Exec. Doc. 1*, part II, 92. In explanation of his actions, Munroe expressed the opinion that the Mexican character was unstable, that the people were generally ignorant and manifested a dislike, "although latent," for Americans, and that a large number of them entertained strong sympathies for the Mexican government and institutions as opposed to those of the United States.

state and territorial forms of government were examined and compared, including the greater expenses which statehood would inevitably entail.[41] Shortly after his selection as senator, Weightman warned Alvarez that the opposition planned "to raise reports of revolution or real disturbances by oppressing the people have the military called out and then argue the unfitness of New Mexico for self govt. and thus defeat the State Govt."[42] Munroe became involved in an extended dispute with Alvarez over the status of the government. The merits of the dispute, interesting though it was,[43] lost their significance because of events in Washington. Even so, Secretary of War Charles M. Conrad saw fit to instruct Munroe "to abstain from all further interference in the civil or political affairs of that country."[44]

Weightman was given his credentials as senator and proceeded to Washington to present the constitution to the Congress and press for the admission of New Mexico as a state. He arrived in the nation's capital only to learn that a few days earlier, September 9, 1850, the act creating the Territory of New Mexico had been approved.[45] Obviously disappointed, Weightman wrote to Alvarez, "It is Mr. Hugh Smith's opinion *as well as mine* that but for the death of General [President] Taylor we would at once have received a State Govt."[46] Still hopeful, he expressed the belief a short time later that "if New Mexico will stick to it she can get a State Govt. It may be delayed for a time but must come—and it may come in the next

[41] Circular (1850), *Miscellaneous Territorial Records*, New Mexico Archives.

[42] July 19, 1850, *Alvarez Papers*, New Mexico Archives.

[43] See particularly the arguments advanced in Alvarez to Munroe, July 13, 1850, 31 Cong., 2 sess., *Sen. Exec. Doc. 1*, part II, 95–98.

[44] September 10, 1850, *ibid.*, 108.

[45] "Organic Act Establishing the Territory of New Mexico," *New Mexico Statutes, 1953*, I, 388–403. Weightman's communication to the Senate and accompanying documents are in 31 Cong., 1 sess., *Sen. Exec. Doc. 76*.

[46] September 14, 1850, *Alvarez Papers*, New Mexico Archives.

session."[47] News that the struggle to achieve a regular government had at last succeeded, although not in the form anticipated, did not reach New Mexico until after McCall had left the territory. If the outcome was unsatisfactory to some, there were many others who fully approved of it. McCall did not comment.

Santa Fe was the headquarters of the Third Infantry regiment, and there McCall settled down to what, for him, soon proved a boring existence. "I am getting very tired of Santa Fé," he complained. "There is nothing in the town to interest or divert the mind: the country around has still less attraction; no beauty of scenery, no game, absolutely nothing but sand-hills and snow-covered mountains." The climate he considered abominable, with hail or a snow storm on the average of once every third day, and strong, cold winds in the intervals. No doubt the fact that he was suffering from neuralgia, as he did periodically, affected his attitude. It was an affliction, he charged, indigenous to Santa Fe.[48] A month later the weather had improved and with it McCall's spirits. He had taken quarters in the home of Juan Sena,[49] a block east of the plaza, where he also ate his meals, trying the effect of a Mexican diet on his neuralgia—that is, "a good dose of Chile Colorado and Ajo" at each meal.[50] It was during this

[47] Weightman to Alvarez, October 18, 1850, *ibid.*

[48] McCall to M———, May 13, 1850, *Letters from the Frontier*, 492–93.

[49] Sena was a descendant of Bernardino de Sena, who came to New Mexico with his foster parents in 1693. Bernardino de Sena prospered, acquiring considerable property, including the site of the structure now known as Sena Plaza, located on Palace Avenue, less than a block east of the Palace of the Governors. Chávez, *Origins of New Mexico Families*, 286. In the will which he drew up in 1758, Sena described his home as a "two story house in this town, containing seven rooms and the corridor on the second floor and nine rooms and a porch in the lower floor." Archivo 860, July 17, 1758, Survey Office, translation in the library of the Museum of New Mexico, Santa Fe. The present Sena Plaza is the home in which McCall found accommodations. It dates from 1831.

[50] McCall to M———, June 11, 1850, *Letters from the Frontier*, 495.

period that he prepared the report for Secretary of War Crawford, as required in his instructions.

The tedium of McCall's existence in Santa Fe was relieved on August 28, 1850, when he received his commission as colonel and inspector general. A week earlier he had been informed by William W. S. Bliss, President Taylor's secretary and son-in-law, that the President had named him for the position.[51] McCall was clearly pleased by the appointment, for he wrote, "He [Taylor] had designated me long before for this office; and his unchanged decision during a long interval, wherein much influence was brought to bear on him in favor of other officers, is certainly highly complimentary." With the commission came orders to make a tour of inspection of the Ninth Military Department, then to report in person to Washington. McCall expected to complete the inspection by the middle of October, and he added, probably with a touch of nostalgia, "I hope to be in Philadelphia by Christmas."[52]

McCall lost no time in beginning the tour, and his final inspection report was dated October 14, 1850. He had completed, as he later put it, "visiting the numerous little forts, garrisons, or camps thinly scattered throughout that ill-starred Territory." He was now free to leave New Mexico, an area in which he had found surprisingly little that pleased him. Retracing the route by which he had come less than a year before, he reached Washington by mid-December. Although he does not say so, it is fair to assume that he was in Philadelphia for Christmas. It was there that he prepared his final report on New Mexico, a report to the Adjutant General's Office in compliance with instructions dated June 24, 1850.[53]

McCall made one other tour of inspection. In 1851 he was ordered to inspect the Division of the Pacific, made up of Military Departments Numbers 10 and 11, and including the present states of Cali-

[51] Bliss to McCall, June 4, 1850, *ibid.*, 523. The commission was dated June 10, 1850.

[52] McCall to M———, August 29, 1850, *ibid.*, 523–24.

[53] *Ibid.*, 525.

fornia, Oregon, and Washington.[54] This he did in 1852,[55] returning to Philadelphia at the end of the tour. In 1853 he was ordered to conduct another inspection of the Ninth Military Department. Brevet Colonel Edwin Vose Sumner,[56] who had been in command of the department since July 19, 1851, was to be replaced by Brevet Brigadier General John Garland[57] in the summer of 1853. It was intended that the inspection be carried out prior to the change in command. The program was disrupted when McCall tendered his resignation from the service on April 22, 1853, giving as his reason the state of his health, which was "not such as to authorize my undertaking this important duty, with the prospect of being able fully to discharge it to my own satisfaction or to the best interests of the service."[58] It would be interesting to know whether his previous experience in New Mexico had anything to do with his decision. The resignation was accepted, and his replacement, Colonel Joseph K. F. Mansfield,[59] accompanied General Garland to New Mexico.

McCall's military career was not yet ended. With the outbreak of

[54] *Ibid.*, 536; and Thian, *Notes Illustrating the Military Geography*, 25.

[55] See McCall's Inspection Report: Department of the Pacific, 1852, Records of the Adjutant General's Office, Record Group 94, The National Archives, Washington, D.C.

[56] Sumner, First Dragoons, was sent to New Mexico to assume command of the department with specific instructions to reduce expenses. He carried out a major revision in the policies of the department. Sumner held command from July 19, 1851, to July 1, 1853. He was also acting governor for a time, following Calhoun's departure on May 2, 1852.

[57] Garland, Eighth Infantry, held command of the department from July 20, 1853, until September 16, 1858.

[58] McCall to Samuel Cooper, April 22, 1853, *Letters from the Frontier*, 536.

[59] Mansfield, inspector general, was a native of Connecticut and a graduate of the United States Military Academy. He served with the Corps of Engineers prior to his appointment to the Inspector General's Department. He died in 1862 of wounds received in the Battle of Antietam. Frazer (ed.), *Mansfield*, xxviii–xxix.

the Civil War he became, on May 17, 1861, brigadier general, United States Volunteers. He served with the Army of the Potomac, and commanded the Third Division, Fifth Army Corps, during the Peninsular Campaign of 1862. On June 30, 1862, his command was engaged at New Market Crossroads, a part of the vast Seven Days' Battles. "In the obscurity of the evening," after the fighting had ended, McCall was taken prisoner by the enemy.[60] He was held prisoner of war at Richmond, Virginia, until August 14, 1862, when he was paroled, then, on August 27, exchanged. Following his release, McCall returned to his home at Belair, near Westchester, Pennsylvania, with a leave of absence for thirty days, in the hope that his health, "which had been impaired by exposure & subsequent imprisonment at Richmond," would improve. A month later he was forced to request an extension because he was "so much reduced & debilitated that [he] could not possibly support a single day in the saddle."[61]

In the succeeding months McCall felt called upon to write a series of letters in defense of the conduct of his command at New Market Crossroads, which had been criticized in the public press.[62] He was particularly concerned when he learned that every brigadier general, other than himself, who had commanded a division of volunteers in the Peninsular Campaign had been promoted to the rank of major general.[63] Although Major General George B. McClellan later recommended that McCall be promoted,[64] no action was taken. McCall's health remained poor. His personal physician stated that he was "laboring under indisposition arising from hepatic derangement, and general debility," and also mentioned an attack of miasmic fever.[65]

[60] Enclosure in McCall to John Cowle, Friday morning, Commission Branch: File M752 of 1863.

[61] McCall to Thomas, September 15, 1862, *ibid.*

[62] McCall to Seth Williams, December 10, 1862, *ibid.*

[63] McCall to Williams, October 11, 1862, *ibid.*

[64] McClellan to Thomas, October 30, 1862, *ibid.*

[65] Certificate of Wilmer Worthington, M.D., September 12, 1862, *ibid.*

On April 3, 1863, McCall tendered his resignation, only to be confronted with new difficulties. He was informed that, by Special Orders 169, he had been mustered out of the service.[66] After further exchange of correspondence his resignation was accepted, postdated to become effective on March 31, 1863.[67] Now, his military career finally at an end, McCall edited for publication, "with the expressed desire of those valued friends for whose eyes alone they were originally intended,"[68] a selection of his private correspondence of the years 1822–53. Included were a few official reports and letters, as well as private correspondence, dating from the months he had spent in New Mexico. McCall died, probably before his book was published, on February 25, 1868, at the age of sixty-five.

McCall's reports are interesting for several reasons. He was in New Mexico at a time when official knowledge of the area was scant, and within the limitations of the subjects which he treated, he made important additions to the available knowledge. His reports represent the most comprehensive information then available to the War Department on such subjects as the composition and attitudes of the population, economic conditions and potential, and possible defense needs. If McCall's information was not always correct, it did embody what was believed to be true of New Mexico at the time. The inspection reports are valuable because they comprise the only general inspection of the posts visited by McCall, except for Santa Fe, all of the others being abandoned within the next two years.[69] The reports throw some light on the military policy followed briefly in New

[66] McCall to Henry W. Halleck, April 21, 1863, *ibid.*

[67] Acceptance of Resignation, Secretary of War Edwin M. Stanton, *ibid.*

[68] *Letters from the Frontier*, *iii.*

[69] In 1851 Major Thomas Swords inspected many of these same posts for the Quartermaster General's Department, with the object of effecting all possible economies in the operation of his department. His report contains much useful information, but it is concerned with only one aspect of the military establishment in New Mexico. See Swords to Jesup, October 25, 1851, and enclosures, 32 Cong., 1 sess., *House Exec. Doc. 2*, 235–53.

Mexico between the close of the Mexican War and the adoption of a permanent policy. They also describe some of the problems and frustrations confronting the military in New Mexico.

The smallness of the garrisons at most of the posts is apparent. At only two, Santa Fe and Cebolleta, did the number of men present exceed one hundred, while at five, fewer than fifty men made up the garrison. The shortage of officers at the posts is even more pronounced. Of the eighty-five officers listed by McCall for the department, ten constituted the headquarters staff. Only thirty-two of the remaining seventy-five were with their assigned companies at the time of McCall's inspection. Of the forty-three who were not, seven were serving at other posts within the department and five were en route from Fort Leavenworth to join their companies. Among the others were one vacancy, two officers under arrest, one serving at the United States Military Academy, three on general recruiting service, a number temporarily absent, and several listed as absent-without-leave. At each of two posts, Taos and San Elizario, only a single officer was present, and at the same two posts there were no medical officers, although at San Elizario a civilian physician was employed. At three of the six posts where dragoon companies were stationed, there were fewer horses than dragoons. At a fourth the horses outnumbered the dragoons by fifteen, but McCall found it necessary to condemn twenty-three of the horses as unfit for service. At a fifth post, Doña Ana, McCall neglected to give the number of horses. Oddly, with all the concern expressed for the quality and condition of the dragoon mounts, there was not a single veterinary surgeon in the department. Such matters as the shortage of forage for the animals, the difficulty of securing firewood at some of the posts, the poor communications between many of the posts, the cost and inadequacy of facilities, and other comparable problems are described.

It is unfortunate that McCall did not like New Mexico better. His reports to Secretary of War George W. Crawford and Adjutant General Roger Jones are reasonably full. His inspection reports, especially those for the posts of El Paso and San Elizario, tend to be brief, reflecting his desire to complete his task and return to the East. In writing his inspection reports, he deviated very little from the form provided in the *General Regulations for the Army*. It is regrettable that he did not conduct his inspection tour at a more leisurely pace and show more initiative in the preparation of his reports.

# IV. McCALL'S REPORT ON CONDITIONS IN NEW MEXICO

SANTA FÉ NEW MEXICO,
July 15th 1850.

*Honorable George W. Crawford,*
*Secretary of War*

SIR,

Since my arrival in New Mexico, having kept in view the instructions with which I was honoured, contained in your letter of November 19th 1849, towit: "It will be instructive (and probably necessary information when the people of New Mexico form a constitution and seek admission into the Confederacy of the States) to have your observations and views on their probable numbers, habits, customs and pursuits of life." And the people of New Mexico having framed and adopted a state constitution, and transmitted it to the Executive to be laid before the Congress of the United States, I have now to submit, in compliance with your instructions, a few remarks, the result of much inquiry, and of such personal observation as could be made while in the regular discharge of military duties.

First, the population of New Mexico is, I am satisfied, less than it has been represented.

According to the statistics presented by Governor Martinez, at the division of the Department of New Mexico into districts in the year

1844, the population, including the Pueblos or civilized Indians, amounted to one hundred thousand.[1]

If, at the period alluded to, the number of inhabitants was not overrated, which is more than probable, it has certainly, since then, diminished in a most unaccountable manner. I have taken pains to ascertain the number of Mexicans, residents of this Department, who at the time of its cession to the United States declared their adhesion to the Republic of Mexico, and of these how many afterwards withdrew their declaration and remained here, and how many actually left our territory, and, of the latter, how many have since returned to make it their permanent home, and I am satisfied that the loss in numbers does not exceed one thousand or, at the utmost, twelve hundred souls.[2] In addition to those above mentioned, a few men of wealth,

[1] General Mariano Martínez de Lejanza was governer of the Department of New Mexico, 1844–45. His report, in which he places the population of New Mexico at 100,064, is printed in translation in Abert, *Report*, 97–99. Martínez' figure is undoubtedly too high, unless it includes the wild Indians. L. Bradford Prince, at one time territorial governor of New Mexico, using the population figures given by Martínez for the districts into which New Mexico was divided, a total of 99,204, concluded that about 7,000 were Pueblo Indians and about one-third were Plains Indians. *Historical Sketches of New Mexico from the Earliest Records to the American Occupation*, 239. This would be reasonably close to the census taken by the United States in 1850, except for the wild Indians, who were estimated at 45,000. By 1860 the population of New Mexico had increased to 93,516, but not until 1870 had it surpassed the hundred thousand mark. In the interim, the Territory of New Mexico had been reduced by half in its extent but had lost none of the area containing European population in 1844.

[2] The state of Chihuahua was particularly interested in encouraging New Mexicans who wished to retain their Mexican citizenship to migrate, offering to receive any number of them. Padre Ramón Ortiz was sent by the Mexican government in 1849 to oversee and encourage the migration.

Initially he received the co-operation of Major Washington. He reported to Governor Angel Trias of Chihuahua: "On the following day

with their peons, have, within the past year, removed to Guadalupé, a settlement on the right bank of the Rio Grande twenty-five miles below El Paso del Norte,[3] where inducements have been held out by

I set out for El Vado county, where it was generally believed that there would be the least number of persons wishing to emigrate to the republic of Mexico. I had barely arrived in the settlements of that country when all its inhabitants appealed to me with enthusiasm, asking me to enlist them and their families among the immigrants to the territory of Mexico. Although they knew that, according to the guarantees of the peace treaty, they would lose all their property, they were willing to lose everything rather than to live in a country whose government gave them fewer guarantees than our own and in which they were treated with more disdain than members of the African race. In this country the total number of families is less than one thousand; and more than nine hundred of them enlisted; the majority of the others failed to do so because the heads of families were absent."

After this auspicious beginning, Ortiz had difficulties with the authorities, various restrictions were placed on his activities, and the earlier cooperation ceased. Donaciano Vigil, secretary of the territory, informed Ortiz that he would not be permitted to visit the various parts of New Mexico to set forth the terms of his commission in person because he was making promises which were too lavish and stirring up too much commotion. There can be little doubt of Ortiz' enthusiasm. He estimated that it would cost the Mexican government 1,653,342 pesos to feed the migrants until they were able to sustain themselves. This he based on the belief that 16,000 families, averaging 5 persons each, which was much greater than the entire Mexican population of New Mexico, were ready to migrate. Carroll and Haggard (eds.), *Three New Mexico Chronicles*, 143–49.

[3] Guadalupe is thirty-three miles below El Paso del Norte (Ciudad Juárez) by the present Mexican National Highway No. 2. In the period following the conclusion of the Treaty of Guadalupe Hidalgo some Mexicans, in order to retain their citizenship, moved from New Mexico into the Mesilla district, west of the Río Grande and south of the line as it was established by the boundary commission in 1850–51. By October, 1852, it was estimated that the population of the district was 1,900, not more than 20 of whom were United States citizens. Bartlett, *Personal Narrative*, II, 386–87.

the Mexican government to bring over to their side the rich and better class of people—the numerical loss thus sustained is scarcely appreciable. In fact, there is no known cause that could have materially reduced the population of New Mexico within the last six years; yet, from positive data, it is very clear that it does not now amount to the number above stated.[4]

Where but little is known, and where in seeking that little conflicting statements are frequently encountered, it is no easy matter to arrive at the truth; therefore, I will not venture the assertion that the population of New Mexico, at the present time, greatly exceeds the quota required to give one seat in the House of Representatives of the United States; and, indeed, so great a portion of the face of the country is made up of rugged mountains and waste plains that it cannot be expected soon, if ever, to receive and support a population in numbers and wealth at all proportioned to its extent of territory.

Besides the native Mexicans, the present population includes of persons born in the United States and in Europe, who have become citizens of the state, at the extent twelve hundred. And of the natives, besides those whom strictly speaking we call Mexicans, there is another distinct and numerous class which seems to invite particular attention; I mean the Pueblo Indians.

Having embraced Christianity under the Spanish rule, the Pueblos were admitted to the rights of citizenship by the Mexican government under Iturbide, and these rights which they have enjoyed to the present time (at least in name) are confirmed to them by the state consti-

[4] McCall was probably correct about the Mexican population. However, James S. Calhoun wrote in 1851, "The population of the Territory has suffered considerable diminuation [*sic*] during the past year." Calhoun to Luke Lea, Commissioner of Indian Affairs, February 16, 1851, Abel (ed.), *Official Correspondence*, 294. Earlier, he had stated that immigration to New Mexico had entirely ceased and that half the Americans who had come there to settle had departed. This he blamed upon failure to control the Indians. Calhoun to Brown, October 12, 1850, *ibid.*, 264.

tution.[5] Under this they are subject to taxation (by legislation) in common with the other inhabitants. It is to be hoped, however, the legislature will, in its wisdom, adopt a mild and conciliatory policy towards these people. Under the present change of government the impressions first made it will be difficult to remove from their minds, and dissatisfaction produced at the outset may ultimately lead to more serious results than would at first glance appear.[6] To explain this it will be necessary to state in what way the Pueblos may be made an element of much good or evil to the state.

[5] Article VIII of the proposed New Mexico State Constitution of 1850 provided:

*Sufragio.*

*Todo varon de edad de veinte-un anos y arriva (Africanos o decendientes de Africanos y Indios barbaros exceptuado) pertenecientes a cualquiera de las clases siguientes quien habran residido en el Estado por seis meses anteriores a alguna eleccion sera jusgado calificado como elector en tal eleccion.*

Those who were eligible to vote were the following: citizens of the United States; persons who had chosen to remain Mexican citizens but, six months prior to any election, renounced their allegiance to Mexico and took an oath to support the United States constitution; and persons of foreign birth who had declared their intention to become naturalized citizens of the United States. The constitution provided specifically that no soldier of the United States Army would be entitled to vote. *Constitución del Estado de Nuevo Méjico*, 12–13. As the Pueblo Indians had been Mexican citizens and as not one of them had chosen to remain a Mexican citizen, the constitution of 1850, since it did not specifically exclude them, accepted them as citizens.

[6] Governor Calhoun, in a message to the territorial House of Representatives on December 20, 1851, stated: "persons have attempted to induce some of the Pueblos to believe, that their rights and privileges, as citizens of this Territory, had been curtailed, which only foreshadowed the end which would be, seizing their lands, and driving them to the forest. Many of these Indians are impressed with the belief, that *they are citizens of the United States, by the terms of her own treaty stipulations, and she cannot now undo it if she would, without an act of perfidy that*

These Indians still carry on an occasional traffic and are careful to maintain a good understanding with the wild Indians. Not only, then, may their influence be used to advantage in controlling and, indeed, in reclaiming several of the least savage of these tribes; but, if at any time the United States find it necessary to chastise an open declaration of hostilities by several of the border tribes—a thing not impossible when a decided effort to restrain their predatory habits comes to be made—they will find valuable auxiliaries in the Pueblos, who count at least twenty five hundred warriors. On the other hand, should the latter from any cause become dissatisfied, either from what they might conceive to be the oppressive bearing of a law of the state, or its maladministration by the petty authorities (for they still look upon the Mexicans with distrust), it would be easy for their parties at different points to unite with the enemy for marauds or for battle without fear of detection.[7]

They have twenty towns or settlements, which contain at least two thousand four hundred families; these, at the moderate computation of four to each family, gives a total of nine thousand six hundred souls, but they probably exceed ten thousand.[8] Each town is a distinct community, having its *gubernador*, or chief, and council, and each community (as a corporation) owns the soil it cultivates. This, a grant

---

*would draw down upon her the deserved scorn and contempt of a whole civilized world."—Journal of the House of Representatives of the Territory of New Mexico*, New Mexico Archives, 83.

[7] The Pueblos had long suffered from the depredations of their wild neighbors, particularly the Navahos, Jicarilla Apaches, and Utes. In general, they had little reason to love or trust their nomadic brethren; yet, in historic times, they had occasionally formed alliances with them against Spaniards or Mexicans. In the various campaigns conducted by the United States Army against the Navahos, some use was made of Pueblo Indians as guides and auxiliaries.

[8] The population of the Indian pueblos was a matter of much speculation at this time. Efforts to take an exact census alarmed the Indians and produced confusing results. See, for example, Calhoun to Lea, December 28, 1850, Abel (ed.), *Official Correspondence*, 280–81.

*Courtesy Woolaroc Museum*

In 1850, Plains Indians, like those pictured in this painting by Elling Williams Gollings, terrorized the people of New Mexico, including the peaceful Pueblo Indians. The United States Army was so ineffectual against the raiders that horses were stolen with impunity from army posts.

*Courtesy New Mexico Tourist Bureau*

Homes of New Mexican Pueblo Indians. *Above*, Acoma Pueblo; *below*, Taos Pueblo.

*Courtesy New Mexico Tourist Bureau*

from the Spanish crown, is embraced within a circle whose radius is a league, the town its center.[9] The Pueblos are intelligent, moral, sober, and industrious, and, generally speaking, they are better off than the lower class of Mexicans.

Many of them in each town speak the Spanish intelligibly, and some of the principal men read and even write the language as far as is required in their simple business transactions.

The "Habits and Customs" of the Mexican portion of the inhabitants do not differ materially from those of Mexicans elsewhere. Yet, in some particulars, changes, the effect of intercourse with our people, have already begun to show themselves—an impression has been made, and perhaps the first steps towards better things has already been accomplished. Here, in Santa Fé, the diminution of filth in the streets, and the improved dress and personal cleanliness of the people, together with the cloaking of immorality, show that precept and example are not altogether thrown away upon them.[10]

The number who are of Spanish blood, unmixed, is small—in the mass, that of the Indian predominates. So, in the mass, the character and disposition of the latter are to a greater or less degree inherited. This is evinced in more than one trait, but it is sufficient to cite their extreme aversion to continued labour. If a Mexican has not inextricably involved himself as the debtor of his employer, and thus through action of the law (Mexican) against debtors become a *peon* for life,[11]

[9] Davis gives an interesting analysis of Pueblo land titles in this period. *El Gringo*, 121–23.

[10] McCall, who obviously disliked New Mexico, was less harsh in his criticism than many who visited it in these years. Lieutenant Colonel Edwin Vose Sumner was, among those who were in a position to influence official opinion, one of the most damning critics of New Mexico. See Sumner to Conrad, May 27, 1852, 32 Cong., 2 sess., *House Exec. Doc. 1*, part II, 23–26. For a discussion of the attitudes of United States citizens see John P. Bloom, "New Mexico Viewed by Anglo-Americans, 1846–1849," *New Mexico Historical Review*, Vol. XXXIV (July, 1959), 165–98.

[11] Peonage continued for some time after the United States had ac-

it is with difficulty he can be kept at work longer than is requisite to earn a few dollars; and, while this lasts, he indulges to the full the luxury of lounging away the hours of the day with his *cigarrito*, and passing the evening in the more exciting amusements of the fandango and the monte table; nor does he resume his task until compelled by want. Being moderate in his appetites, he requires but little to subsist on, and, therefore, is constrained to labour *as little*.

The lower class are as ignorant as idle, and even among their superiors education is woefully neglected.

From this it may be inferred that no great improvement in the moral condition of the present generation can be expected from the introduction of our institutions, which they can neither understand nor appreciate. It is to the coming generation we must look for this; and, therefore, the introduction of primary schools, at as early a day as practicable, is a consideration of much interest.

Of their "pursuits of life" their manufactures, perhaps, stand lowest on the scale; they are certainly primitive in their character. Yet this is not so much to be attributed to a deficiency of aptness and manual skill or dexterity, as to the want of proper instruction and better models, with more continued and systematic application. Gradual improvement in this branch may therefore be looked for, if their natural indolence can be overcome or their love of gain be stimulated

---

quired New Mexico. Davis described it in the 1850's in *El Gringo*, 231–33. Peonage was abolished by an act of Congress on March 2, 1867.

As soon as knowledge of the law reached New Mexico, the territorial governor issued the following proclamation: "Now therefore I, Robt. B. Mitchell, Governor of the Territory of New Mexico, in pursuance of the foregoing act of Congress, do hereby proclaim all persons free within the Territory of New Mexico, who are held to service or labor by any statute or custom heretofore in force in said Territory (except on conviction for crime.) All persons holding peones or other persons to service or labor against their will and in violation of the foregoing law will be severely dealt with."—*Santa Fe Weekly Gazette*, April 20, 1867.

A year later the Santa Fe *New Mexican* announced that "These laws have been but indifferently observed." La Farge, *Santa Fe*, 56.

through the influence of our own enterprising countrymen. The establishment of maufactories [*sic*] would do much to accomplish both, and by fixing the price of labour at a fair rate would probably prove to be the great lever that could be used in overturning the present system of *peon*-age.

The cheapness of wool (which will in time be improved in quality, as well as reduced in price) will, *at once*, lead to the erection of factories for making carpets, blankets and the courser cloths, and they will not only supply the wants of the state itself but, to some extent, the adjoining departments of Mexico. These fabricks will, likewise, eventually become important articles of traffic with the large tribes of mountain and prairie Indians.

The course woolens, if, with the exception of the head-workmen Mexican operatives can be used, may be afforded here at prices to preclude competition, for, independently of the cost of transportation, the price of wool and the price of labour are, here, from one-third to one-half less than in the United States.

To a moderate extent iron works may also be profitably established. Iron is abundant and of fair quality, as is the coal, which is more or less bituminous, and will answer to reduce the ore. The heavy cost of transportation from the United States will, it is probable, soon call attention to this subject.

At present but little attention is paid to mining for two reasons; a want of capital if not a want of enterprise among the people, and an inherent fear of "*los Indios*." There is, however, reason to believe that the mines may hereafter become the principal source of wealth to the state. The mines of New Mexico have always been represented as rich in gold and immensely productive to the Spaniards, until repeated incursions of hostile Indians caused them to be abandoned. The localities of these mines are, at this time, for the greater part unknown, the wild tribes who inhabit the supposed gold-regions having prevented their exploitation. And for the same reason, under present circumstances their exploration is beyond the reach of private enterprise. Nothing, therefore, can be satisfactorily known of the richness or poverty of the state in this respect until its vast mountain regions are thoroughly and scientifically explored. With this view, it would be well if a topographical engineer were associated with an able practical geologist in order that the government might receive full reports, with accurate maps both geographical and geological, of the whole country. For this purpose there would be required a military escort of sufficient strength to enable the party to push its examination to the most remote parts of the state, now the constant haunts of Indians.

Formerly, of the profitable pursuits of New Mexico, stock-raising stood high upon the list; and although now sadly reduced by the continued inroads of the Nabajoes and Apaches it will again, when protected from their marauds, yield large profits to the proprietors. There are in New Mexico grazing lands of great extent, where countless flocks and herds may be reared at a very trifling expense. They require neither stabling nor forage during the winter, the nutritious gramma, a species of grass found on the mountain sides and the adjoining uplands, affording abundant sustenance during that season. The climate too is well adapted to all kinds of stock, particularly sheep, which, owing to the dryness of the atmosphere, are almost exempt from rot and other diseases common in low countries. Some twenty or five and twenty years ago, before the hand of the Redman had fallen so heavily upon them, the people of this state, as well as Chihuahua, sent annually to the City of Mexico vast numbers of sheep* [*The Chavez connexion, consisting of three or four families residing below Albuquerque, are known to have sent as many as 200,000 sheep to the city in one year.[12]—McCall's footnote.] as well

[12] The Chávez family had many members, dating back to Pedro Durán y Chávez, who was in New Mexico at least as early as 1600. In the mid-nineteenth century various Chávezes lived in the towns of Los Chávez, Belen, Los Padillas, Isleta, Atrisco, and elsewhere south of Albuquerque. Other Chávezes were scattered throughout the settled portions of New Mexico. Chávez, *Origins of New Mexico Families*, 19, 321–26. It is doubtful that sheep in the numbers mentioned by McCall were ever driven from New Mexico to Mexico City in a single year. The principal market for New Mexican sheep was Chihuahua; however, flocks of as many as 20,000 head were occasionally driven as far as

as cattle and mules. At this day not one thousand are sent from districts that formerly furnished their hundreds of thousands—such has been the rapacity and the relentless spirit of hostility of the Nabajoes and Apaches.

The hill sides and the plains that were in days past covered with sheep and cattle are now bare in many parts of the state, yet the work of plunder still goes on! The predatory operations of the two tribes just mentioned are even now carried on in the close vicinity of our military posts; the shepherds are pounced upon and shot with arrows to prevent their carrying information, and with their spoil the Indians dash at speed to the mountains and are beyond reach before the loss is known. In this way they (I mean now the Apaches only) run the flocks from seventy to one hundred miles in twenty-four hours. And, consequently, out [of] ten thousand sheep that may be started, probably not more than one thousand will reach their destination. As the overdriven animals falter from exhaustion those that do not fall dead by the wayside are lanced as the Indians pass to prevent their falling again into the hands of the Mexicans. Thus the destruction is usually ten fold the gain of the Indians. The Apache is satisfied with that, because all his care is to supply his present wants. The more provident Nabajoe is more careful, because his principal object is to increase his stock at home. Within no more than three months past between fifteen and twenty thousand sheep and several hundred head of cattle and mules have been driven from the Rio Grande above Socorro and from the vicinity of [Las] Vegas, and several shepherds killed, with entire impunity by the two tribes already named.* [*Since the above was written an official report has been received that a flock of sixteen thousand had been carried off from the Puerco opposite Cibolletta.—McCall's footnote.] They were on several occasions pursued by the troops, but without success.

It is only necessary to free the mountains bounding the valley of

Durango and Zacatecas. A few cattle also were driven to southern markets, and woolen goods and peltries also entered into the trade. Moorhead, *New Mexico's Royal Road*, 45.

the Rio Grande from the incursions of these Indians in order to increase again, in a few years, the stock to its former numbers.

Then wool of improved quality, besides supplying the home consumption, would be sent to Missouri and bring large returns, and horned-cattle, mules, etc., raised at little or no expense would secure large profits at the same market.

I place agriculture last, or as the least productive of wealth of the three principal industrial pursuits of New Mexico (viz: mining, stock raising, and agriculture), but I do so rather in reference to the past history and the future prospects of the state than to its present circumstances. Formerly, under the Spanish government, mines were the most productive of wealth. Towards the close of that era, and during the early period of the independence of Mexico, the immense droves of horses and mules, the herds and flocks which covered the face of the country, constituted the chief riches of this department.[13] Of both these, in succession, the inhabitants of New Mexico have been despoiled by their more warlike borderers, and, therefore, at this day, their soil is almost all that remains to them. Its produce, through sufferance of the Indians,* [*The Nabajoes said on a recent occasion that their only reason for not exterminating the New Mexicans long-ago, was that it was [to] their interest to keep them as their shepherds. —McCall's footnote.] has saved them from starvation during the inflection of a twofold scourge, but it has not nor will it ever make them rich. Such is the history, the past and the present.

The future of New Mexico, it is to be hoped, will disclose another picture—the Indians subdued, the hill-sides white with flocks, and the neglected mines again yielding up their hoards of the precious metals. And then, the cultivation of the soil, although I believe it will always supply the wants of the inhabitants, will be productive of less wealth to the state than either of the other pursuits. Because, were its products ten times what they ever can be, the isolated position of the state and its entire want of the common and requisite facilities of transportation,

[13] There had never been "immense droves of horses and mules" in New Mexico, and cattle were not really numerous until the expansion of the open range cattle industry in the post–Civil War period.

either by water-communication or otherwise, would render the products of agriculture, in whatever excess above the home consumption, unavailable for exportation. And here it may not be inappropriate to give the opinion of many persons here with whom I have conversed respecting the navagableness of the Rio Grande. Although no accurate knowledge is professed to have been derived from close examination of the great bend of the Jornada [del Muerto], yet its course has with extreme difficulty been followed throughout over steep mountains and ragged cliffs that overhang the water; and judging from the appearance of the river in its rapid and irregular descent through this pass, a distance of near one hundred and fifty miles, the opinion entertained was very decided that loaded boats would not be able to make the passage in safety, even at the highest stage of water—at low water it would be perfectly impracticable. And above the Jornada, it will be borne in mind, lie more than three-fourths of the arable land of the river (within the state) and at least nine-tenths of that of the state at large.

In [the] future, as heretofore, it is probable that to the narrow valley of the Rio Grande (the "*river-bottom*") will be confined the greater part of the strictly agricultural portion of the state. The affluents of the great river, the Pecos on the east and the Puerco on the west, have along their courses large tracts of good land, but the want of timber on the first and the too frequent occurrance of a partial or total want of water on the last are serious hinderances to their improvement.

There are spots on each where, but for the danger to be encountered from Indians, isolated settlements might be made to advantage, but these would add but little to the total amount.

The best lands on the Rio Grande are between Piña Blanca and the Jornada del Muerte in a narrow strip on either bank of the river that would measure, following its meanders, about one hundred and eighty miles. These lands, the bottom lands, vary in depth from one-half of a mile to two miles and a half, but probably do not exceed, on an average, one mile.

The soil is light, but where within reach of irrigation is inriched by the fructifying waters of the river, and produces abundant and almost unfailing crops of wheat, corn, beans, and onions.

The uplands, even on the very borders of the river and although the soil be good, are unproductive, for the reason that irrigation is impractical in the ordinary way. If, by boring, water in sufficient quantity for irrigation could be got, many large tracts of uplands, now worthless except for grazing, would possibly become as productive as the bottoms, but this, in both respects, is problematical.

At points where bodies of this land are found sufficiently large to warrant the expense another mode, more eligible, may be adopted. The fall of the river in its passage through this part of the state, being about two and a half feet to the mile, the distance it may be necessary to bring the water from above is calculated thus, a large "acéquia" or canal opened five or eight miles above would throw its brances [*sic*] in every direction over land from twelve to twenty feet above the level of the river at the point cultivated.

On the march from El Paso del Norte to Santafé the river lands were carefully noted, and a rough estimate made of the amount, at present, in cultivation, say thirty-two hundred acres, and as much more cultivable still vacant, while there is along the river bank at least forty-five thousand acres worthless for agricultural purposes.

Twelve miles above Don' Aña commences the noted Jornada, crossing the high table-land that fills the great western bend of the river, a stretch of ninety miles without water.* [*At a point twenty-five miles from the north end of the Jornada, by taking a trail (impracticable for wagons) is found at the distance of six miles westward the Ojo del Muerto,[14] or Dead Man's Spring, where there is running water; but the fatigue of the animals, occasioned by this extra march of twelve miles, is not compensated by the draught of water, and most trains, unless they can command time to lie by here, push on to the end of the journey without halting. During the rainy season two or three pools may be found, containing perhaps water enough for 250

[14] The Ojo del Muerto, located in the mountains west of the Jornada, was a favorite haunt of the Apaches. Fort McRae was established near the spring on April 3, 1863.

or 300 animals, not more, and this may not last three weeks after the rain ceases.—McCall's footnote.]

Around this bend impassable mountains close in upon the river banks as far as Fray Cristobal,[15] eighteen miles below Valverde,[16] and from Don' Aña to Lopez,[17] a distance of one hundred and forty miles, there is not a human habitation, that of Val Verde having been abandoned many years since in consequence of overflow.

From the north end of the Jornada to Piña Blanca there is at present under cultivation about sixty miles of bottom land with an average depth of one mile, giving sixty square miles, or thirty-eight thousand four hundred acres; of cultivable land, unimproved, about fifty square miles, or thirty-two thousand acres; and of land uncultivable, the greater part entirely sterile, about seventy square miles, or forty-four thousand eight hundred acres.

The different qualities of land, it will be understood, are, in greater or less bodies, interposed amongst each other along the whole line, though the best lands and in the largest bodies lie between Lopez and Algodones.

On the right or west bank of the river, following its meanders, there may be from El Paso to Piña Blanca about forty-seven square miles, or thirty thousand two hundred and eight acres now under cultivation; of good land, vacant, one hundred and eighty miles, or

[15] Fray Cristóbal was located at the northern end of the Jornada del Muerto and was a much-used camp site. It was the last place where water was certain to be available before entering the Jornada. At one time a rancho had existed near by but it had been abandoned because of Indian hostilities. Fray Cristóbal had never been the site of a permanent settlement. Carroll and Haggard (eds.), *Three New Mexico Chronicles*, 196, n. 338.

[16] Valverde, some twenty miles above Fray Cristóbal, was also an important camp site and former hacienda, abandoned in the 1820's because of Indian depredations.

[17] Luis Lopez, about fifteen miles above Valverde, was originally an hacienda destroyed during the Pueblo Revolt of 1680. Reoccupied following the reconquest, it developed into a small settlement, lying on both sides of the Río Grande.

one hundred and fifteen thousand two hundred acres; and of land waste, or fit only for grazing, two hundred and three square miles or one hundred and thirty thousand acres.

Here, also, on the right bank of the river the good, bad, and indifferent lands are intermixed in tracts of various sizes along the route.

In addition to the foregoing there are in isolated tracts many considerable bodies of arable land, the principal of which are here enumerated.

First, the beautiful valley of Taos, begirt almost by the Rocky Mountains, their spurs and other detached peaks. The valley may be from twenty-five to thirty miles in circumference, and may contain immediately on the margins of the several streams that unite near the town of (San Fernandez de) Taos, forming the Rio de Taos, and thence to its debouch in the Rio Grande, about fifteen thousand acres now in cultivation and ten thousand acres, arable, vacant. The remainder, though the soil is generally good, lies too high for irrigation in the ordinary way, even supposing that the streams afforded enough water, which is doubtful.[18]

Passing from the valley a spur of the Rocky Mountains there is from La Joya[19] to Cañada[20] a stretch along the Rio Grande of about fifteen miles, with an average depth of two miles, say twenty thousand acres, of good cultivable land, little of which is improved.

Crossing the Rio Grande at Cañada we ascend the Rio Chamas to the town of Abiquiu, adjoining which the river bottom is cultivated for about three miles with an average width of one and [one] half,

[18] First Lieutenant Joseph H. Whittlesey, who was assistant quartermaster at the Post of Taos, described the valley as "about thirty miles in length, and from three to ten in breadth." Many streams crossed it, and agriculture was carried on by "artificial irrigation." Virtually all of the available water was used, so that little expansion of agriculture could be expected. Whittlesey to Brent, September 10, 1849, 31 Cong., 2 sess., *Sen. Exec. Doc. 1*, part II, 297–98.

[19] La Joya is the present Velarde.

[20] Santa Cruz de la Cañada, near where the road leading south to Santa Fe left the Río Grande.

or twenty-eight hundred and eighty acres. The unimproved lands on this stream, equally good in quality and position, amount to thrice that quantity—in this estimate both banks of the river are included.

Recrossing the Rio Grande there will be found at Rayado and Moro Town some twenty thousand acres of good land, about one-tenth of which is improved; at the former a portion of the land lies high, but may be irrigated by bringing the water some miles.

Around Los Vegas, Upper and Lower Tecoloté, and Barclay's trading house,[21] there may be one hundred thousand acres, of which nearly one-fifth is improved.

On the Pecos River at the towns of Pecos, San José, San Miguel, Anton Chico, etc., probably six thousand acres [are] in cultivation, and thrice that amount of arable land [is] vacant.

Of several of the last named bodies of land it should be remarked that doubt exists whether the streams on which they lie will afford a sufficiency [of water] to irrigate the whole of what is actually within reach of their waters.

Returning, westward, we have on the Rio de Santa Fé, below the town, not more than five thousand acres in cultivation. All that around, still vacant, is worthless for agricultural purposes. And from Cañada to Piña Blanca, along the river, there is but little good land on this side. The lands on the Pecos as far as yet settled are included in the above estimates. Below the settlements there is timber at but two points, these are the Bosque Redondo, or Round Forest, and the Bosque Grande, or Great Forest. The latter, in or about the parallel of Valverde, extends along the river for fifteen miles, with a breadth of eight or ten miles, including both banks. Sixty miles above is the former, lying equally on both banks, with a diameter of ten miles. Each has good timber in abundance, but it is impossible to say what quantity of land adjoining either is fit for the plough, and they are

[21] Barclay's Fort was erected in 1849 by Alexander Barclay (an Englishman previously employed at Bent's Fort) and Joseph B. Doyle, who were associated in the firm of Barclay and Doyle. It was located on the south side of the Mora River near the present town of Watrous. Bieber (ed.), in Webb, *Adventures in the Santa Fé Trade*, 133, n. 176.

the only points on the Pecos below the Anton Chico settlement where wood enough for fuel is found.

The Puerco and its western tributary the Rio San José, the Rio de Jemez, and the country thence along the Rio Grande to the mouth of the Rio Chamas, have some small tracts of land in cultivation, principally by Pueblos. I have been unable to ascertain the amount from any reliable source and, therefore, have not included it in the estimate. But it is believed, as mentioned above, that the frequent sinking of the Puerco in deep sands, under which upon hard clay it follows its course for miles, reappearing at intervals in the form of pools, until finally lost entirely before reaching the Rio Grande, will prevent its ever adding much to the agricultural produce of the state.

On the headwaters of the Arkansas, I have been told by old trappers, there is a beautiful country of great extent, where the land, well watered and well timbered, is sufficiently level for farming. They expressed the belief that good crops of wheat and corn might be raised without irrigation, the rains being seasonable and sufficient.[22]

More minute examination of this country will be necessary to determine its character and value.

I shall now proceed to recapitulate and sum up what may be considered the agricultural districts of New Mexico, not including any portion of the state now held by wild Indians.

| | LAND NOW IN CULTIVATION. | LAND CULTIVABLE, NOW VACANT. |
|---|---|---|
| Left or east bank of Rio Grande | *Acres* | *Acres* |
| From El Paso to Don' Aña | 3,200 | 3,200 |
| From Fray Cristobal to Peña Blanca | 38,400 | 32,000 |
| Right or west bank of Rio Grande | | |
| From El Paso to Peña Blanca | 30,280 | 115,200 |

[22] McCall's reference to the headwaters of the Arkansas is not clear. The river rises in South Park, an extensive area lying at about 9,000 feet altitude, which is adapted to grazing but not to agriculture. In any case, it was not included within the limits of the territory as established in 1850.

| | | |
|---|---|---|
| Valley of Taos | 15,000 | 10,000 |
| On the Rio Grande<br>From La Joya to Cañada | 2,000 | 18,000 |
| Valley of Chamas<br>at Abiquiu | 2,880 | 8,840 |
| Rayado and Morotown | 2,000 | 18,000 |
| Los Vegas, Upper and Lower<br>Tecoloté, and<br>Barclay's Trading House | 20,000 | 80,000 |
| Pecos, San José, San Miguel,<br>and Anton Chico | 6,000 | 80,000 |
| Santa Fé | 5,000 | |
| Total number of acres | 124,760 | 303,240 |

From the foregoing statement, based upon close personal observation, and much minute inquiry, it would appear that more than one-half of the arable land, either improved or vacant, as far as now known with any degree of certainty, lies in the immediate valley of the Rio Grande.[23]

[23] Captain Thomas L. Brent, assistant quartermaster, who was stationed in the Department of New Mexico, 1848–50, described the arable lands of the Río Grande Valley somewhat differently: "The valley of the Rio Grande, or that part of it which may be considered as available in supplying the wants of the troops in New Mexico, extends from Taos . . . to a point about 50 miles south of El Paso. The distance between these two points may be safely estimated at about 500 miles. The width of the valley varies from 300 yards to two miles; I allude to the cultivable portion of it. Throughout the whole extent of the valley, irrigation is indispensable for the production of crops of any kind of grain; and from Taos to Socorro . . . little or no addition to the irrigible [*sic*] land can be made. The supply of forage, therefore, is at its maximum, unless some increase may be obtained by improved agricultural methods. Below Socorro, on both sides of the river, (with the exception of about 80 miles, where the river runs through a deep fissure or cañon,) the bottoms afford a considerable quantity of fine land, which can be subjected to cultivation, particularly from Doña Ana to within six miles of El Paso, a distance of

The method adopted in estimating, it is true, is rude, but neither time nor opportunity admitted of a more regular and satisfactory examination. The figures, I may assert with confidence, are not too high, nor do I believe they will be found very greatly below the truth with respect to the lands specified. What amount of farming lands there may be in addition to these, further examinations will determine.

In looking at the past in the history of New Mexico, it is clear that the fruits of labour in the principal pursuits of life above noticed have, up to the time of the cession of the territory to the United States, been blighted by the presence of formidable tribes of Indians who still infest the country. And it would from certain indications appear that the future prosperity of the state, to arise from the steady, uninterrupted prosecution of these pursuits, will in a great measure depend on the impression now to be made on these Indians.

It may be apprehended that if they are not in the beginning impressed with the ability and the settled purpose of the United States to chastise those who plunder and murder its citizens, if acts of this kind, now of almost monthly occurance [*sic*] and utterly beyond the power of the present military force to check, are continued longer unpunished, the Indians will hold us in the contempt with which they now look upon the Mexicans, whom they have wantonly robbed and murdered for two centuries past. And the inevitable consequence will be, sooner or later, a war, more or less general, with the surrounding tribes.

This subject appears to be so closely blended with those to which my attention has been directed that I trust a few remarks on the present strength and temper of these Indians may not be unacceptable to the Department. The information has been gathered piece-meal, and therefore may be regarded as the collective knowledge of several persons who have seen much of the different tribes.

Of the eight tribes of wild Indians who inhabit the mountains and plains of New Mexico and the contiguous country, the Nabajoes and

---

about 60 miles."—Brent to Jesup, October 9, 1850, 31 Cong., 2 sess., *Sen. Exec. Doc. 1*, part II, 292–93.

Apaches are the most formidable as enemies, the most troublesome as neighbors.

The first are, with [the] exception of the Moqui, the most civilized; they are without exception the most wealthy of all. They are not warlike nor so bold in attack as the Apaches, but they are numerous, well aquipped [*sic*], and occupy a country well fortified by nature. Their country, extending from the San Juan to the Gila, with a breadth of one hundred and fifty miles, consists chiefly of mountains and high tablelands, and is full of fastnesses. Their possessions consist of large stocks of horses, mules, horned cattle, and sheep, which are, perhaps, extravagantly represented by persons who have had intercourse with them, as numerous beyond calculation, many times more so than those of all New Mexico at present. There may be great extravagance in all this, but it is well known that these Indians do possess stock more or less. If such be the case, and they are supposed to have retained one out of ten, or even out of every twenty, of the countless flocks and herds they have driven off from the Rio Grande within the last twenty years to increase their home stock, their progeny would in less time have swelled the amount to extravagant numbers. Although they have no permanent villages, they cultivate the soil to a considerable extent, making periodical visits to their fields at planting and harvest times. In this way they make a sufficiency of grain for all their wants, besides a few vegetables and fruits. They are said to be intelligent and industrious, and their manufactures, blankets and course cloth, in their neatness and finish go far to prove this, these articles being made (of wool of their own growing) not only for their own use, but for traffic also, to a large amount.

For some years past they are believed to have steadily increased in numbers and to count, now, about eighteen hundred lodges, which, at six per lodge, would give ten thousand eight hundred souls.

From the aptness of these Indians and the advancement they have made in the arts of civilization, it occurs to the mind that they might with proper management be induced to settle themselves permanently as the Pueblos have done, after which they might be advantageously employed in an attempt to reclaim their more wild and savage neighbors. And the accomplishment of an object so important would seem worthy of notice.

The forays which the Apaches make upon the Mexicans are incited by want; they have nothing of their own and must plunder or starve. This is not the case with the Nabajoes. They have enriched themselves by appropriating the flocks and herds of an unresisting people and cannot offer the plea of necessity.

In the first place, before anything can be done with this people, it is believed it will be indispensable to open the communication with them in their own country, in the presence of a sufficient military force to impress them seriously with the weight and importance of the conference. That the object is not an idle "talk," a treaty such as they have been in the habit, from year to year, of making with the New Mexicans, to be continued in force only until their own immediate objects are quietly attained, but a treaty the violation of which will bring upon them war in all its severity [must be impressed upon them]. Then (the treaty being concluded), let the first offense be so punished as to prove that we are in earnest! Forbearance exercised towards the Nabajoes would be mistaken humanity, and the blood of our own citizens would be the fruits of it. It would be dealing with them too much in the style they have been accustomed to, and the only effect would be to excite their contempt for us.

But I am satisfied that the presence of a strong military force in their country (the Nabajoes muster over two thousand warriors) would ensure the observance of any treaty it might be important to make with them. Their theivish propensities could then be controled [*sic*], and they might in a short time by judicious management be induced to give up their roving habits and settle themselves in permanent towns in the vicinity of their fields. They could with little labour live well on the increase of their flocks and the bountiful product of their soil, which with little attention gives growth to noble crops of wheat as well as corn. Nor would the change of life to them be very great.

If the Nabajoes are first secured, and their chiefs enlisted in our cause, their influence may at once be brought to bear upon the other tribes. They entertain the most friendly relations with their northern neighbours, the Utahs,[24] as do the latter with the tribe adjoining on the east, the Jicarilla Apaches, and by the last the communication is kept up with the several bands of their own tribe on the east of the state, and so on to the Gila bands on the south. And here if the Gila Apaches prove refractory, the Nabajoes may be brought against them without difficulty, for they are far from friendly now, and frequently have a brush when they meet.

To an end so desirable the Pueblos of the state might in the first place be well employed in bringing about the reformation of the Nabajoes, although, at present, they are not friendly.

The Moqui Indians, who live to the southwest of the Nabajoes,[25] are weak in numbers and are too remote to give annoyance to the state, were they so disposed. They have, however, no such disposition, but, on the contrary, are pacific, honest, and hospitable and are, besides, the most civilized of the western Indians. They always proved themselves good warriors in their former contests with the

[24] The "most friendly relations" between the Navahos and the Utes may be questioned. Ruth M. Underhill states that the Utes had been engaged in warfare against the Navahos for centuries. *The Navajos*, 116. Certainly they felt free to run off Navaho stock, raid their fields, and steal their women and children. In the campaign conducted by Colonel Kit Carson against the Navahos in 1863–64, the Utes were willing spies and auxiliaries for the army. They expected to keep the women and children as well as the plunder which they captured. Carson recommended that they be permitted to do so as the only way to recompense them for their valuable service. Carson to the Assistant Adjutant General, July 24, 1863, *War of the Rebellion: A Compilation of the Official Records of the Union and Confederate Armies*, Series 1, XXVI, part 1, 232. General James H. Carleton, in command of the department, forbade the Utes to take captives, although he permitted a bounty to be paid for captured horses, mules, and sheep. Carleton to Carson, August 18, 1863, *ibid.*, 235.

[25] Today the Hopi (Moqui) Indian Reservation is completely surrounded by the Navaho Indian Reservation. The Hopi pueblos are still where they were in McCall's day, which was west, rather than southwest, of the Navaho country.

Nabajoes and Apaches, and, though much reduced in numbers by their more powerful enemies, were never subdued.

The cultivation of a friendly understanding with them might be repaid at some future day by their services in various ways, as guides, etc., in the event of a war with either of their old enemies. The Moqui live in permanent villages, cultivate large farms, have a large amount of stock, and make blankets and cloths from wool of their own growing. The number of their lodges is about three hundred and fifty, which at seven per lodge would give a population of twenty-four hundred and fifty souls.

On the north of the Nabajoes are the Utahs, occupying the territory between the San Juan and the head of the Arkansas, a rugged country but well stocked with game. They have neither permanent villages nor cultivated fields, and subsist chiefly on game. They are a warlike people and much attached to a wandering life, frequently extending their excursions to California.[26] Altogether they amount to four or five thousand, though there are rarely at a time more than one thousand immediately on the borders of the state. These people do not extend their forays further south than Abiquiu, Taos, and Morotown. And in these they are often united with the Jicarilla Apaches. In event of an active campaign being set on foot for the purpose of punishing the outrages committed recently by the latter, the Utahs would undoubtedly render them great assistance covertly, and, at the same time, send in to inform us of their determination to remain neutral. It is not probable however they would openly join them.

Adjoining the Utahs on the northeast are the Sheyennes and Arapahoes, who range from the head waters of the Arkansas eastward upon the plains. They subsist entirely upon the buffaloe, commit no depredations, are friendly to the white man; though in the event of a war with other tribes could not perhaps be depended upon. Together they amount to about three thousand five hundred souls.

The eastern part of New Mexico, up to the Rio Pecos, is a part of the range of the Comanches, and they visit these grounds at least once

[26] It is doubtful that the Utes ever frequently extended their excursions into California.

a year, generally after the breaking up of their quarters near the sources of the Brazos and Trinity Rivers of Texas. They ralely [*sic*] commit depredations in New Mexico, and their movements are principally of interest to the state from their intimate connexion with the Apaches. They meet the latter on the Pecos, and there concert their campaigns into Chihuahua and Sonora. From these departments they annually bring off large numbers of mules, and often from Durango, into the center of which they sometimes make their way in company with the Mescaleros (Apaches). And from these departments they also bring off many prisoners.

Again, on their return, they halt at the Pecos, and are now met by the New Mexican traders [the Comancheros]. Their mules are many of them exchanged with the latter for arms and ammunition, cloths and paint, etc., etc. The remainder are driven with them, on their return, and their meat eaten until they again enter the buffaloe range.

Their prisoners are said to amount to large numbers. They consist principally of women and children, though men are often brought over. A New Mexican, living at San Miguel, recently returned from a large camp of Comanches and Apaches on the Pecos, stated that in the camp of the former there were almost as many Mexican slaves, women and children, as Indians. It will be a difficult matter to induce them to restore these prisoners. And until this unlicensed trade is broken up, their predatory incursions into Mexico can never be checked. The Comanches, divided into three bands, have in all upwards of twelve thousand souls.

The Kayuguas,[27] who occupy the country west of the Brasos, are rarely seen on the borders of New Mexico. They do not exceed two thousand souls.

Lastly, the several bands of the Apaches. These Indians, owing to their numerical strength, their bold and independent character, and their immemorial predatory habits, will, it is to be apprehended, prove more difficult to reclaim or subdue than any other of the, strictly speaking, New Mexican tribes.

From the earliest accounts we have of them, they have been re-

[27] The Kiowas, who were often allied with the Comanches.

garded by their kindred tribes as mountain robbers. On the Gila, at the period of the Spanish conquest, they were in the habit of despoiling the fields of their more industrious and pacific neighbours, the Moqui. By these they have latterly been successfully resisted. But the inhabitants of Chihuahua and Sonora are still groaning under their relentless spoliations. They complain bitterly, but continue to submit without resistance.

The Apaches, divided into six bands, inhabit the country enclosed between the eastern chain of the Rio Grande mountains and the River Pecos, from the northern to the southern boundary of New Mexico, and on the south the country bordering on the Gila River, thus completing the chain by uniting with the Utahs on the north and with the territory of the Nabajoes on the west.

Of the different bands, the Jicarilla Apaches, on the extreme north, are one of the smallest, but, at the same time, one of the most troublesome of the tribe. They have latterly committed more murders on our people than all the others together. Ranging from the upper Arkansas to the Canadian, their trail crosses the Independence and Santafé road between the Point of Rocks[28] and the Wagon Mound or Santa Clara Spring,[29] and this ground is known as the scene of several recent and deplorable tragedies.[30] They have suffered severely in two or

[28] Point of Rocks is located on the Cimarron branch of the Santa Fe Trail, about twenty miles east of the Canadian River crossing.

[29] Santa Clara Spring was about two miles northwest of the present town of Wagon Mound.

[30] There were two tragedies. In September, 1849, a small party—including Dr. John M. White, who was a Santa Fe merchant, his wife, and his small daughter—was attacked by Jicarilla Apaches at Point of Rocks. The eleven male members of the party were killed, and Mrs. White, the child, and a Negro female servant were taken captive. When efforts were made to rescue them, Mrs. White was killed by an Indian woman. The Congress appropriated fifteen hundred dollars to ransom the daughter, but neither she nor the servant was recovered. It was believed that the child, at least, had been killed. A vivid account of the massacre and subsequent rescue attempts is found in the correspondence of Indian Agent Calhoun. See especially Calhoun to Brown, November 2, 1849; and

three conflicts with our troops during the past year, and are supposed now to number less than one hundred warriors, four hundred souls. They, as well as all the other bands of this tribe, have no permanent villages, no fields of grain, and, fearing collision with the stronger tribes that roam the buffaloe plains, the Jicarillas depend for their subsistence chiefly on the success of their marauding parties.

This band is considered as incorrigible, and it is believed they will continue to rob and murder our citizens until they are exterminated. I know of no means that could be employed to reclaim them.

Next in succession, southwardly, are the White Mountain Apaches, numbering one hundred and fifty warriors. They are in close communication with the Sacramento Apaches, who have about the same number of warriors. These two bands inhabit the White and Sacramento Mountains, and together they range the country extending north and south from the junction of the Gallinas with the Pecos to the lower end of the Jornada del Muerto. They continue to drive off the stock and to kill the Mexican shepherds both in the vicinity of Vegas and along the Rio Grande from Sandival's[31] to Don' Aña.

Next come the Apaches Mescaleros, consisting of two bands, under the chiefs Marco and Gomez; the former, the more northerly, having two hundred warriors; the latter four hundred. They hold the country east of the Rio Grande from the Guadelupe Mountains to Presidio del Norte. These two bands are the strongest, and the most warlike, and fearless of their tribes. They have rarely molested the inhabitants of New Mexico north of El Paso. Nor were they unfriendly to the

November 30, 1849; and Lea to Calhoun, November 18, 1850, in Abel (ed.), *Official Correspondence*, 68–69, 88, 269.

The other incident occurred at Wagon Mound in May, 1850. Some ten or eleven persons, the entire party accompanying the mail from the East, were killed, the mail bags cut open, and the mail destroyed or scattered. Again, the Jicarilla Apaches were the perpetrators. See Ambrose E. Burnside to James N. Ward, May 23, 1850; Calhoun to Brown, May 24, 1850, in *ibid.*, 198–99, 206, and related correspondence.

[31] Sandoval is located on the west bank of the Río Grande between Albuquerque and Bernalillo.

United States citizens whom they met on the road until a feeling of hostility was aroused by the infamous attack of Glanton,[32] an American citizen, in the pay of the government of Chihuahua on a part of Gomez' band in 1849. They have, however, for years, in conjunction with the Comanches, committed fearful havock in Chihuahua and Sonora, and like them have carried off women and children, though not by any means to the same extent.

These bands have no manufactures whatever, and, having no agriculture and but little game in their own country, they subsist in a great measure on the meat of horses, mules, and sometimes cattle driven from Mexico by their foraging parties. They are not, however, altogether without a farinaceous food. A kind of cake or paste is made from the mesquite bean, and the root of the maguay plant is roasted and eaten.

The Gila Apaches, subdivided into three or four smaller bands,

[32] John Glanton was a native of Tennessee who fled to Texas after committing a murder in his home state. He served in the Mexican War, though not with honor. Mustered out of the army in 1848, he settled in San Antonio. Whether he murdered several of the local citizens, as a California newspaper later charged, or merely indulged in lesser crimes, he found it desirable to leave Texas. He moved to the Mexican state of Chihuahua, where he sought to make an honest living collecting Apache scalps, for which the state government offered a handsome bounty. He became *persona non grata* there when it was ascertained that some of the scalps he and his henchmen turned in belonged to Mexicans rather than Apaches. There can be little doubt that Glanton's killing of Apache women and children led the Apaches to seek reprisal against Americans generally. Glanton and his followers made a last move to the Yuma crossing of the Colorado River. There he took over by force the ferry business already in operation, and proceeded to defraud the emigrants and abuse the Yuma Indians. He was later accused of robbery and murder. The Yumas put up with Glanton for a time, then killed him and all but three of his associates. Douglas D. Martin, *Yuma Crossing*, 138–52; Arthur Woodward, *Feud on the Colorado*, 20–30; and Jefferson Van Horne to the Assistant Adjutant General, Santa Fe, September 10, 1849, 31 Cong., 1 sess., *Sen. Exec. Doc. 24*, 34.

make their home (if an Apache can be said to have a home) on the Gila River. Their foraging parties sometimes make their appearance on the Rio Grande near Don' Aña, but by far the greater portion of their supplies are brought from Chihuahua. They are bold and independent and together muster about four hundred warriors.

To take into view the different bands collectively, as a tribe, and the extent of country held by the tribe; to consider their restless habits, their aversion to permanent villages and the labour of agriculture; at the same time bearing in mind the scarcity of game throughout [a] great part of their country, and, therefore, the temptation, in fact the almost necessity to poach upon their neighbours; and it would seem like the undertaking of a tedious task to attemp to reclaim the Apaches. It is true it will require time to subdue their propensity to plunder, to controle their movements, to settle them in permanent villages, and to induce them to commence the cultivation of the soil; and until this is effected they must continue to plunder, or they must starve. Still it may be possible to accomplish all this, by judicious management, in a few years' time. During at least the early part of this period it would, of course, be necessary to feed these Indians, to give them cattle and sheep and to encourage the rearing of them, to employ suitable persons (New Mexicans would be the best as the Apaches understand their language) to teach them how to prepare their fields and plant their corn for the first year or two. And the greatest difficulty, perhaps, would be found in carrying out this part of the scheme, to overcome the pride of the Apache warriors, who think any pursuit but those of war and the chase beneath their dignity.

From the following little incident may be drawn very fair conclusions as to the present condition and temper of the Apaches.

In March last, Mr. F. X. Aubrey,[33] on his way from San Antonio

[33] Francis Xavier Aubrey (Aubry) was one of the great pathfinders of the West. His accomplishments in covering great distances in record times made him something of a legend in his own lifetime. In the course of his trips, he constantly sought out new and shorter routes, some of which were adopted by emigrants and freighters. Aubrey was killed by Richard H. Weightman, as the result of a quarrel, in Santa Fe on August

to El Paso, with a train of wagons, fell in with Marco's band near the Lympia River.[34] The former had with him near sixty men, which perhaps had some influence on the character of his reception. An amicable meeting, however, took place, and some mules were obtained from the Indians.

In the "talk" held between the parties, Mr. A[ubrey] told Marco that the United States desired to be on friendly terms with him, and that consequently he must not allow his people to kill our citizens or carry off their stock. This he promised to do. He was then told he must also give up plundering the Mexicans. After a long pause, he replied, "I had supposed that my Brother was a man of good sense. Has he, then, seen between the Pecos and the Lympia game enough to feed three thousand people! We have had for a long time no other food than the meat of Mexican cattle and mules, and we must make use of it still, or perish." He said subsequently, "If your people will give us cattle to feed our families, we will no longer take from the Mexicans."

If these people were maintained in idleness they would, perhaps, remain quiet, but whether they could be induced to take upon themselves the task of providing for their future subsistence by their own manual labour is a question that nothing but actual experiment will solve.

The whole of the Indians of the country are ignorant of the power of the United States, and also of its views as regards themselves. And it would do much to enlighten them as to the policey [*sic*] of our Government, if delegations from the Pueblos and the principal wild tribes were called to the United States. A journey through the States and a visit to our principal cities would impress them as to the means and resources of the country to carry on a war.

---

18, 1854. Brought to trial for murder, Weightman was found not guilty on the ground that he had acted in self-defense. Twitchell, *Leading Facts of New Mexican History*, II, 305–308; and Ralph P. Bieber and Averam B. Bender (eds.), *Exploring Southwestern Trails*, 59–61.

[34] The Limpia River, or Creek, rises in the Davis Mountains, in West Texas, and flows east, its waters eventually entering the Pecos.

If, however, by such means as have been referred to, these people may not be reclaimed, it is very certain that a considerable augmentation of the armed force will be required to controle them.

Within the last hour, information of a perfectly reliable character has been received that near [Los] Padillas, about seventy miles south of Santa Fé, seven thousand sheep were driven off by Nabajoes a few days since, and a few miles lower on the river six hundred, the shepherd of the last flock being pierced with fourteen arrows.

I have the honor to be [etc.]
GEORGE A. MCCALL

(Copies of the state constitution in the Spanish and the English language enclosed herewith.)[35]

P.S. The returns in the office of the Secretary of [the] Territory show the following number of votes polled in the recent elections. No estimate of the population can be made from them as the number entitled to vote who *did not* vote is unknown.

| | |
|---|---|
| Number of votes polled for the constitution | 8,371 |
| Number of votes polled against the constitution | 39 |
| | 8,410 |
| For Governor | Votes |
| Connelly | 4,604 |
| Baca | 2,706 |
| | 7,310 |
| For Lieutenant Governor | |
| Alvarez | 4,586 |
| St. Vrain | 3,465 |
| | 8,051[36] |

[35] These documents are not filed with the report and are not reproduced herein. The English version of the constitution was published in 31 Cong., 1 sess., *Sen. Exec. Doc. 74*.

[36] The opposing candidates for governor were Dr. Henry Connelly and Francisco Tomás Cabeza de Baca; for lieutenant governor, Manuel Alvarez and Ceran St. Vrain.

N.B. The following is believed to be a pretty accurate estimate of the strength of the Apaches and also of the other New Mexican Indians. I am aware that the Apaches and Utahs are, by some persons, set down as above ten thousand each, and the Pueblos at from ten to fifteen, but I feel confident they have been overrated.[37]

| | *Warriors* | *Souls* |
|---|---|---|
| Apaches, Jicarillas | 100 | 400 |
| White Mountains | 150 | 600 |
| Sacramento Mountains | 150 | 600 |
| Mescaleros: Marco's band | 200 | 1,000 |
| Mescaleros: Gomez's band | 400 | 1,800 |
| Gila band (3 or 4 subdivisions) | 400 | 1,600 |
| Total of Apaches | 1,400 | 6,000 |

*Wild Indians of New Mexico.*

| | | *Lodges* | *Souls* |
|---|---|---|---|
| West of Rio Grande. | 1. Nabajoes | 1,500 | 10,000 |
| | 2. Moqui | 350 | 2,500 |
| North of the State | 3. Utahs, on the state line | | 1,000 |
| | Utahs, far west | | 4,000 |
| | 4. Sheyennes | 300 | 2,000 |
| | 5. Arrapahoes | 300 | 1,500 |
| East of Pecos | 6. Comanches | 2,500 | 12,000 |
| | 7. Kayuguas | 400 | 2,000 |
| West of Pecos and South of State | 8. Apaches | 1,400 | 6,000 |
| | Grand Total | | 41,500[38] |
| | Not including west Utahs | | 37,500 |

G. A. McC.

[37] McCall's figures deviate very little from those provided by Charles Bent four years earlier, except for the Navahos, to whom Bent assigned a population of only 7,000.

[38] The total should be 41,000.

# V. McCALL'S INSPECTION REPORTS

*Santa Fe*

No. 1.

Inspector General's Office,
SANTA FÉ, NEW MEXICO,
August 31st 1850.

COLONEL,

I have the honor to report for the information of the General-in-Chief that in obedience to instructions from the Adjutant General's Office, dated Washington, June 24, 1850 (received the 28th instant), I have this day completed the inspection of the troops and staff departments of the army at this post.

The town of Santa Fe, the Head Quarters of the 9th Military Department, is garrisoned by B and D Companies of the 2nd Artillery, and D Company of the 3rd Infantry. It is also the Head Quarters of the 3rd Regiment of Infantry.

The officers present and absent are,

Head Quarters of the Department

Major and Brevet Colonel John Monroe,[1] 2nd Artillery, commanding [the] 9th Military Department and also the Post of Santa Fé since October 23, 1849.

[1] See Appendix A for a listing of all military personnel mentioned in McCall's reports. It should be noted that McCall occasionally misspelled names.

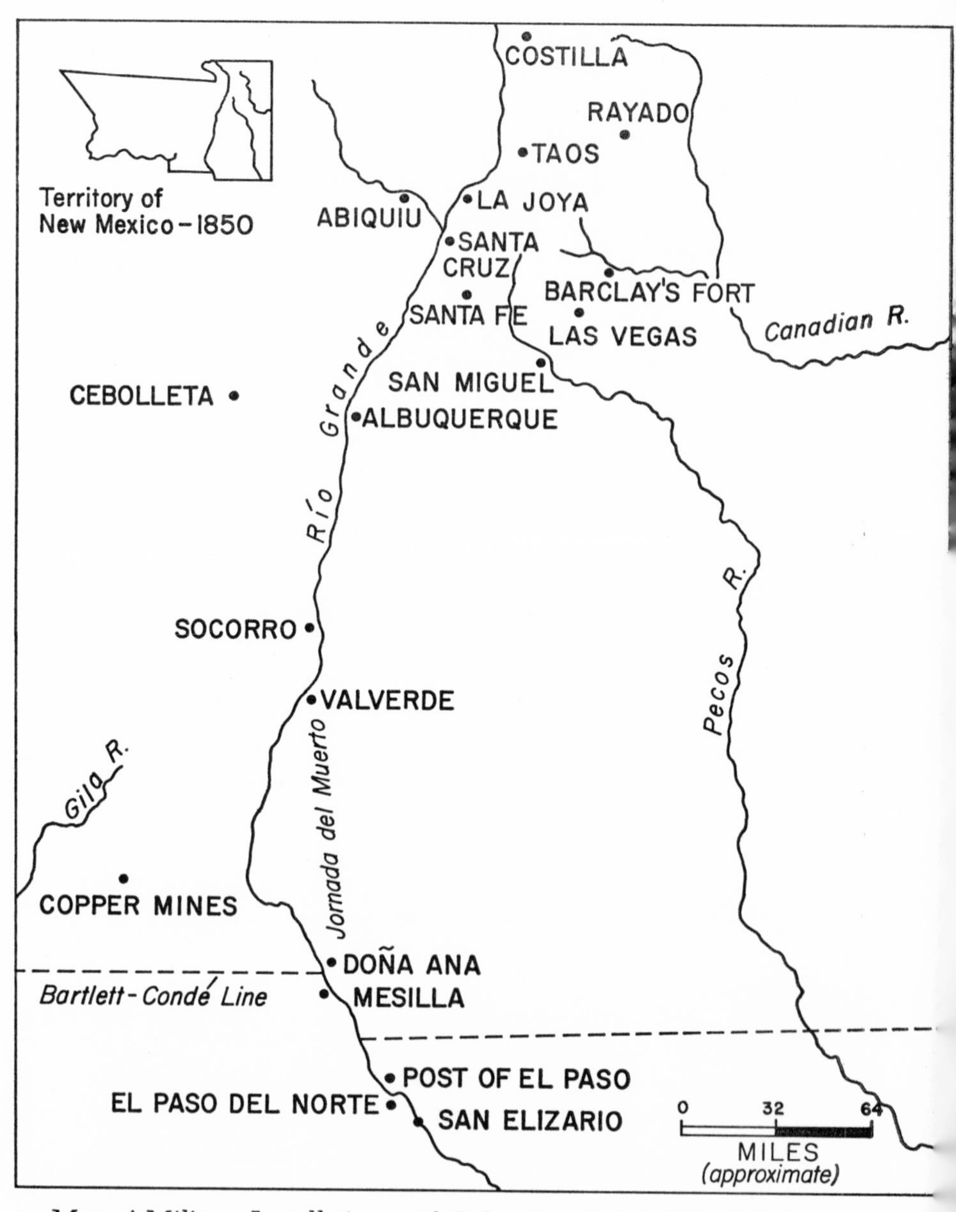


*Map of Military Installations and Other Locations in New Mexico in 1850.*

1st Lieutenant L. McLaws, 7th Infantry, acting Assistant Adjutant General of [the] department since October 23, 1849.

Captain L. C. Easton, Chief Assistant Quarter Master of the department since July 12, 1850.

Captain A. W. Reynolds, Assistant Quarter Master of the post.

1st Lieutenant F. J. Thomas, 3rd Artillery, Chief Assistant Commissary of Subsistence of the department.

Surgeon Charles McDougall, United States Army.

Major Francis A. Cunningham, Paymaster, United States Army.

Major John J. Hagner, Paymaster, United States Army.

1st Lieutenant J. H. Simpson, Topographical Engineers, on leave for six months for the benefit of his health.

Brevet 2nd Lieutenant John J. Parke, Topographical Engineers.

Head Quarters of the 3rd Regiment of Infantry.

Colonel J. B. Many, 3rd Infantry, absent, sick, since October 14, 1843.

Lieutenant Colonel E. A. Hitchcock, 3rd Infantry, absent without leave since June 30, 1850.[2]

Major W. R. Jouett, 3rd Infantry, nothing definite known.[3]

Major [ ] a vacancy.[4]

[2] Ethan Allen Hitchcock was promoted to a full colonelcy, Second Infantry, on April 15, 1851. He was named commander of the Pacific Division on April 19, 1851, and assumed his command on July 9. Thian, *Notes Illustrating the Military Geography*, 25. Although McCall lists him as absent-without-leave, he was not mentioned in the Post Returns of Fort Marcy at any time during the year 1850. "Post Returns of Fort Marcy, New Mexico, 1849–1894," Records of the Office of the Adjutant General, The National Archives, Washington, D.C.

[3] William R. Jouett became lieutenant colonel, Second Infantry, on January 31, 1850. Prior to McCall's inspection he had departed to join his new regiment, which was stationed in California. Jouett does not appear in the Post Returns of Fort Marcy at any time in 1850. *Ibid.*, and Heitman, *Historical Register*, I, 584.

[4] The vacancy was created when McCall was appointed colonel, In-

Captain and Brevet Major Gouverneur Morris, 4th Infantry, on duty with the 3rd Infantry by assignment, commanding [the] Regiment since August 29th 1850.[5]

2nd Lieutenant and Brevet Captain B. E. Bee, 3rd Infantry, Adjutant.

Regimental Quarter Master A. W. Bowman, 3rd Infantry, on detached service, Assistant Quarter Master at El Paso.

B and D Companies, 2nd Artillery.

Captain and Brevet Lieutenant Colonel Horace Brooks, D Company, 2nd Artillery, commanding [the] Batallion since July 11, 1850.

Captain and Brevet Major H. L. Kendrick, B Company, 2nd Artillery.

1st Lieutenant and Brevet Captain H. A. Allen, D Company, 2nd Artillery, on leave of absence for four months since July 15, 1850.

1st Lieutenant and Brevet Major J. J. Peck, B Company, 2nd Artillery, on leave of absence for six months since August 30, 1850.

1st Lieutenant Charles Griffin, B Company, 2nd Artillery.

2nd Lieutenant J. Nones, D Company, 2nd Regiment Artillery.

1st Lieutenant and Brevet Captain W. B. Blair, D Company, 2nd Artillery, on detached service, Assistant Commissary of Subsistance since March 16, 1847.

2nd [Lieutenant] L. Beall, B Company, 2nd Artillery.

D Company, 3rd Regiment Infantry.

Captain N. C. Macrae, D Company, 3rd Infantry, commanding Newport (Kentucky) Barracks, since September 4, 1848.

1st Lieutenant and Brevet Captain G. Sykes, D Company, 3rd Infantry, [on] general recruiting service since July 15, 1850.

2nd Lieutenant and Brevet 1st Lieutenant H. B. Clitz, D Company,

---

spector General's Department. The appointment was dated June 10, 1850, and reached McCall on August 28, 1850.

[5] Actually, Gouverneur Morris was promoted to the rank of major and transferred to the Third Infantry on January 31, 1850. Heitman, *Historical Register*, I, 727.

3rd Infantry, on duty at [the] Military Academy since August 28, 1848.[6]

Brevet 2nd Lieutenant L. H. Marshall, 3rd Infantry, commanding Company D since July 15.

W. R. Shoemaker, Military Store Keeper attached to Ordnance.

W. H. Reed, Chaplain.

Total of Artillery Battalion (B and D Companies, 2nd Artillery) present, 100.

Total of Artillery Battalion (B and D Companies, 2nd Artillery) absent, 1.

Total of D Company, 3rd Infantry; present, 50; absent, 1.

Total horses in [the] Artillery Battalion, 12.

Herewith is submitted, under separate heads, the report required by the 56th Article of the General Regulations for the Army.[7]

[6] Henry B. Clitz, who had been brevetted for meritorious conduct in the Battle of Cerro Gordo, was assistant instructor of infantry tactics at the United States Military Academy. *Ibid.*, 311; and "Report of the Secretary of War," 31 Cong., 2 sess., *Sen. Exec. Doc. 1*, part II, 365.

[7] Article LVI of *The General Regulations for the Army of the United States* (1847 edition), provided:

"It is through this department that the Secretary of War and the Commanding General are to be made acquainted with the actual state and condition of the army, and, more especially, the character and proficiency of the officers.

"It is therefore made the duty of the Inspector-General critically to inspect, as often as the Secretary of War or the Commanding General may direct, every branch connected with the military service, including the armories, arsenals, military posts, the departments of the staff, the department of the Commissary-General of Purchases, and the troops in general. At the conclusion of an inspection . . . the Inspector-General will forthwith make a report of the same to the Commanding-General; and at the end of a tour . . . the Inspectors-General will make and transmit to the Commanding-General, to be laid before the Secretary of War, reports of all that may have passed under their observation during their in-

Officers in command of Brigade, Regiments, corps, or military posts.

Major and Brevet Colonel John Monroe, 2nd Artillery, has been in command of the 9th Military Department since the 23rd October 1849. This officer has, at the same time, held the command of the Post of Santa Fé[8] since the 23rd October 1849. The instruction and the discipline of the troops, however, has been left exclusively to the senior officers of their respective corps (Artillery and Infantry) present at the post, and to them exclusively is due the credit for putting their commands in order.

Officers of the Army in general.

The officers at the post, generally, understand their duties well and are attentive and efficient in the performance of them.

Brevet Lieutenant Colonel Brooks has been but a short time in command of the Artillery Battalion, but he has been active and zealous in his efforts to advance the instruction of his command. Their previous instruction did not go beyond the school of the piece; their proficiency so far is due to Brevet Major Kendrick. The want of horses has heretofore been a great drawback to the improvement of these

---

spection. These reports will embrace the information required, under the following heads, viz . . . ."

There follow paragraphs 971 through 992, providing detailed instructions for the information to be included in the inspection reports. Pp. 179–85. McCall's original reports number each section to correspond to the paragraphs of Article LVI. The numbering has been omitted here.

[8] McCall does not mention Fort Marcy in his report, although it was an active post at the time, commanded by Major John Munroe. Fort Marcy was established in August, 1846, immediately after United States troops occupied Santa Fe. It was located on an elevation, some 650 yards northeast of the plaza, and overlooked the entire town. As originally designed, it was "computed for a garrison of 280 men." William H. Emory, *Notes of a Military Reconnoissance, from Fort Leavenworth in Missouri, to San Diego, in California*, 30 Cong., 1 sess., *House Exec. Doc. 41*, 32. Fort Marcy was a genuine defensive work, the only one in the department, and contained no quarters for the garrison, which was accommodated in the town. Santa Fe was garrisoned until 1894.

companies in the exercises and manouvres of field Artillery. They have also been partially drilled in the schools of the squad and company in Infantry tactics.

Each company has in its possession one six-pounder gun, with caisson, harness, etc., complete; one twelve-pounder field howitzer, complete; and three mountain howitzers; with fifty-six rounds of ammunition for each gun and field howitzer, and sixty rounds for each mountain howitzer. The manouvres were executed in a very creditable manner, when it is taken into consideration that on yesterday was the first time an attempt has been made in the school of the battery since these companies have been in New Mexico. The 3rd Infantry, under the command of Brevet Lieutenant Colonel McCall from March 26 to August 28. Captain and Brevet Major Morris, 4th Infantry, has been assigned to duty with the 3rd Infantry. He assumed the command of the Regiment on the 29th instant.

Non-Commissioned Officers, Musicians, and Privates.

In both the Artillery and the Infantry they are obedient. In the Infantry they are very well instructed in the schools of the squad and company; they are extremely attentive to their personal appearance; and the non-commissioned officers are prompt and efficient on duty. The number of men in the ranks, in either corps, corresponds with the returns.

Regimental and Company Books.

The regimental books of the 3rd Infantry are regularly, accurately, and neatly kept. Those of the companies are in the form and manner prescribed by the regulations.

Quarter Masters, Pay Masters, and Commissaries of Subsistence, and all disbursing officers of the Army.

The senior Assistant Quarter Master of this department arrived in Santafé on the 11th of July 1850, and has the superintendence of his department in New Mexico. He has shown himself to be zealous in promoting the interests of the service during the short period he has been here.

Captain Reynolds, who is the post quarter master at present, but who has been performing the duties of Chief Assistant Quarter Master of the department since the 15th of April last, informs me that the means hitherto employed to procure funds frequently fail; the mode adopted was to draw on the Quarter Master at St. Louis and dispose of his drafts to the merchants or others who wished to remit.

The last sum received was obtained in Chihuahua[9] by Captain Bowman, Assistant Quarter Master. The quarter master here has now on hand $55,368, while he has outstanding debts to the amount of $52,100. He informs me the department is often largely in debt and is therefore unable to compete with individuals in the purchase of corn, etc. at the proper times; that in consequence he must purchase at second hand and pay high prices; that a sufficiency of funds cannot be obtained here, but should be brought from the States.

His funds are in his own keeping. His accounts are regularly kept and duly transmitted.

The Paymaster, Major Cunningham, informs me that he has not

[9] Chihuahua was the center of an important silver mining district in northern Mexico. It was founded, probably in 1705, as a result of the silver discoveries in the vicinity. A mint was authorized in Chihuahua, as in a number of other mining centers, in order to encourage mining by avoiding the expense and delay involved in sending the silver to Mexico City for coinage. The mint in Chihuahua was closed temporarily in 1818, but was reopened sometime after the termination of the independence movement in Mexico. In 1839 it was leased to a John Jennison and Associates for a period of fifteen years at an annual rental of 250 pesos, plus the salaries for an assayer and an inspector. Gold, silver, and copper coins were minted in quantity. During the Mexican period in New Mexico, funds were sent from Chihuahua to pay the presidial troops in Santa Fe, and much of the silver which entered into the Santa Fe trade had its origin in Chihuahua. The mint continued to be operated by lessees until 1874, when it finally reverted to government control. Matías Romero, *Memoria de Hacienda y Crédito Público Correspondiente al Cuadragésimoquinto Año Económico*, 393–94; Francisco R. Calderón, *La República Restaurada, La Vida Económica*, 174; Gregg, *Commerce of the Prairies*, 302; Moorhead, *New Mexico's Royal Road*, 198; and Humboldt, *Ensayo Político*, III, 307, n.

the slightest difficulty in getting his drafts, to any amount he may require, cashed either here or at Taos. And that in his opinion it was unnecessary to bring money here from the States.

The troops at all the stations in New Mexico have been paid to include the month of June last. His funds, likewise, are in his own possession.

The Chief Assistant Commissary of Subsistence of the department also informs me that the heaviest disbursements during the ensuing year will be paid in drafts on the United States.

### Ordnance Department.

Captain W. R. Shoemaker, Military Store Keeper, who has charge of the ordnance depôt of this military department, is active and industrious, and competent to the discharge of the duties required of him. The ordnance and ordnance stores in his possession are kept in a good state of preservation. All the stores that have been estimated for by Colonel Monroe, since he has been in command of the department, have been received at Santa Fé.

### Medical Department.

Surgeon McDougall, who arrived at Santafé July 11, 1850, has, since his arrival, been very sedulous in the discharge of the many duties devolving on him. He reports the supply of medicines recently received here for distribution in the department to be by no means adequate to the demands. In some particulars his requisitions have not been filled.[10]

### Repairs of Forts, Quarters, Barracks, Magazines, &c.

Colonel Monroe and his acting Assistant Quarter Master occupy the building that was, under the Mexican government, the Palace of the Governor. This building has been repaired from time to time. Floors have been laid, etc., by the Quarter Master's Department. No further repairs are considered necessary at present. The troops are likewise in barracks built by the Mexican government. All other offices and quarters for officers are rented.[11]

[10] See Appendix B.

[11] McCall does not give the amount paid for the rental of officers' quar-

The stables and corrals, the wagon yards, etc., have been fitted up by the Assistant Quarter Master upon ground claimed as the property of the government.[12]

Arms.

The two batteries in possession of the Artillery companies are in good order and are complete, including carriages, limbers, caissons, harness, etc.

These companies are armed partially with the musketoon,[13] recently received. At my request, Lieutenant Colonel Brooks made

---

ters and offices in Santa Fe at the time of his inspection. According to a statement prepared by Captain Langdon C. Easton in July, 1851, the sum of $645 per month was being expended for rentals at that time. This did not include the cost of quarters for Dr. McDougall, which were rented from Captain Alexander W. Reynolds. By this time James S. Calhoun was territorial governor and had moved into the Palace of the Governors. Major Munroe and Lieutenant McLaws were no longer housed there, but were living in quarters rented from María Gertrudes Barcelo, the famous "La Tules," proprietress of Santa Fe's outstanding gambling establishment. "Statement of buildings rented by the Quartermaster's Department at the Post of Santa Fe, New Mexico," 32 Cong., 1 sess., *House Exec. Doc.* 2, 242.

[12] Barracks for the troops, stables, corrals, and other facilities were located north of the Palace of the Governors, approximately in the area now bounded by Palace Avenue and South Federal Place and Grant and Washington Avenues. This was the same area which had accommodated military structures during the Spanish and Mexican periods.

[13] The musketoon was a short-barreled weapon, forty-one inches in over-all length. The musketoon mentioned here was probably the .69 caliber weapon adopted in 1847 for the use of the dragoons, artillery, and sappers. Berkeley R. Lewis, *Small Arms and Ammunition in the United States Service*, 49. See also Charles E. Chapel, *Guns of the Old West*, 62–64; and Carl P. Russell, *Guns on the Early Frontiers*, 173. In actual use in the West the musketoon proved unsatisfactory, for a variety of reasons. Colonel Mansfield, in 1853, criticized it strongly and recommended that it be dropped. Frazer (ed.), *Mansfield*, 65–66.

trial of this arm, the target being placed at one hundred and one hundred and fifty yards, and the result was favourable to the accuracy of its fire. The percussion musket in possession of the Infantry was also tried by D Company, 3rd Infantry, and the regularity and accuracy of its fire was also very satisfactory. The arms of this company are in high order.

Clothing and Equipments.

In both corps the clothing conforms to the regulations. It is of good quality and of the prescribed pattern.

Forage.

The production of forage within reach of this post is equal to the demand, but speculators have possession of it, and corn is now held at six dollars the fanega (2½ bushels), or $2.40 per bushel.[14] The Quarter Master's Department is paying sixty dollars per ton for hay, and one and three-quarters cents per pound for fodder. From midwinter until the grass and fodder were fit to be cut, there was a great deficiency in long forage; wheat straw, the sole dependence, could only be got at extravagant prices and in quantities that did not meet one-fourth of the demand.

[14] As is true of many Spanish units of measurement, the meaning of "fanega" varies, depending both on the time and the area. Corn, apparently, was even scarcer in 1851 than in 1850, the price in July ranging from $6.00 to $15.00 per fanega. Samuel Ellison to Easton, July 4, 1851, 32 Cong., 1 sess., *House Exec. Doc. 2*, 251–52. However, by 1853, the price had dropped to from 75 cents to $1.40 per bushel. Frazer (ed.), *Mansfield*, 35, 45, 47, 49, 51, 56. An estimate of the amount of corn the army expected to be able to purchase in New Mexico in 1850 was prepared by Captain Thomas L. Brent. It came to only 78,425 bushels. The table is of interest because the total is broken down into the amounts expected from the various towns, including some of the Indian pueblos. 31 Cong., 2 sess., *Sen. Exec. Doc. 1*, part II, 301. The census of 1850 reported a corn production of 365,411 bushels and a wheat production of 196,516 bushels. *Seventh Census of the United States*, 1007.

Subsistence Department.

The supplies for this department, derived from the Atlantic States, are and must be, from very many causes, irregular in the time of their arrival. Again, a twelvemonth in advance it is very uncertain what number of troops the commissariat of New Mexico may be required to subsist. And thus it is that the data on which estimates should be based are so variable a character as to render it exceedingly difficult to escape one extreme in avoiding the other.

The Chief Assistant Commissary of Subsistence at this depôt reports that the supply now arriving is considerably short of his estimates, and that he has sent in by express to have the deficiency supplied this autumn if possible.

With the consent of the Commissary General of Subsistence, he has entered into contracts for the supply of flour from wheat grown in this country. The delivery of this flour has just commenced. It is dark, coarse, and sometimes gritty; but it is made from new wheat, is sound, and has not been objected to by the troops stationed here. Yet, it is not to be compared with flour received from the States if sound.

Besides flour, salt and beans, as portions of the ration, may be supplied here from the products of the country.

Quarters and Barracks.

Those occupied by the Artillery Battalion are not well arranged for the comfort of the men. They are in tolerable order.

The quarters occupied by the Infantry company are better, and are kept in fine order.

The Quarter Master Department has here for the distribution of supplies from the depôt to the different posts of the department fifty-six wagons and three hundred and thirty-five mules.

Wood for fuel (under contract) is delivered at Santafé for $3.50 per cord, or at a distance of four miles from the post at $1.50 per cord. The wood is pine and it is estimated that two cords are equal to one of good oak or hickory, and it is so issued.

[The] Greater part of the forage bought is transported by the quarter master eighteen miles on the average.

I have the honor [etc.]

GEORGE A. MCCALL, *Inspector General*

*Lieutenant Colonel W. G. Freeman, A.A.G.*
*Head Quarters of the Army, New York.*

[Received November 9, 1850.]

## *Abiquiu*

No. 2

Inspector General's Office,
ABIQUIU, NEW MEXICO,
September 3rd 1850.

COLONEL,

Agreeably to instructions from the office of the Adjutant General of the Army, dated June 24th 1850 (received at Santa Fé on the 28th ultimo), I have the honor to report, for the information of the General-in-chief, that I have this day inspected the troops and the staff departments at this post.

The town is occupied by D Company of the 2nd Regiment of Dragoons. The officers of the command, present and absent, are,

Captain and Brevet Major L. P. Graham, 2nd Dragoons, commanding company and post.

1st Lieutenant and Brevet Major O. F. Winship, 2nd Dragoons, absent, Assistant Adjutant General, United States Army.

2nd Lieutenant N. C. Givens, 2nd Dragoons, absent on leave until 21st September 1850.

Brevet 2nd Lieutenant Charles W. Field, 2nd Dragoons, acting Assistant Quarter Master and acting Assistant Commissary of Subsistence.

Assistant Surgeon H. R. Wirtz, United States Army.

The total of the company present is 48; of horses 36.

There are on temporary detached service twelve non-commissioned officers, etc., and twelve horses.

I herewith submit, under distinct heads, the report required by the 56th Article of the Regulations for the Army.

Officers in command of —— Military Posts.

Under the command of 1st Lieutenant Charles Griffin, 2nd Artillery, the company (D of the 2nd Dragoons) arrived at Abiquiu on the 27th January 1850 and the post was then established. Lieutenant Griffin remained in command of the company and post until relieved by Major Graham on the 20 July following. From what I have been able to learn, this officer appears to have discharged his duties with zeal and ability, and to have paid such attention to the instruction of the company as the character of the service, the frequent detachment of large portions of the company on escort and other service, did admit of.

Major Graham, who has been in command since July 20, has, for reasons above stated, had but little opportunity to improve the discipline of the Company or the condition of the horses.

Officers of the Army in general.

The officers at the post appear to understand their duties and are intelligent and zealous in the performance of them. Unanimity and respect for each other, to all appearance, prevail among them, and the staff and company officers appear to be sober and active and to afford their superior officer that support which he is entitled to require from them.

Non-Commissioned Officers, Musicians, and Privates.

They are obedient, but are not perfectly instructed in the prescribed drill, although they have been drilled in the school of the platoon as frequently as other duties required of them have allowed. Their personal appearance, as far as regards health, is good; with respect to dress, etc., it is not remarkably neat, which is owing in some measure to their clothing being much worn. The non-commissioned officers are generally prompt and efficient.

The numbers in the ranks correspond with the returns.

Officers, Non-Commissioned Officers, Musicians, and Privates of Cavalry.

They understand tolerably well the exercise of the sword and carbine. They are now armed with the musketoon but have no prescribed drill for the manual of this piece. They have no pistols. The officers are fine horsemen.

Company Books.

The company clothing and descriptive books are kept in the form and manner prescribed by regulations; the former is brought up to April last, since which date there has been no issue of clothing, the latter is brought up to the present date. The order book is incomplete, owing to the fact that certain orders have not been received from Department Head Quarters.

Quartermasters, Paymasters, and Commissaries of Subsistence.

The acting Assistant Quarter Master appears to have discharged his duties (since arrival at the post, July 20, 1850) in a satisfactory manner. His accounts are brought up to the 31st of August, and with accuracy and regularity. His funds are in his own hands. They are obtained on requisitions on the senior Assistant Quarter Master at Santafé, from time to time, as necessary to meet the expenses of the post.

This officer is likewise acting Assistant Commissary of Subsistence, and the same remarks are in like manner applicable to the latter department.

Paymaster Hagner, United States Army, has arrived here this day and will (tomorrow) pay the troops to include the 31st August.

Medical Department.

Assistant Surgeon Wirtz, United States Army, arrived at this post, which had previously been without a medical officer, on the 26th August last. There is no hospital at the post, and the supply of medicines is small. The sick, at this time six in number, are treated in quarters.

The climate of this region of [the] country is considered a very healthy one (the only cases of disease now existing being venerial), yet I have recommended the immediate establishment of a hospital with a suitable ward, etc., etc.

Veterinary Department of Cavalry.

[There is] No veterinary surgeon at the post.

Repairs to Quarters, Barracks, &c.

Here there are no quarters, barracks, or other buildings the property of the United States Government. The expense of all the rented quarters for officers and soldiers, the storehouses, stables, etc., amount to $183 per month.[15] They are the common adobe (sun dried brick) houses of the country. Such alterations tending to promote the health and comfort of the troops, all were practacable without expense to [the] government, have been made.

Arms.

The musketoon and sabre are in serviceable state, but not in a high order.

Clothing and Equipments.

The clothing until very recently has been deficient in quantity, and, therefore, that in use does not, in all instances, strictly conform to regulations. A supply, recently received, for one company, sixty-one strong, for one year, is now in store, but is not yet issued or fitted to the soldier. The quality of this supply appears to be good.

Cavalry Horses.

Many of them, although of sufficient height, are not of the proper figure for Dragoon horses for service in this country. They want strength and activity and, consequently, are not well suited, in general, for the particular service required of them. They are neither perfectly trained, nor are they generally, in good condition. Indeed, no small part of their number are unfit for a week's scouting in the neighbouring mountains. This defect, low condition, may be ascribed, perhaps, equally to the broken constitution of the horses by previous hard service and to the present want of good forage.

Forage.

It may be calculated that, after the present year, a sufficient supply of corn, or at least of corn and wheat, for one company of eighty-five

[15] By the summer of 1851 the cost of renting quarters for one company of dragoons at Abiquiu had risen to $280 per month. Swords to Jesup, October 25, 1851, 32 Cong., 1 sess., *House Exec. Doc. 2*, 235.

horses, with the requisite number of mules or work animals, may be had from the produce of the valley of the Chamas, in which Abiquiu is situated, and at a cost, delivered at the post, of $3.00 per fanega (2½ bushels). At the present time, however, it is with extreme difficulty that old corn can be procured of good quality or in sufficient quantity at from $4 to $5 the fanega. Long forage, hay or a substitute for it, is still, if possible, more difficult, at present, to obtain, and this is a difficulty more likely to continue for years to come than the one first mentioned.

There are no good grazing grounds in this vicinity, and the supply of grass (for hay) that may be gathered from the margins of cultivated fields, where only it is fit to be cut, is but trifling. The corn fodder is much of it consumed by the rancheros, themselves, in a green state; and wheat straw, the chief dependence, is altogether insufficient to supply a full company the year round with the full ration.

Still, with all these together, it is thought that one company may be maintained here, notwithstanding there may occur intervals during which it may not be practicable to furnish the full ration from the produce of lands within a reasonable distance.

### Subsistence Department.

Hitherto there has been with one exception, the period of high water in the Rio Grande, no difficulty in getting forward supplies of subsistence from the depôt at Santafé. The repetition of this may be guarded against, in future, by throwing forward supplies at the proper time.

Of the ration, the flour is principally of wheat grown in the country. At present it is indifferent, being neither fine nor free from grit. It is asserted that these objections will shortly be removed, being ascribed to the newness of the mills, which have but recently gone into operation. It is yet to be proven, however, that this mode of supplying the troops is preferable in any respect to that of furnishing them from the States.

The salted meats (pork and bacon) are of excellent quality.

The fresh meats (in summer mutton, in winter beef) are good; there being, however, no market for beef beyond the consumption of the troops, it cannot be furnished except in winter.

The ration is sufficient for the proper wants of the troops.

Quarters and Barracks.

Are in a fair state of cleanliness. The interior arrangements are not according to prescribed regulations but are as good as the original plans of the buildings would admit of being made.

Miscellaneous.

The locality of the town of Abiquiu has some advantages in a military point of view; it is in close vicinity of the country frequented, on the north by the Utah, on the west by the Nabajo Indians. Both these tribes have for ages been in the habit of making occasional marauds in the valley of the Chamas. Yet in our present relations with these people, a single company of Dragoons, or even half a company at the present organization, total strength eighty-five, is thought will be a sufficient garrison.

Abiquiu is distant by a good wagon road from Santa Fé about forty-eight miles.[16] From Taos, by a mule trail, crossing the intervening mountains, in a course tolerably direct, about forty-five miles.[17] Either of these routes may be accomplished, the former with wagons, the latter with light packs, in two days. There is also a line of communication between Abiquiu and Taos by way of San Juan where

[16] The road from Santa Fe to Abiquiu was approximately the same as the present highway, the distance now being forty-five miles.

[17] A mule trail between Taos and Abiquiu of only forty-five miles would indeed be "tolerably direct," since the straight-line distance between the two places is approximately forty-five miles. None of the maps of the period show the trail referred to, nor is there any such direct route today. If the trail existed, it probably crossed the Río Grande at Cieneguilla (Pilar), a little below the mouth of the Taos River. In describing the roads and trails leading to and from Taos, First Lieutenant Joseph H. Whittlesey made no mention of any direct connection with Abiquiu. Whittlesey to Brent, September 10, 1849, 31 Cong., 2 sess., *Sen. Exec. Doc. 1*, part II, 298.

there is a good ford, to La Joya, with wagons. At the latter point, the supplies are packed on mules, and the Taos Mountain[18] is crossed by a rough trail, which continues over rocky hills, in all, a distance of twelve miles; there again by wagons to Taos. The whole distance is not far from seventy-five miles.[19]

In addition to these lines of communication, there is a practicable wagon road the whole way to Taos through a gorge east of Taos Mountain. By this route the distance is increased to one hundred and five miles, and it requires two days more to accomplish it than the last.[20]

[18] The Taos Mountain here mentioned should not be confused with the Taos Mountains which lie northeast of the town and pueblo of Taos. McCall's Taos Mountain is a spur of the Sangre de Cristo Range which runs west to the Río Grande. It is sometimes called the Picuris or the Embudo Mountains.

[19] It is possible to go by highway over a portion of this route, dropping down along the Chama River from Abiquiu, crossing the Chama and the Río Grande near San Juan Pueblo, then proceeding north along the east side of the Río Grande to La Joya (Velarde). Here the present highway and the older route part company. The older route left the river at La Joya and, according to the Parke map (1851), ran northeast to Embudo Plaza, the present Dixon, then turned north across the mountains. The Abert map (1846–47) does not show the route across the mountains. The present distance by highway from Abiquiu to Taos is about sixty-five miles.

[20] The Parke map shows a road or trail running east from La Joya to Tramps, there turning north, and going through Picuris and Ranchos de Taos to Taos. Lieutenant Whittlesey described the roads leading to Taos from the south: "The roads to and from this place over the mountains may be described as follows: The direct road to Santa Fe, seventy five miles, runs north and south along the Del Norte, or within a few miles of it. At fifteen miles from Taos begins the ascent of the mountain, which rises precipitously to a great elevation and is crossed in a distance of ten miles. It is altogether impracticable at present for carriages . . . . From La Joya to Santa Fe, the road, although bad, is practicable for wagons. At La Joya comes in the wagon-road from Taos, which, to accomplish a distance of thirty-five miles, makes a circuit of nearly one hundred, and is

During about two months of the year, usually June and July, the fords of the Río Grande at Cañada, on the route between Abiquiu and Santa Fé, and at San Juan, between Abiquiu and Taos, are impracticable owing to high water.

For the transportation of supplies of subsistence, forage, and fuel (wood) the acting Assistant Quarter Master has forty mules and six wagons. Forage is brought from distances varying from two to fifteen miles, wood about three miles.

I have the honor [etc.]
GEORGE A. MCCALL

*Lieutenant Colonel William G. Freeman, A.A.G.*
*Head Quarters of the Army, New York.*

[Received November 9, 1850.]

*Don Fernandez de Taos*

No. 3.

Inspector General's Office,
DON FERNANDEZ DE TAOS, NEW MEXICO,
September 6th 1850.

COLONEL,

In pursuance of instructions from the Adjutant General's office, dated Washington, June 24, 1850 (received at Santafé on the 28th ultimo), I have the honor to report for the information of the General-in-chief, that I have this day made an inspection of the troop and the departments of the staff at this post.[21]

H Company of the 3rd Infantry constitutes the garrison. The officers of this company present and absent are,

Captain W. H. Gordon, 3rd Infantry (temporarily absent on duty at Santafé), is the permanent commander of the company and post.

---

exceedingly difficult, not more than half loads being carried when transportation is attempted by this road."—Whittlesey to Brent, September 10, 1849, 31 Cong., 2 sess., *Sen. Exec. Doc. 1*, part II, 298.

[21] The post at Taos was established in 1847, following the Taos uprising which resulted in the death of Governor Charles Bent, Captain John H. K. Burgwin, and others. It was maintained until the establishment of Cantonment Burgwin in 1852.

1st Lieutenant A. J. Williamson, H Company, 3rd Infantry, absent without leave since August 15, 1850.

2nd Lieutenant and Brevet 1st Lieutenant J. N. Ward, H Company, 3rd Infantry, on detached service at Socorro, commanding A Company, 3rd Infantry, since [June 12, 1850].[22]

2nd Lieutenant A. Jackson, G Company, 3rd Infantry, on temporary duty with H Company, acting Assistant Quarter Master and acting Assistant Commissary of Subsistence.

Total of the company present, 44. Absent, sick at Santafé, 4.

Herewith is submitted under separate heads, the report called for by the 56th Article of the General Regulations for the Army.

Officers in command of —— Military posts.

The former garrison, a squadron of Dragoons under [the] command of Brevet Major Grier, 1st Dragoons, having been removed to Rayado, Captain Gordon was ordered here with his company and assumed command of the post on the 16th July last. The company has been well instructed in the schools of the squad and company. For this much credit is due to Lieutenant Williamson, who while with the company showed much zeal in establishing its discipline and advancing its knowledge of the drill.

Officers of the Army in general.

Lieutenant Jackson, the acting Assistant Quarter Master and Assistant Commissary of Subsistence, [is] at present the only officer at the post. [He] appears to understand his duties, which are well performed, as well in command of the company as in the staff departments.

Non-Commissioned Officers, Musicians, and Privates.

[They] Are generally obedient and well instructed in the prescribed drill. They are very attentive to their personal appearance, and the non-commissioned officers discharge their duties promptly

[22] The date is not given in the manuscript; in his report of the inspection of the Post of Socorro, however, McCall states that Lieutenant Ward assumed command of his company at Socorro on June 12, 1850.

and correctly. The numbers in the ranks correspond in every respect with the returns.

Company Books.

The company clothing book is brought up to the close of the second quarter, the descriptive book to the present date. The order book is not regularly kept nor up to date.

Quarter Masters, Paymasters, and Commissaries of Subsistence.

The acting Assistant Quarter Master having arrived at the post within the present quarter has not as yet rendered any returns for this post. He has on hand a balance due the United States of $450, which is in his own possession.

The same officer is acting Assistant Commissary of Subsistence, of which department he has funds to the amount of $1,600, which is also in his own keeping. The active duties of both these departments appear to be carefully discharged.

Paymaster Hagner, United States Army, has paid this company to include the 30th June 1850.

Medical Department.

There is no medical officer at this post, no hospital nor medicines, nor is there a practising physician in the town. The nearest officer of the medical department of the army is at Rayado, a distance of forty-five or forty-eight miles over a mountainous and very rugged country.[23] The sick are, therefore, necessarily sent to Santafé, a distance (by the only wagon road from this post thither) of one hundred and ten or more miles, over a rough country for much of the way. A

[23] The straight-line distance between Taos and Rayado is approximately forty-five miles. As McCall stated, part of this is over very rugged country. Even today the shortest route between the two, part of it by primitive road, is sixty-five miles. Whittlesey wrote: "The roads to Las Vegas, El Moro, El Rayado, &c., on the other side of the mountains, are mere bridle-trails along the beds of mountain torrents. A road leads from this place to the Ocaté [Creek] just practicable for empty wagons, and there joins the Bent's Fort road to the States."—Whittlesey to Brent, September 10, 1849, 31 Cong., 2 sess., *Sen. Exec. Doc. 1*, part II, 298.

short time since, six men were sent to hospital in this way, one of them suffering under fever of typhoid characters. A supply of medicines and hospital stores for the post was forwarded from Santafé by Dr. McDougall some weeks since, but owing to some cause not explained, it was stopped at Cañada, where I am informed it still lies.

### Repairs to Quarters, Barracks, &c.

There are no quarters or other buildings at this post the property of the government. Quarters for officers and soldiers, storehouses, stables, etc., are rented in the town; these are the usual adobe dwellings of the country. The total expense of the buildings and corrals rented for these purposes is $120 per month.[24]

### Arms.

The arms are in a perfectly serviceable state, and are very well cleaned and preserved.

### Clothing and Equipments.

The clothing of the company is of the regulation pattern. There is none on hand for issue, but that in possession of the men is still, in general, in excellent condition. A years' supply for a company fifty-two strong, for one year, is invoiced, en route from the Atlantic States.

### Forage.

Forage, the produce of the valley of Taos, is purchased here by the Quarter Master as wanted. A supply of corn and wheat for a squadron of Dragoons, one hundred and seventy horses, together with officers' horses and the requisite number of draught animals may always be had. The average price paid for corn and wheat is $3.50 per fanega (2½ bushels), though it sometimes rises as high as $5. For long forage, wheat straw is the principal dependence, there being no grass fit for hay in the vicinity. Corn fodder may be got, but not in any quantity, much of it being used green, and much of it

[24] By the summer of 1851 the cost of rentals in Taos had increased to $135 a month, the post still being garrisoned by one company of infantry. Swords to Jesup, October 25, 1851, 32 Cong., 1 sess., *House Exec. Doc.* 2, 235. This was a smaller increase than that occurring at most posts.

destroyed by bad management of the rancheros in curing and taking it in. It is not probable, however, that large quantities of forage will ever be required for the maintenance of troops here. It is valuable, however, the grain only, as being within reach of any cavalry force that may be stationed at Rayado, whither [it] may be transported on pack animals.[25]

Subsistence Department.

The acting Assistant Commissary of Subsistence draws his supplies from a depôt established by the senior Assistant Commissary of Subsistence of the 9th Department at La Joya, distant thirty-six miles. With pack mules, a supply can thence be obtained, by crossing the Taos Mountain, in four days, or with wagons, by turning the Taos Mountain on its eastern slope, in eight days, distance sixty-five miles.[26]

Thirty days subsistence for the present force is now on hand. Of this, the flour is made in the country. In quality it is tolerable, being made of new wheat, and now sound, but it is course and not free from grit.

For the purpose of supplying the mills, more wheat was planted in this valley this spring that [*sic*] usual, and consequently less corn, and the price of corn has therefore risen. Thus the amount saved in the Commissary Department by purchase (by contract) of New Mexican flour, if any, is perhaps doubly lost by the Quarter Master Department through the advanced price of corn. This appears to be the result the present year. It may not continue to be so in future years.[27]

[25] Swords reported in 1851, "All the grain for the animals [at Rayado] had to be brought across the mountains from Taos, a distance of forty miles, on pack-mules, costing $2.50 per bushel." *Ibid.*

[26] Whittlesey had reported earlier in the year that his supplies were transported from La Joya to Taos by contract, at less expense than by public train. Whittlesey to Brent, April 21, 1850, 31 Cong., 2 sess., *Sen. Exec. Doc. 1*, part II, 300.

[27] Whittlesey blamed the shortage of flour on the fact that "The amount of wheat sold and manufactured into whiskey of a most deleterious nature is about 10,000 bushels, in favorable years. This amount being

Quarters and Barracks.

Are in a very good state of cleanliness. The interior arrangements are as near those prescribed by regulations as the plan of the building will allow.

Miscellaneous.

The town of Don Fernandez de Taos may be considered a proper station for a small force, say half a company of Infantry (present organization of eighty-four total), of which two non-commissioned officers and ten privates might be mounted. The inhabitants of the Valley of Taos are the most turbulent in New Mexico, and the Indians of the Pueblo of Taos, three and one-half miles north of Don Fernandez, still entertain a smothered feeling of animosity against the Americans, which it is well to keep under. But the force above specified is considered sufficient to enforce all police regulations and keep these people quiet.

As the base of operations of a strong cavalry force against either the Utahs or Jicarillea Apaches, it has nothing to recommend it; but, on the contrary, many obstacles of serious character interpose themselves among the surrounding mountains on the north and northeast to check and retard an advance into the enemies' country. (As a strategic point on this portion of the frontier of New Mexico, Rayado possesses many advantages over Taos. See report respecting Rayado.) From Taos to Santa Fé there is a good wagon road as far as the base of the stony hills north of the Taos Mountain, fifteen miles, thence over these hills and the mountain, twelve miles with pack animals, whence wagons may again be taken to Santafé. This route is accomplished in five days, distance eighty miles. The Taos Mountain may, however, be turned on the east with wagons and the march made in six and [one] half days, the distance being about one hundred and ten miles. For transportation of subsistence, forage, and fuel the acting Assistant Quarter Master has two six-mule teams and wagons,

withdrawn from the necessities of consumption, seems to me to call for legislative action to stop the pernicious traffic." Whittlesey to Brent, September 10, 1849, *ibid.*, 298.

and one two-mule team and cart. Wood for fuel is hauled about ten miles. He has three horses for express and escort service.

I have the honor [etc.]

GEORGE A. MCCALL, *Inspector General*

*Brevet Lieutenant Colonel William G. Freeman, A.A.G.*
*Head Quarters of the Army, New York.*

[Received November 9, 1850.]

*Las Vegas*

No. 4.

Inspector General's Office,
LAS VEGAS, NEW MEXICO
September 13th 1850.

COLONEL,

In obedience to orders from the Adjutant General's Office, dated Washington, June 24, 1850 (received at Santa Fé on the 28th ultimo), I have the honor to report for the information of the General-in-Chief that I have this day inspected the troops and staff departments of the army at this post.[28]

The garrison consists of K Company, 2nd Dragoons, and G Company, 3rd Infantry.

The officers present and absent are,

Captain and Brevet Lieutenant Colonel E. B. Alexander, 3rd Infantry, commanding the post.

Assistant Surgeon Thomas A. McParlin, United States Army.

Captain Croghan Ker, K Company, 2nd Dragoons, at Albuquerque in arrest since May 11, 1850.

1st Lieutenant and Brevet Major T. H. Brooks, G Company, 3rd Infantry, on detached service, aide-de-camp to Brevet Major General Twiggs.

1st Lieutenant A. Pleasanton, K Company, 2nd Dragoons, en route from Fort Leavenworth to join his company.

[28] The Post of Las Vegas was established on October 2, 1849. Troops had been stationed temporarily at Las Vegas on several occasions prior to that date.

2nd Lieutenant A. D. Tree, K Company, 2nd Dragoons, Adjutant, 2nd Dragoons, since May 21, 1849.

2nd Lieutenant A. Jackson, G Company, 3rd Infantry, on detached service at Taos, New Mexico.

2nd Lieutenant John Buford, A Company, 2nd Dragoons, commanding K Company, 2nd Dragoons.

Brevet 2nd Lieutenant S. M. Barton, 3rd Infantry, commanding G Company, 3rd Infantry.

Total present K Company, 2nd Dragoons, 51; on detached service, 12; horses present, 47; detached, 12.

Total present G Company, 3rd Infantry, 41; absent 2.

I submit herewith, under separate heads, the report required by the 56th Article of the General Regulations for the Army.

Officers in command of —— Military Posts.

Brevet Lieutenant Colonel E. B. Alexander, 3rd Infantry, on duty as Major of the Regiment by assignment, arrived at Las Vegas and assumed command of the post, relieving Brevet Captain Judd, 3rd Artillery, on the 23rd April 1850.

The troops now here arrived also at recent and different periods, viz: G Company, 3rd Infantry, March 15, 1850; K Company, 2nd Dragoons, June 3, 1850. Since the arrival of Lieutenant Colonel Alexander he has attentively discharged his duties and paid proper attention to the instruction of his command.

The Dragoon Company (K) had, previously to its arrival here, been stationed at Cibolletta, New Mexico, under [the] command of its captain, C. Ker. On the 11th March last the captain was placed in arrest by the commanding officer of the department, and Brevet 1st Lieutenant John Adams of I Company, 2nd Dragoons, was detached from his company at Taos to command this company, which command he held from the 15th May till the 10th of August last. On the 10th August, 2nd Lieutenant J. Buford, A Company, 2nd Dragoons, was assigned to duty with this company. He relieved 1st Lieutenant Adams, and has retained the command of it until the present date.

The company has been regularly drilled since its arrival at Vegas and is now well instructed in the school of the platoon.

G Company, 3rd Infantry, was commanded by Brevet 1st Lieutenant J. N. Ward, H Company, 3rd Infantry, from March 5 till June 1, 1850, when he was relieved by Brevet 2nd Lieutenant S. M. Barton, 3rd Infantry. This company has been well drilled for some months past in the schools of the squad and company.

Officers of the Army in general.

The officers at the post understand their duties well and are very zealous in the performance of them. They are sober and active and afford the commanding officer all the support he could require of them; there is also unanimity and respect for each other.

Non-Commissioned Officers, Musicians, and Privates.

They are obedient and well instructed in the prescribed drill. The non-commissioned officers are generally efficient. The numbers actually in the ranks correspond with the returns.

Officers, non-commissioned officers, Musicians,
and privates of Cavalry.

Those of K Company, 2nd Dragoons, are properly instructed and are tolerably expert in the exercise of the sword, carbine, and pistol. They have just received the musketoon and revolver (pistol), but they have not the manual for these arms. The officer commanding the company is a fine horseman.

Company Books.

The books of both these companies are regularly and accurately kept, and in the form prescribed.

Quartermasters, Paymasters, and Commissaries of Subsistence.

The acting Assistant Quarter Master (Lieutenant Buford) has been in the performance of the duties of the department, at this post, but a few weeks. During this period he has performed his duties in a satisfactory manner in every respect. He has no accounts made out. He has funds in his hands to the amount of $400, obtained on requisitions on [the] senior Assistant Quarter Master.

The same officer is the acting Assistant Commissary of Subsistence, and the same remarks will apply to the discharge of his duties in this department. For this department funds are likewise received on requisition on the senior Assistant Commissary of Subsistence at Santafé. Requisition has been made for [the] fourth quarter of [the] present year, but the money has not yet been received.

Ordnance Department.

The acting ordnance officer of the post is Lieutenant Buford. He has in charge two six-pounder bronze guns, complete, and accoutrements for the same. One twelve-pounder howitzer, complete, and accoutrements for same. And twenty-five rounds of ammunition for each piece of ordnance. These pieces are not in very good order, although serviceable.

Medical Department

The officer of this department, at this post, appears to be very faithful in the discharge of his duties. There is a very good hospital and a sufficient supply of medical and hospital stores, and the sick, eleven in number at this time, appear to be well attended.

Veterinary Department of Cavalry.

[There is] No veterinary surgeon at the post.

Repairs to Quarters, Barracks, &c.

There are no quarters or other buildings the property of the Government at this post. Quarters for officers and soldiers, storehouses, stables, and corrals for work animals are rented in the town. The total cost of these is $260 per month.[29]

Arms.

The musketoon, revolving pistol, and sabre of the Dragoons and

[29] By the summer of 1851 the cost of rentals in Las Vegas had jumped to the sum of $439 per month. Part of the increase can be accounted for by the addition of a second company of dragoons to the garrison. "Statement of quarters, &c., hired at Las Vegas," 32 Cong., 1 sess., *House Exec. Doc.* 2, 251.

the percussion musket of the Infantry are cleaned and preserved in a proper manner.

Clothing and Equipments.

The clothing conforms to the regulations. The Infantry company has on hand a supply for fifty-two men for one year. That for the Dragoons has not yet been received.

Cavalry Horses.

They have generally been well selected and are now in good condition, as far as regards flesh, but some eight or ten of them have been hitherto either completely broken down or severely injured in service, and they are, consequently, although well looking under the saddle on parade, utterly unfit for a rough campaign in the Indian country.

Forage.

The forage required for the troops stationed here is bought by the acting Assistant Quarter Master from time to time as required. And the probability is that corn will be as high as $5 the fanega (2½ bushels) before the new crop is fit to be fed. The prospect of this crop is that in addition to the wants of the inhabitants it will not suffice to feed more than from one hundred and fifty to one hundred and seventy head of horses during the year. The crop of the valley of Vegas is here referred to. All the wheat of this valley is already engaged by the millers at Morotown (St. Vrain and company), but the mill will furnish a considerable supply of bran, and there will be no difficulty in providing long forage for the same or a larger number of horses. It is thought that, hereafter, more land will be brought into cultivation, and that the crop of corn will be much encreased [*sic*]. This cannot be calculated on with any certainty. The only thing certain is the supply of long forage, for the grazing in the vicinity is uncommonly fine and of great extent.

The consumption of corn at this post is very great, and a large depôt should be established either here or in the vicinity. The consumption is caused by troops and government trains passing and repassing. Frequent and large demands are made, often as high as five hundred bushels at a time, for Vegas is considered the point of departure upon the journey across the plains, and here the outfit is completed. Again they come from the east, and on approaching the end of their long journey they find their animals exhausted and send in for succour. Thus, large supplies of forage have at times to be sent out as far as the Cimeron to enable trains to accomplish their march, which without relief would be doubtful.[30]

Subsistence Department

There is in store nearly one years subsistence for the present command, with the exception of salted meat and vinegar, of the former a few months supply, of the latter there is none. Flour is received (under contract) from the mills at Moratown, twenty-five miles distant. The quality of the provision is, in general, good. With respect to flour some remarks have been made in the reports of inspections at Taos, etc., but at this post no complaint is made by the troops as to its quality.

Quarters and Barracks.

Are in good order, sufficiently large and airy, and in most respects better than those at the several posts previously inspected.

Miscellaneous.

A small military post, either here or at some adjacent point on the Fort Leavenworth road, is important, *principally as a depôt* from

[30] Major Swords, whose duty it was to secure a reduction in the cost of the Quartermaster's Department in New Mexico, wrote of the use of corn as forage: "But scarce as forage was, I could not but be struck by the profuse and extravagant manner in which it was used. To the mules I had with me, I did not think it necessary to feed a grain of corn during the whole trip, except when I was obliged to stop in the towns, where there was no grazing, yet they kept in good order; and although this may not always be the case, I found that not a train started, no matter for what distance, that was not well supplied with grain, which, from not using nose-bags, was generally throwm [*sic*] on the ground, and a large portion of it wasted; the animals preferring the sweet and nutritious grasses of the country, to the hard, flinty Mexican corn."—Swords to Jesup, October 25, 1851, 32 Cong., 1 sess., *House Exec. Doc.* 2, 239.

which supplies coming from the east may be diverted, perhaps to Rayado, but more certainly to those posts in the Rio Abajo country which are furnished from the same source, that is all above the Jornada del Muerto, Albuquerque, Cibolletta, and Socorro.[31] A wagon road has been made from this point, by way of Anton Chico, to Albuquerque and thence to the last named posts. At present these posts are supplied from the depôt at Santafé by way of Albuquerque. It is asserted that a shorter and better road to Albuquerque may be had by way of Anton Chico than by way of Santa fé. In support of which I may cite the instance of Dr. Connelly's train, just arrived from the east, taking that route in preference.[32]

For anything more than a depôt, there would appear to be little to recommend the occupation of this place. It is distant sixty miles from the border of the country of the Jicarilla Apaches on the north, and at least one hundred miles from that of the White Mountain Apaches on the south.

Both these bands, it is true, pass by Las Vegas in their periodical visits to each other, but they pass, usually, at a distance so far east of the town as to be beyond observation, and in small parties.

For all the advantages of support or cooperation in Indian warfare, it is too far (sixty miles) from the Post on the Rayado, and it is also out of the usual line of march of the Comanches when they visit New

[31] Fort Union, located about twenty-five miles northeast of Las Vegas, was established on July 26, 1851. The supply depot was moved from Santa Fe to Fort Union even before storehouses had been erected. It remained the principal supply depot for the area for many years, declining in importance after the railways were built into New Mexico. Once Fort Union had been established, it became the junction point for the Cimarron and Mountain branches of the Santa Fe Trail. Fort Union was abandoned in 1891.

[32] Dr. Connelly's train, to which McCall refers, had run into difficulties on its return from the States loaded with merchandise. The Jicarilla Apaches had stolen some eighty or ninety of Connelly's mules, forcing the train to lie over until additional animals could be obtained. Calhoun to Brown, August 30, 1850, Abel (ed.), *Official Correspondence*, 255–56.

Mexico. The latter either direct their course to the headwaters of the Arkansas or low down upon the Pecos. The proper disposition of the cavalry force on the eastern frontier of New Mexico would seem to be at Rayado and on the Pecos, below the junction of the Gallinas with that river. At each of these points a squadron of Dragoons with half a company of Infantry might be posted to advantage. It is an unnecessary expense to occupy any post in this country solely with Dragoons—the horse, here, costs more than the man.[33] But at Vegas there need not be more than one company of Infantry (one-half mounted), simply for escort service, and to guard the depôt, and to support the civil authorities here and at San Miguel.[34]

Barclay's trading house, or fort as it is called, situated at the point where the Bent's Fort road and the Cimeron road come together, and eighteen miles from Vegas, has been much extolled as an advantageous position, both for the location of a depôt and the establishment of a military post. But there are undoubtedly objections to this position which should not be passed unnoticed.

In the first place, as a depôt, every article of supplies destined for any military post in New Mexico, except Rayado, must of necessity pass through the town of Las Vegas. Those intended for Rayado should be detached from the train, without unloading, at the Point of Rocks.

[33] The cost of keeping a horse is not estimated, but in 1851 the cost of keeping a mule for one year on grain, exclusive of other forage, was placed at $320. "Estimate of the cost of the keep of one mule," 32 Cong., 1 sess., *House Exec. Doc.* 2, 241.

[34] San Miguel remains today a small town, located on the Pecos River, some three miles south of National Highway 84–85, between Las Vegas and Santa Fe. Although the present highway bypasses San Miguel, the Santa Fe Trail ran through it. In the Mexican period it was a more important town than Las Vegas, which was not established until 1835, serving as the county seat of San Miguel del Bado County, which included Las Vegas, and as a port of entry for the Santa Fe trade, although the customs were actually collected in Santa Fe. Twitchell, *Leading Facts of New Mexican History*, II, 15, n. 13; and Moorehead (ed.), in Gregg, *Commerce of the Prairies*, 77, n. 17.

More ample and better storehouses may be rented in Vegas, at less expense. Indeed, were Barclay's to be occupied for this purpose, large storehouses would have to be built outside the work.

Of this fort the outer walls are a square of sixty-four yards, with semicircular bastions or towers at two opposite angles. Against the north wall is a range of two-story buildings, against the south wall one of one-story. Detached from the east and west walls are one-story buildings, and between these and the walls are sheds for horses. The buildings, either for quarters or for storehouses are one room deep, about fifteen feet in the clear. The whole structure is of adobe, with roofs of the same. Mr. Barclay demands $20,000 for the fort, together with 700 *varas* of land fronting on the water (the Mora) and extending back to the hills; [he] would probably take $15,000. The rent he fixes at $2,000 per annum.

As a military station it would accommodate comfortably not more than one company of Dragoons with their horses, and furnish the requisite store rooms.

It is in the midst of an extended plain, gradually sloping to the center. Being perfectly bare of trees or brushwood, no movement of troops could possibly take place without being known; for the Indians, when about to make a foray into the settlements, closely watch the avenues to and from the military posts on that portion of the frontier. And any military force moving from this point to unite with those at Rayado, on the border of the Jicarilla country, must travers an open plain for forty miles, a view of which is commanded from distant mountains and hills the entire distance. The same is the case on the route to Vegas, eighteen miles.

At Barclay's, wood for fuel and timber for building are more distant than at Vegas. At the latter, wood for fuel is delivered at $2.50 per cord.

I have the honor [etc.]

GEORGE A. MCCALL, *Inspector General*

*Lieutenant Colonel W. G. Freeman, A.A.G.*
*Head Quarters of the Army, New York*

[Received November 9, 1850.]

*Rayado*

No. 5.

Inspector General's Office,
RAYADO, NEW MEXICO,
September 16th 1850.

COLONEL,

In obedience to instructions from the Adjutant General's Office, dated Washington, June 24, 1850 (received at Santa Fé on the 28th ultimo), I have the honor to report for the information of the General-in-Chief that I have this day inspected the troops and staff departments of the army at this post.

The garrison consists of G and I Companies of the 1st Dragoons.

The officers present and absent are,

Captain and Brevet Major William N. Grier, I Company, 1st Dragoons, commanding [the] post since May 27, 1850, on temporary duty at Taos.

Assistant Surgeon D. L. Magruder, United States Army, joined August 21, 1850, on temporary duty at Taos.

Captain R. S. Ewell, G Company, 1st Dragoons, en route from Fort Leavenworth to join his company.

1st Lieutenant Joseph H. Whittlesey, I Company, 1st Dragoons, Assistant Commissary of Subsistence and acting Assistant Quarter Master.

2nd and Brevet 1st Lieutenant John Adams, I Company, 1st Dragoons.

2nd Lieutenant and Brevet 1st Lieutenant O. H. P. Taylor, G Company, 1st Dragoons, commanding company since September 12, 1847.

Total present, G and I Companies, 41.

Total absent G and I Companies, 31. (25 of G Company in California)

Total horses present, 44.

Total horses absent, 5.

Herewith is submitted under separate heads the report required by the 56th Article of the General Regulations for the Army.

Officers in command of —— Military Posts.

This squadron of Dragoons, previously stationed at Taos, arrived at this place, under orders for temporary service, on the 24th May 1850. On the 1st August the commanding officer was ordered by the commander of the department to establish himself here and provide supplies for one year. Brevet Major Grier, who has commanded this squadron since April 1, 1850, has been in command of this post from the date it was established to the present time. He appears to have discharged his duties with much zeal and ability.

Less attention, however, appears to have been paid to the instruction of the troops in the prescribed drill, in consequence of the increased fatigue duty incident to the establishment of a new post, and also in consequence of having been previously to the arrival of the squadron here on repeated hard service in the Apache country. To these causes may be added the greatly reduced numbers of the squadron. The drill, therefore, in the school of the squadron is by no means perfect.

Officers of the Army in general.

The officers in general appear to understand their duties and to perform them with zeal. They are active and efficient on field service. And at the post serve in harmony together.

Non-Commissioned Officers, musicians, and privates.

They appear to be obedient, but are not well instructed in the prescribed drill. Their appearance is that becoming hard service rather than parade duty. The numbers correspond with the returns.

Officers, Non-Commissioned Officers, musicians, and privates of Cavalry.

They are more expert in the exercises of the sword, carbine, and pistol than proficient in the drill of the squadron. The officers are all good horsemen.

Company Books.

Are regularly kept and brought up to [the] present date.

Quarter Masters, Paymasters, and Commissaries of Subsistence.

The Assistant Commissary of Subsistence is also the acting Assistant Quarter Master. He is very active, capable, and efficient as a Quarter Master. His funds, received as required from the senior Assistant Quarter Master at Santa Fé, are in his own keeping.

In the Commissary Department similar remarks are applicable. The sales to officers supply the necessary funds in this department.

The troops have been paid by Major Hagner to include the 30h June.

Ordnance Department.

Brevet Major Grier, in charge of the ordnance at the post, has one six-pounder gun, complete, and one mountain howitzer, complete, together with fifteen rounds of ammunition for each piece.

Medical Department.

Assistant Surgeon Magruder, United States Army, joined August 21st 1850. There is at the post no hospital and but a small supply of medicine. The sick (at present one) are treated in quarters.

Dr. Magruder left this post, under orders for Taos, on the 15th instant, to attend the troops at that post, among whom some cases of severe illness had occurred, there being no army medical officer at Taos, nor any practizing [*sic*] physician in the town.

Veterinary Department of Cavalry.

There is no veterinary surgeon at the post.

Repairs to Quarters, Barracks, &c.

There are no quarters or other buildings belonging to the government at this post. Since their arrival here the troops have been in tents. The officers are now in quarters, and in a few weeks there will be quarters completed for the whole of the present force, or for one full company. The quarters now in preparation for the troops were originally intended by the builder, Mr. Maxwell,[35] for his private dwelling.

[35] Lucien B. Maxwell, a native of Kaskaskia, Illinois, got his first taste of the Far West as an employee of Bent, St. Vrain and Company. Later he was employed as a hunter by John C. Frémont on two of his expedi-

The price of quarters, when completed, for officers and men, stables, etc., will be $200 per month.[36]

Arms.

Halls carbines, the common holster pistols, and sabres are in good service order.

Clothing and Equipments.

Very little clothing has been on hand for many months and, consequently, that in possession of the men, in many cases, does not conform to regulations. I Company has just received a supply of clothing for sixty-one men for one year. It is of good quality. G Company has not received the supply estimated for, but the commanding officer of the company has been notified by the senior Quarter Master at Santafé that his company may be supplied from that depôt on his requisition.

Cavalry Horses.

They were when purchased of rather inferior description, very

tions, on both of which Kit Carson served as guide. Following the expedition of 1842, Maxwell went to New Mexico, engaged in trapping, and made his home in Taos. In 1844 he married Luz Beaubien, daughter of Judge Charles Beaubien. Beaubien, together with Guadalupe Miranda, owned the vast Mexican grant which, with the addition of the Sangre de Cristo Grant, eventually came to be known as the Maxwell Land Grant. Maxwell gained possession of the entire grant, through inheritance and by buying out the other heirs and claimants. He settled at Rayado Creek in 1847, building there an adobe mansion which Paul A. F. Walter described as "of some forty rooms," and Jim Berry Pearson calls "a twenty-room manor house." This, presumably, was the structure rented as quarters for the troops at Rayado. When Fort Union was established in 1851, Maxwell moved to Cimarron, where he erected a new house similar to his house on the Rayado. The house on the Rayado is now on the Philmont Boy Scout Ranch and is still in use. Walter, "New Mexico's Pioneer Bank and Bankers," *New Mexico Historical Review*, Vol. XXI (July, 1946), 211; and Pearson, *The Maxwell Land Grant*, 4–11.

[36] By 1851 the rental cost had increased to $3,400 per year. Swords to Jesup, October 25, 1851, 32 Cong., 1 sess., *House Exec. Doc. 2*, 235.

many of them having been picked up in the country, obtained from emigrants, etc., in a half broken down condition.

All the horses present are reported serviceable, but it is solely because no better can be got. Few of them are of sufficient strength and activity to perform the service required of them, and in evidence of this it may be stated that on more than one occasion the Apache Indians, when almost within the grasp of this squadron, have escaped through the better bottom and speed of their horses.

Most of these horses have been on hard service in this country for about two years, and much of that time in the mountains, a service that soon tells upon our horses. Nearly half of them are knee-sprung or otherwise injured in the limbs.

The horses brought out with this squadron in 1846 were soon after sent home and a remount of mules substituted. Again, with [the] winter of 1847–8, the squadron was mounted on horses; most of those now present have been in service since July 1848. Few horses in this service last longer than three years.

Forage.

The acting Assistant Quarter Master has made arrangements to supply one company, eighty-five strong, and the requisite number of draught animals. This officer states that by giving immediate notice, before the crops are disposed of, he could secure enough of corn for a full squadron.

Hay of fair quality, in any quantity, may be cut (of the native grass) within four miles of the post. It costs this season (under contract) $20 per ton; but, with proper arrangements, may next year be had for $10 per ton. Corn cannot be had for less than $5 the fanega (2½ bushels), for the reason that an unusual quantity of land in this region has this year been put in wheat. The Assistant Quarter Master at this post informs me that if notice were given this autumn of the amount of corn that would be required here for the next year, persons in the neighborhood would be induced to put in cultivation in the spring new land enough to produce the double of the present crop, and that a considerable reduction in price would follow.

Subsistence Department.

There is on hand for the number of troops now present about three months supply of subsistence. Every article except flour is received from the depôt at Santa Fé.

Flour is received from the Moratown mill, forty miles distant. Although course and gritty, this flour being made of new wheat is not objected to by the troops. The ration is found to be sufficient.

Quarters and Barracks.

The troops are in tents. The police of the camp is good.

The Quarter Master has for the uses of the post two six-mule teams and wagons and two four-mule etc., etc., eighteen pack mules and saddles, and four horses for express service.

Miscellaneous.

The settlement of Rayado, at the base of the Rocky Mountains, and on the rapid stream of the same name, was undertaken, within the country of the Apaches, by two well known mountain men, Maxwell and Kit Carson. It is here that the squadron of Dragoons commanded by Major Grier are now encamped.

The many advantages which this position (or one quite near it) possesses as the site of a military post are worthy of notice.

Rayado is about forty-five miles east of Taos; it is close to the border of the great plains, yet well screaned [*sic*] from observation; while from the high ground in its rear it commands an extensive view. It is, thus, near the range of the Comanche and other wild tribes of the prairie, and, at the same time, covers better than any other point the line of highly fertile though yet unsettled lands that stretch along the base of the mountains and border the numerous streams which gush from their sides, even from the Raton spur to the town of Las Vegas. It is within striking distance of the wintering places of the Apaches on [the] Red River (Canadian), and of the prairie tribes on the headwaters of the Arkansas. It is the point from which, should either of these tribes cross the mountains and penetrate into the Valley of Taos, their retreat might most certainly be cut off.[37] It is on the line of a projected road from the Big Timbers, on the Arkansas below Bent's Fort, to Santa Fé, which it is believed will afford a shorter and an easier route, with more water, grass, and wood. And it is within three miles of the present Bent's Fort road, at a point forty miles below the Raton spur of the Rocky Mountains. If the post were pushed forward into the prairie it would then be easily turned by the Indians.

In fine, this position, in a military point of view, appears to be, in every respect, a most eligible site for a frontier post—with a garrison of at least a squadron of Dragoons and a detachment of half a company of Infantry.

The lands on the neighbouring stream will support a population of several hundred families, and these lands will soon be taken up if security is afforded by the presence of a sufficient military force. The increased produce of grain, etc., would soon reduce the expenses of the post some 50 per cent.

Pine timber for building, of good quality (the P. Brachyptera), is abundant within four or five miles of any point that may be selected, not far distant from that now occupied. Wood for fuel is abundant and at hand. The grazing lands in the vicinity are extensive, and afford hay for the cutting.

In establishing a permanent post here or elsewhere, the adobe or sun-dried brick will be found, probably, the best building material the country affords. It is the most easily and expeditiously obtained;

[37] The traditional route taken by the Comanches in approaching the northern settlements in New Mexico, whether for trade or plunder, was across the Sangre de Cristo Mountains by way of Sangre de Cristo Pass. The approach from the east was commonly up the Huerfano River, across the pass, then into the San Luis Valley, essentially where United States Highway 160 enters the valley today. From this point, raids were launched against such settlements as Taos, Ojo Caliente, and Abiquiu. See Frazer, "Governor Mendinueta's Post on the Cerro de San Antonio," *University of Wichita Studies* (No. 49), 1. The Post of Rayado was not so located that it could deter Indian incursions by this route. Fort Massachusetts was established at the eastern base of Mount Blanca, in the San Luis Valley, in 1852, in part to guard the Sangre de Cristo Pass route.

it is fit for laying (when of the proper and approved size and form) in four days after being moulded; it is equally durable and less expensive than bricks; and when faced with a coating of lime-plaster is as comfortable as a building of brick or stone.

Should a permanent post be established here, the provisions and heavy stores from the east, destined for this point, should be packed separately at Fort Leavenworth and the wagons detached from the train at the Point of Rocks, on the Cimeron road, distant from this point forty-five miles over a level prairie. Or, at least, [they should be] deposited at Barclay's or Vegas (see report No. 4) and not, as at present, carried to the general depôt at Santa Fé to be distributed, causing an unnecessary transportation of two hundred miles; which, owing to the price of corn and the generally high rate of expenses here, costs as much, or nearly as much, as the transportation from Fort Leavenworth to the Point of Rocks.

Among the advantages of this post, not hitherto mentioned, should be noticed the salubrity of the climate, the winters being more mild, it is said, than those at Santa Fé, and the ease, in consequence, with which a movement of troops may be made at any season of the year.

I have the honor [etc.]

GEORGE A. MCCALL, *Inspector General*

*Lieutenant Colonel W. G. Freeman, A.A.G.*
*Head Quarters Army, New York.* [Received November 9, 1850.)

P.S. In the body of this report is [*sic*] was omitted to remark that there are twenty-five rank and file of G Company, 1st Dragoons, in California. This detachment went out as the escort of Colonel Collier,[38] and has been so reported since July 12th 1849. As they are

[38] James Collier was appointed collector of the port of San Francisco. He was escorted to California by a detachment of the First Dragoons, under the command of Brevet Captain Herman Thorne. Also under the protection of the dragoons was a party of emigrants. Thorne, a dragoon private, and a Mexican were drowned while crossing the Colorado River. Fort Thorne, New Mexico, established in 1853, was named for Captain Thorne. Collier arrived in San Francisco in November, 1849. Collier to

still born [*sic*] on the rolls of the company, without any known prospect of their return to it, it is respectfully suggested whether it would be better to transfer them to some company there, in order that the one here may be filled up.

Repectfully,
G. A. M.

*Albuquerque*

[No. 6.]

Inspector General's Office,
ALBUQUERQUE, NEW MEXICO,
September 29th 1850.

GENERAL,

In accordance with instructions, I have the honor to submit, herewith, a report of inspection of the troops at this post.[39]

The garrison is F Company, 3rd Infantry. Total present, 48.

Officers present and absent ,

Major M. S. Howe, 2nd Dragoons, commanding post since August 1st 1849.

Assistant Surgeon John Byrne, United States Army.

Captain and Brevet Lieutenant Colonel J. H. Eaton, F Company, 3rd Infantry, absent on detached service since July 25, 1849.

1st Lieutenant S. B. Schroeder, F Company, 3rd Infantry, en route from Fort Leavenworth to join his company.

2nd Lieutenant C. B. Brower, F Company, 3rd Infantry, commanding company and acting Assistant Quarter Master and Assistant Commissary of Subsistence.

William M. Meredith, November 13, 1849, 31 Cong., 1 sess., *House Exec. Doc. 17*, 24; Calhoun to Brown, January 17, 1850, Abel (ed.), *Official Correspondence*, 100; and Amiel W. Whipple, *The Whipple Report* (ed. by E. I. Edwards), 61–62.

[39] The Post of Albuquerque was established on November 17, 1846. Troops were withdrawn in 1851, but the town was regarrisoned and became department headquarters in 1852. The post was discontinued on August 23, 1867.

Officers in command of —— Military Posts.

Since the 1st August 1849, this post has been under the command of Major Howe, and has been, during the greater part of this period, the station of H Company, 2nd Dragoons (now at Cibolletta). With the view of reoccupying this post by a company of Dragoons, the commander of the department has retained Major Howe in command. The latter appears to have paid due attention to the discharge of his duties, and to the maintenance of a good discipline and police at this post.

Officers of the Army in general.

The only company officer present, Lieutenant Brower, as far as was made apparent in the course of the inspection and subsequent drill, has a fair knowledge of his duties as a company officer.

Non-Commissioned Officers, musicians, and privates.

Are obedient and tolerably well instructed in the prescribed drill. Their personal appearance is good. The numbers with ranks correspond with the returns.

Company Books.

Are regularly kept, and are brought up to the present date.

Quarter Masters, Pay Masters, Commissaries of Subsistence, &c.

The acting Assistant Quarter Master and Assistant Commissary of Subsistence has his accounts brought up to the close of the past quarter. In the Quarter Master Department he has on hand funds to the amount of $60, in the Subsistence Department, $75; these amounts are in his own hands. Small sums are received as required from the senior Assistant Quarter Master and Assistant Commissary of Subsistence at Santafé.

Ordnance Department.

There are at the post two mountain howitzers, but the carriages of these pieces are unfit for service in the field. There is but a small supply of ammunition on hand.

Medical Department.

The medical officer appears to discharge his duties very faithfully. The hospital is well situated and is kept in fine order, and the sick are well attended. The supply of medicines and stores on hand is reported to be sufficient for the wants of the present garrison.

Repairs to Forts, Quarters, Barracks, &c.

There are no quarters or other buildings at the post belonging to the government. The amount of rents paid for quarters for officers and men, for hospital, for store houses, etc., etc., is $165 per month.[40]

Arms.

The arms (percussion musket) accoutrements, etc., are properly cleaned and well preserved.

Clothing and Equipments.

The supply of clothing on hand is sufficient for present wants. It is of the prescribed pattern and of good quality.

Forage.

In ordinary seasons the lands in the vicinity of Albuquerque will afford, after supplying the demands of the inhabitants, about 25,000 fanegas of corn, and, at present, Santa Fé and Cibolletta draw considerable supplies from this section of the country. The price at this time is about $4 the fanega (2½ bushels). Grazing lands are also extensive in the vicinity, and large supplies of hay, in ordinary seasons, may be cut on these lands.

Subsistence Department.

There are on hand supplies for about forty days; all these are procured from the depôt at Santafé. They are of good quality, with the single exception of the candles. These were made in the country, by

[40] The cost of rented facilities in Albuquerque had increased to $275 a month by the summer of 1851. At that time the garrison had been enlarged, as anticipated by McCall, by one company of dragoons. "Quarters occupied at the post of Albuquerque, New Mexico," 32 Cong., 1 sess., *House Exec. Doc.* 2, 244.

contract. They are of tallow and are of bad quality. A better quality might, I believe, be procured in the country, but a considerable loss will almost always accrue from the issue of tallow candles to troops in warm climates.

Quarters and Barracks.

These are kept in a very fair state of cleanliness, and as nearly in conformity to regulations as the character of the buildings will admit.

Miscellaneous.

It is the expressed intention of the commanding officer of the 9th Department to reoccupy this post with the company of Dragoons now at Las Vegas. I do not, however, see the necessity for a larger force at this point than may be sufficient to guard a depôt of forage. For this purpose a platoon of Infantry (forty-two rank and file) would be ample. But Bernallio, twenty-five miles above, is preferable as a depôt, being more central in the principal corn district. As far as I can perceive, the only object in keeping Dragoons here, is that they may be conveniently supplied with forage. It may also be contended that this is a central position from which mounted troops may be sent in an emergency, with sufficient celerity, either to the north or the south. Experience, however, has demonstrated the contrary of this. Mounted troops, even when their horses are in the best condition, have rarely been able to overtake the marauders and strip them of their plunder, when the act was committed in their own vicinity. The troops, to render essential service, must be posted within the Indian territory. But on this subject I shall have the honor to speak more fully in my general report. At present, I will only add that I do not consider it important that the military post at this place should be continued. A guard for the depôt at Bernallio would be all that I believe to be necessary.

I am very respectfully [etc.]

GEORGE A. MCCALL, *Inspector General*

*Major General Roger Jones, Adjutant General, U.S.A.*
*Washington City, D.C.* [Received December 26, 1850.]

*Cebolleta*

[No. 7.]

Inspector General's Office,
Cibolletta, New Mexico,
October 1st 1850.

General,

In obedience to instructions, I have the honor to submit, herewith, a report of inspection of the troops at this post.

The town of Cibolletta is at present garrisoned by,
H Company, 2nd Dragoons—total 56; horses 41.
I Company, 3rd Infantry—total 51.

Officers present and absent,

Captain and Brevet Lieutenant Colonel D. T. Chandler, I Company, 3rd Infantry, commanding company and post since September 3, 1850.

Assistant Surgeon William A. Hammond, United States Army.

Captain William H. Saunders, H Company, 2nd Dragoons, in arrest.

1st Lieutenant E. K. Kane, H Company, 2nd Dragoons, Assistant Quarter Master, absent.

1st Lieutenant J. C. McFerran, I Company, 3rd Infantry, absent at San Elizario since July 1, 1850.

2nd Lieutenant and Brevet 1st Lieutenant J. N. G. Whistler, I Company, 3rd Infantry, acting Assistant Quarter Master and Assistant Commissary of Subsistence, on detached service since September 24, 1850.

2nd Lieutenant William D. Smith, H Company, 2nd Dragoons, commanding company.

Officers in command of Military posts &c.

This town was occupied and a military post established on the 1st December 1849, by Captain C. Ker, 2nd Dragoons, with his Company K, 2nd Dragoons. This officer remained in command until relieved and placed in arrest by Major M. Howe, of the same regiment, on May 1, 1850, when Brevet 1st Lieutenant John Adams of I Company, 1st Dragoons, was ordered from Rayado and placed in command of the company and post. This officer remained in command until the last of May, when K Company was relieved by H Company, under command of 2nd Lieutenant J. Buford, Jr., and the former company proceded to Albuquerque. On the 22nd July 1850, Lieutenant William D. Smith, 2nd Dragoons, relieved Lieutenant Buford in command, and five days afterwards, in obedience to department orders, marched his Company H to Albuquerque, leaving a small guard with the sick and stores. Again on the 3rd September the post was reoccupied by its present garrison (H Company, 2nd Dragoons, and I Company, 3rd Infantry), under Brevet Lieutenant Colonel Chandler.

Thus, during a period of ten months, the post has experienced many changes in garrisons as well as commanders. This frequent change of officers in command of companies, often young and inexperienced and without the same interest in the company that they would naturally feel in that to which they are permanently attached, is proved in this instance, as in many others that have come under my immediate observation, to be exceedingly detrimental to the service. The high discipline of the company declines and, as a consequence, the property in its charge (horses, arms, etc.) suffers in proportion. It cannot, therefore, be expected that I found H Company, 2nd Dragoons, in high order.

The captain of this company (Captain Saunders) joined it on the 24th August last, and was placed in arrest by Brevet Lieutenant Colonel Chandler on the 11th September. Lieutenant Smith, also recently joined, is now in command of it. He appears to be using his best efforts to restore its discipline, etc., etc. But the troops, since their arrival here, have been much occupied in repairing quarters, and little attention has been paid to the drill.

Officers of the Army in general.

The officers of the post appear to understand their various duties, and, in time, an improvement may be expected, if further continual changes are not made.

Non-Commissioned Officers, Musicians, and Privates.

The Dragoon company is not well instructed. The Infantry company is tolerably well instructed in the schools of the squad and company, and its non-commissioned officers are good. The numbers correspond with the returns.

Officers, non-commissioned Officers, and privates of Cavalry.

The officers are well instructed; the rank and file are not.

Company Books.

The books of both companies are regularly kept, those of the Infantry company neatly, those of the Dragoon company less so.

Quarter Masters, Commissary of Subsistence, &c.

The officer discharging these duties is absent in command of an escort, conducting the Bishop of Durango,[41] to the Indian town of Azunia.[42] Lieutenant Colonel Chandler, who is in temporary discharge of the duties, informs me that no accounts or returns have been made since the arrival of his command at this post, less than a month since. Funds are received as required from the senior Assistant Quarter Master and Assistant Commissary of Subsistence at Santafé.

[41] Bishop José Antonio Laureano López de Zubiría y Escalante, the twenty-third bishop of Durango, was born on July 4, 1791, at Arizpe, Sonora. He became bishop of Durango on September 29, 1831. Pastor Rouaix, *Diccionario Geográfico, Histórico y Biográfico del Estado de Durango*, 513. Bishop Zubiría made three visits to New Mexico, the first in 1833, the second in 1845, and the last in 1850. Angélico Chávez, *Archives of the Archdiocese of Santa Fe, 1678–1900*, 187. John Russell Bartlett, who met Bishop Zubiría at El Paso del Norte, on his way back to Durango, commented, "In his journey north of El Paso . . . the Bishop received every attention from the civil and military authorities, and was furnished with escorts by the latter through such portions of the country as could not be traversed in safety without. His gratitude for this kindness was warmly expressed." *Personal Narrative*, I, 147. New Mexico remained a part of the Diocese of Durango until July 19, 1850, when the Vicariate Apostolic of New Mexico was created by Pope Pius IX. News of this event apparently did not reach either New Mexico or Durango until 1851. Chávez, *Archives*, 114, 118.

[42] Azunia is a variant of Zuñi. It is not included in Frederick Webb Hodge (ed.), *Handbook of American Indians North of Mexico*.

## Medical Department.

The Assistant Surgeon appears to be very faithful in the discharge of his duties. His hospital is kept in very good order, and is well supplied with medical and hospital stores. His supply is sent by Surgeon McCormick, from New Orleans. The medicines, etc., have been very carefully and securely put up.

## Repairs to Quarters, &c.

There are no quarters or other buildings belonging to the government at this post. Such repairs as were deemed requisite to the hired quarters, etc., have been made.

## Arms.

The Dragoons have fifty-four cavalry musketoons and thirty Colts revolving pistols. These arms are new, just issued. The arms of the Infantry company, the same they had in use before coming to New Mexico, are in good order.

## Clothing and Equipments.

The Dragoons have not received their clothing regularly for a long time. They are, consequently, very imperfectly uniformed. The clothing of the Infantry is better.

## Forage.

The price of corn here, now, is from $4 to $5 per fanega (2½ bushels) at the distance of forty-five or fifty miles, whence it is transported at the expense of the Quarter Masters Department. A contract for 2,000 fanegas has been made; a greater supply could not be commanded. At the town of Azunia, seventy-five miles distant, corn is said to be abundant; but it is always difficult, sometimes impossible, to obtain it from these Indians, even when their granaries are full to overflowing, so provident are they and so apprehensive of a year of want and famine, which, owing to the destructive work of a species of grass-hopper that occasionally appears, is sometimes severely felt throughout the country. They are supposed to have on hand at this moment at least two years supply of corn; yet, it is quite uncertain whether the Quarter Master will be able to obtain a bushel from them.

Subsistence Department.

A department order requires that sixty days supplies be always kept on hand. There is now in store twenty days [supply] only. In the usual state of the roads, supplies may be had by sending an express to Santafé in from nine to ten days, from Albuquerque in from three to four days. The supply on hand is of good quality. Mutton is abundant in the vicinity. Beef is not so abundant and commands a high price.

Quarters, Barracks, &c.

[They] Are in a tolerable state of cleanliness. Those of the Infantry are the better of the two. Repairs are now going on in both.

Miscellaneous.

As a military post, Cibolletta is of some importance, in as much as two Nabajo trails pass through gorges in the mountains at a few miles distance from the post. There is another from Azunia, sometimes used by the Nabajoes. The latter, leading to the Rio Abajo country (much subject to the depredations of the Nabajoes), may be intersected at a distance of thirty miles from this post by a practicable cavalry route, and the Indians cut off, if timely information of their presence in the lower country is sent to the commanding officer, the Indians having to make by the trail from the lower country in question a circuit of sixty miles to reach the same point.

Wood for fuel is abundant at the distance of two miles, and is cut and brought in by the troops.

Grazing grounds are good at the distance of four miles; hither the horses and mules not at work are now daily driven.

The Quarter Master had thirteen six-mule teams and wagons for the service of the post. This number is not sufficient to keep the post supplied with subsistence from Santafé in addition to the work of bringing in forage, wood, etc. Trains are consequently, at times, sent from Santafé.

I am, very respectfully [etc.]
GEORGE A. MCCALL, *Inspector General*

*Major General R. Jones, Adjutant General, U.S.A.*
*Washington City, D.C.* [Received December 26, 1850.]

*Socorro*

[No. 8.]

Inspector General's Office,
SOCORRO, NEW MEXICO
October 5th 1850.

GENERAL,

Agreeably to orders from your office, I have the honor to submit, herewith a report of inspection of the troops at this post.[43]

E Company, 2nd Dragoons, total, 54; horses, fit for service, 46; unfit 23.

A Company, 3rd Infantry, total, 35.

Officers present and absent,

J. F. Hammond, Assistant Surgeon, United States Army.

Captain and Brevet Colonel Charles A. May, E Company, 2nd Dragoons, absent on sick leave since August 9, 1850.

Captain and Brevet Colonel L. S. Craig, A Company, 3rd Infantry, absent on general recruiting service.

1st Lieutenant and Brevet Captain T. Jordan, A Company, 3rd Infantry, absent, Assistant Quarter Master.

1st Lieutenant and Brevet Captain R. P. Campbell, E Company, 2nd Dragoons, commanding company and post since August 1, 1850.

2nd Lieutenant and Brevet 1st Lieutenant J. N. Ward, G Company, 3rd Infantry, commanding A Company, 3rd [Infantry], and acting Assistant Quarter Master and Assistant Commissary of Subsistence.

Brevet 2nd Lieutenant B. H. Robinson, E Company, 2nd Dragoons, joined July 21, 1850, under orders to relieve Major Steen at Don' Aña, in command [of] H Company, 1st Dragoons.

[43] The Post of Socorro was established in 1848 and abandoned in 1851.

Officers in command of —— Military Posts.

Brevet Colonel May joined his company on the 26th of August 1849, and remained in command of the company and post until the 9th August 1850. The garrison was reinforced on the 21 May 1850 by A Company, 3rd Infantry, under 2nd Lieutenant T. J. Mason, 3rd Infantry, who was drowned in crossing the Rio Grande the same day, thus leaving Colonel May, the only officer at the post, in command also of the Infantry company. Brevet Captain Campbell arrived on the 1st August and relieved Lieutenant Ward (who had been detached from Las Vegas, and assumed command of A Company, 3rd Infantry, on the 12th June 1850) in command of the Dragoon company, Colonel May being sick. Captain Campbell, now commanding the post, appears zealous to improve the discipline and efficiency of his company.

Officers of the Army in general.

Understand their duties, are intelligent, and active. Lieutenant Ward, in particular, is a very efficient officer, and discharges his numerous duties, commanding [the] company, acting Assistant Quarter Master, and Assistant Commissary of Subsistence, with great asiduity [*sic*] and judgment.

Non Commissioned Officers, Musicians, and Privates.

Those of the Infantry company are well instructed. The Dragoons are less perfect.

Company Books.

Of both companies are regularly and well kept in the form prescribed by regulations.

Quarter Masters, Commissaries of Subsistence, &c.

These duties are discharged by the officer acting in these departments in a very satisfactory manner. His books and accounts are kept with apparent accuracy. His funds are in his own possession when on hand, but at present there are outstanding debts to the amount of $5,000, and estimates for the fourth quarter of the present year for forage, a years supply, $30,000 has not yet been received.

Medical Department.

The hospital is sufficiently commodious for the present garrison. The supply of medicines and hospital stores is sufficient for present wants. The sick are carefully attended.

Arms.

Of both companies [are] in good service order.

Clothing and Equipments.

The Dragoons have just received one years supply of clothing for sixty-one men, of the old pattern. The Infantry company is deficient in clothing as well as in camp and garrison equipage, for which requisitions have been made.

Cavalry Horses.

The horses have, generally speaking, been well selected for size and strength, but, either from the influence of the climate, or from hard usage or want of proper forage, have much degenerated since their arrival in New Mexico. Indeed, horses brought here, particularly from the more northern states of the Union—for instance, Missouri and Illinois—have to undergo acclimation before they are fit for hard service; and, if actively employed in mountain service within twelve months after their arrival, are apt, if not completely broken down, to be so far injured as never entirely to recover their original strength and healthiness. This will be apparent when the fact, above stated, is considered, viz: that of sixty-nine horses of this company, brought to this country less than eighteen months since, twenty-three, or one-third, are now reported unfit for service.

Forage.

Corn is now selling for $4 the fanega (2½ bushels), and at this price more cannot be got within a reasonable distance (of the present crop) than will suffice for one full company (eighty-five) of Dragoons and their teams (two), say one hundred animals. During the winter of 1847–8 corn was as high as $12 the fanega, and it is the opinion of the acting Quarter Master that it will reach that price before the coming spring. Wheat is at $4 the fanega. A supply of this for fifty animals in addition to the above might now be secured.

Hay is $50 per ton; fodder $20 per ton. The latter, in the condition in which it is received, is worth about half the same quantity of hay. One hundred tons have been delivered at the grazing camp, fifteen miles below the post, and fifty tons at this post; this includes both hay and fodder. Hay cannot be cut here until after the fall rains; the above quantity could not well be increased in a dry season, like the present. This will not feed more than about eighty animals at the rate of three-fourths of the ration per day. There are at the post, including Quarter Master's teams, express horses, etc., one hundred and twenty-seven animals.

Subsistence Department.

There is now on hand about forty days supply. A train sent hence to Santa Fé (one hundred and fifty miles) can return with a supply in twelve days. Flour is brought in to the post in small quantities by the inhabitants, and purchased by the Acting Commissary of Subsistence at eight cents per pound. In this way a supply for four full companies of eighty-five each might now be had. A contract exists for the supply of this post from the mills at Moratown. Beans may also be had, now, in great abundance. Beef cattle are also easily obtained in the vicinity.

Quarters and Barracks.

Are clean and well arranged.[44]

Miscellaneous.

It may be well to keep a garrison at this post, say eighty men, one-half mounted, to protect the settlement and the general grazing camp of the department. Though should barracks be built by the govern-

[44] McCall does not give the cost of rented quarters in Socorro. In the summer of 1851 it amounted to $290 per month for one company of dragoons, the infantry company no longer being stationed there. "Report of quarters hired at the post of Socorro, New Mexico," 32 Cong., 1 sess., *House Exec. Doc.* 2, 245.

ment, there will be found at one or two points (from twenty to thirty miles lower on the river) more eligible positions.[45]

Wood (pine) is delivered under contract at the distance of fifteen miles for $3 per cord. From this point it is hauled in by the Quarter Master.

I am very respectfully [etc.]
GEORGE A. MCCALL, *Inspector General*
*Major General R. Jones, Adjutant General, U.S.A.*
*Washington City, D.C.* [Received December 26, 1850.]

## *Doña Ana*

[No. 9.]

Inspector General's Office
DON' ANA, NEW MEXICO,
October 10th 1850.

GENERAL,

In obedience to orders, I have the honor to submit, herewith, a report of inspection of the troops at this post.

H Company, 1st Dragoons, total present, 54.
B Company, 3rd Infantry, total present, 43.

Officers present and absent,

Captain and Brevet Major E. Steen, 1st Dragoons, commanding company and post.

[45] Fort Conrad, located about twenty-four miles south of Socorro, on the right side of the Río Grande at the foot of Valverde Mesa, was established on September 8, 1851. In 1851, Major Swords wrote of Socorro: "Although as high as two dollars and fifty cents per bushel was paid for corn, and some of it had to be hauled a distance of forty miles, this had been considered an advantageous place for keeping surplus stock; there being in charge of the acting assistant quartermaster fourteen horses and eighty mules besides those in service with the dragoons, and in addition to ninety mules sent there from Santa Fé. A contract had been made for the delivery of four hundred tons of hay at thirty-nine dollars and eighty-five cents per ton. In consequence of the scarcity of forage, resort was had last spring to feeding green wheat in its growing state, thus cutting short the crop of the year."—Swords to Jesup, October 25, 1851, 32 Cong., 1 sess., *House Exec. Doc. 2*, 237.

Assistant Surgeon P. G. S. Tenbroek, United States Army.
Captain and Brevet Major O. H. Shepherd, 3rd Infantry, absent without leave since September 2, 1850.
1st Lieutenant and Brevet Captain A. Buford, H Company, 1st Dragoons, absent en route from Fort Leavenworth.
1st Lieutenant John Trevitt, B Company, 3rd Infantry, commanding company [and] acting Assistant Quarter Master and Assistant Commissary of Subsistence.
2nd Lieutenant S. Sturges, H Company, 1st Dragoons, absent en route to join his company from Fort Leavenworth.
2nd Lieutenant L. W. OBannon, B Company, 3rd Infantry.

Officers Commanding ——— Military Posts.

This post was established by Major Steen on the 1st August 1849, with H Company, 1st Dragoons. On the 6th December 1849, the garrison was reinforced by B Company, 3rd Infantry. Major Steen has shown much zeal in the performance of his duties, particularly in several expeditions against the Apache Indians in the Sacramento Mountains and on the River Gila, in which he had several engagements with them, and was once severely wounded.

Officers of the Army in General.

The officers all understand their duties well and are zealous in their performance. They have afforded the commanding officer all the support he required.

Non-Commissioned Officers, Musicians, and Privates.

Are well instructed in the prescribed drill. Their personal appearance is very good; and the non-commissioned officers are prompt and efficient.

Officers, Non-Commissioned Officers, Musicians, and Privates of Cavalry.

They are fine riders, are expert in the use of their arms, and well drilled in the prescribed evolutions (schools of the platoon and squadron). Taken all together, it affords me pleasure to say that this company is in better order than any I have seen in this department.

Company Books.

Are regularly and accurately kept in the form and manner prescribed. This is the case in both companies.

Quarter Masters, Commissary of Subsistence, &c.

The officer in charge of this department is very zealous and attentive in the performance of his duties. His accounts are kept with accuracy and regularity. His funds are in his own possession, and now amount to about $7,000 in the Quarter Master Department and $85 in the Commissary Department. He draws on the Quarter Master at El Paso for funds as they are needed.

Medical Department.

The Assistant Surgeon appears to be attentive to his duties. The hospital is in good order and the supply of medicines and hospital stores are sufficient for present wants.

Repairs to Quarters and Barracks, &c.

There are no buildings belonging to the government at this post. The rents for eight months past have been at the rate of $260 per month, and will shortly be increased to $335.[46]

Arms.

The Dragoons have the carbine, the infantry the percussion musket; both are in a serviceable state and are well cleaned and preserved.

Clothing and Equipments.

Are of good quality and sufficient for present wants.

Cavalry Horses.

This is the best troop of horses that I have seen in the department. They are now in good condition, although many of them have been from four to five years in service, and some of them much longer. The average durability of Dragoon horses now in this department, I

[46] The cost of rentals at Doña Ana had increased to $362 per month by the summer of 1851. The garrison remained unchanged. "Report of quarters rented at the post of Doña Ana, New Mexico," *ibid.*, 246. Apparently the charge had been increased twice in less than a year.

have found, has not exceeded *three* years. This is to be attributed in some measure to their being purchased sometimes in emergencies and without a sufficient field for selection being open to the officers purchasing, as is the case in this part of the country. On this subject, I shall, in obedience to your instructions of [the] 24th June last, give my views more fully in a subsequent report.

Forage.

The present price of corn here is $5 the fanega. The supply to be obtained in the vicinity is sufficient for the demands of the post.

Hay is $50 per ton, fodder $40. Of these a sufficient supply is on hand. A much larger amount of forage could not be procured in the vicinity this year; the next, however, it might be doubled by making arrangements in time with the Mexicans who are now preparing to bring new lands into cultivation on the opposite side of the river, about seven miles below Don' Ana.[47] If encouragement were given to these people, this new settlement would in a few years furnish much that [is] required by the troops at this post.

Subsistence Department.

Flour is delivered here, under contract, at eleven cents per pound; brought from the States the cost is about seventeen cents per pound.[48] This flour is of good quality (better than that made at the mills at Moratown) and there is in store one years supply for the present command (say one hundred strong). All other parts of the rations (except fresh beef) are from the depôt at El Paso, sixty-two miles distant. Beef cattle are abundant in the vicinity. Beef is delivered at six cents per pound.

Beans may be got, now, at from $1.75 to $2 per bushel. Those brought from the United States cost, including the expense of transportation, $9 and upwards.

[47] The area opposite and below Doña Ana was the Mesilla district.

[48] The contract for delivering flour to the three southern posts was held by Simeon Hart, who had erected a small mill on the left bank of the Río Grande, opposite El Paso del Norte, in 1849. Strickland, "Six Who Came to El Paso," *Southwestern Studies*, Vol. I (Fall, 1963), 37.

Quarters and Barracks.

Are in very good order, and as near the regulations as circumstances will admit. These remarks apply equally to both companies.

Miscellaneous.

I consider this position an important one for a Dragoon force. It has always been a favorite crossing place for the Apaches from the east to the west and returning.

The grazing lands are at convenient distances, and horses may always be kept in good order here.

I am, very respectfully [etc.]
GEORGE A. MCCALL, *Inspector General*

*Major General R. Jones, Adjutant General, U.S.A.*
*Washington City, D.C.* [Received December 26, 1850.]

*El Paso del Norte*

[No. 10.]
Inspector General's Office
EL PASO DEL NORTE, NEW MEXICO,
October 12th 1850.

GENERAL,

I have the honor to transmit, herewith, a report of the inspection of the troops at this post.[49]

E Company }
K Company } 3rd Infantry, total present, 81.

Officers present and absent,

Captain and Brevet Major J. Van Horne, 3rd Infantry, commanding post.

Assistant Surgeon Lyman Stone, United States Army.

Captain and Brevet Major W. S. Henry, K Company, 3rd Infantry, absent on general recruiting service since August 26, 1850.

[49] United States forces occupied El Paso del Norte in 1847, during the Mexican War, but the permanent post, located on the United States side of the Río Grande, was not established until September 8, 1849. It was evacuated in 1851 and reoccupied in 1854. For a history of the post see M. H. Thomlinson, *The Garrison of Fort Bliss, 1849–1916.*

1st Lieutenant and Brevet Major I. B. Richardson, on leave of absence since October 10, 1850.

1st Lieutenant and [Brevet] Major D. C. Buell, K Company, 3rd Infantry, absent, Assistant Adjutant General.

2nd Lieutenant and Brevet Captain B. E. Bee, K Company, 3rd Infantry, absent at regimental head quarters, Adjutant.

2nd Lieutenant J. D. Wilkins, E Company, 3rd Infantry, commanding Company E.

2nd Lieutenant W. H. Wood, C Company, 3rd Infantry, commanding K Company, 3rd Infantry.

1st Lieutenant and Brevet Captain A. W. Bowman, Regimental Quarter Master, on duty as Assistant Commissary of Subsistence and acting Quarter Master at the post.

Officers Commanding ——— Military Posts.

Major Van Horne has been in command of this post since September, 1849. The companies here, at present, are well instructed. Company K recently arrived from San Elizario, has been commanded during twelve months past by Lieutenant Wilkins. This company has been drilled to manouvre and manage a section of battery, consisting of three mountain howitzers, and acquitted itself well on drill.

Officers of the Army in general.

Are intelligent and understand their duties very well.

Non-Commissioned Officers, musicians, and privates.

Are well instructed in the drill. Their personal appearance is soldierlike. The numbers in the ranks correspond with the returns.

Company Books.

Are regularly and neatly kept, and are up to the present date.

Quartermasters, Commissary of Subsistence, &c.

The duties in these departments appear to be performed in an efficient and satisfactory manner. Funds are procured on drafts on the Quarter Master General of the Army, on the Deputy Quarter Master General at New Orleans, either here or in the city of Chihuahua. In the last place, it is represented, any amount required for this or the upper posts, may, in this way, be procured free of cost to [the] government. This officer has on hand in Quarter Master Department funds to the amount of $10,000, and the Subsistence Department, $20,000. These are in his own possession.

Ordnance Department.

Lieutenant Wilkins, acting ordnance officer, has three mountain howitzers and five hundred rounds of ammunition, together with a sufficient supply for small arms.

Medical Department.

The duties of this department are ably performed. The wards are comfortable and the sick carefully attended.

Repairs to Quarters, Barracks, &c.

The buildings used as quarters, storehouses, hospital, etc., are hired at the rate of $350 per month. This includes ground enough for a garden.[50]

Arms.

In possession of both companies are in fine order.

Clothing and Equipments.

A full supply is on hand and is of good quality.

Forage.

From six to seven thousand fanegas of corn, one years supply for two hundred animals, may be commanded here. The price at present varies from $4 to $6 the fanega. Last year $8.50 was given. The supply will increase with the population of this section of the country, but there is little prospect of its doing so very rapidly.

Subsistence Department.

There is in store eight months supply for the present garrison;

[50] The quarters occupied opposite El Paso del Norte were rented from Benjamin Franklin Coons, one of the early settlers of the area. In July, 1851, the rental for the property occupied by the post was still $350 for the quarters and garden, but with an additional $60 for a storehouse. "Report of persons and articles employed and hired at El Paso del Norte," 32 Cong., 1 sess., *House Exec. Doc.* 2, 250.

should that part of the train now at the Guadalupe Mountains[51] get in without loss, there will be sufficient for one year. Flour, made in Chihuahua, of fair quality, is delivered here at eleven cents per pound. Beans of excellent quality may also be got in the vicinity. The Assistant Commissary of Subsistence reports that beef cattle may be got from Texas at *cheaper rates* than from Chihuahua. This may be the case at present, owing to the fact that nearly the whole of the latter state has been swept of its stock by the Apaches; and how long this condition of things may continue it is impossible to foresee.

Quarters and Barracks.

Are in good order and well arranged.

Miscellaneous.

I do not consider it important that a strong garrison should be maintained here. This has heretofore been the principal crossing place on the route to and from the city of Chihuahua, etc. But at present the lower road, crossing at the Presideo of San Elizario (twenty-two miles below), is preferred by all heavy trains, as it avoids the Sand Hills on the former route. To occupy both these positions appears to be unnecessary, and of the two I consider San Elizario the more important. The only service required of, or that can be required of Infantry here is to give security to the Mexican town on the opposite bank of the river. As a depôt, San Elizario is preferrable, as the old presideo would afford ample storeroom without cost to [the] government.[52]

[51] The Guadalupe Mountains lie in both Texas and New Mexico. The "upper road" from San Antonio to El Paso ran by way of Waco (Hueco) Tanks and Guadalupe Pass, an area which was a favorite lurking place of the Indians, who often attacked supply trains and the mail carriers in the Guadalupe Mountains.

[52] The usefulness of the Post of El Paso became most apparent after it had been evacuated in 1851. In the following two years, 1851–53, it was reported that some eighteen persons had been killed within the general area of El Paso and San Elizario, large quantities of livestock stolen, and other depredations committed by the Indians. See the statement drawn up by

Fuel here, by contract, is $9 per cord. Timber for building must be hauled from the mountains sixty or seventy miles.

I am, very respectfully [etc.]
GEORGE A. MCCALL, *Inspector General*
*Major General R. Jones, Adjutant General, U.S.A.*
*Washington City, D.C.* [Received December 26, 1850.]

*Presidio de San Elizario*

[No. 11.] Inspector General's Office
PRESIDEO DE SAN ELIZARIO, NEW MEXICO,
October 14th 1850.

GENERAL,

In obedience to instructions, I have the honor to submit, herewith, a report of inspection of troops at this post.[53]

C Company, 3rd Infantry, total 44.

Officers present and absent,

---

Judge Joel L. Ankrim, in Frazer (ed.), *Mansfield*, 70–75. Ankrim urged the re-establishment of the Post of El Paso.

[53] The Presidio of San Elizario, officially named the *Presidio de Nuestra Señora del Pilar y Gloriosa San José*, was established by Spain in 1773 and was located on what was then an island in the Río Grande. It remained in Mexican hands after Texas won its independence and was first occupied by the United States on September 15, 1849. The garrison was withdrawn in September, 1851, but the presidio was retained by the government for some time thereafter, funds being spent for the repair of the buildings as late as 1857. During the Civil War it was occupied for a time by the Confederacy and later by Union troops.

Second Lieutenant William H. C. Whiting, Corps of Engineers, described the island in 1849: "But the greatest abundance and best cultivation is found on La Isla, the fertile island of the Rio Grande, below El Paso, about thirty miles in length, from four to eight broad, and studded with the little towns of Isleta, Socoro [*sic*], and San Elezano [*sic*]. This island now belongs to the United States, a change greatly rejoiced in by its denizens, but extremely disliked by the Mexican government."—Whiting to Totten, June 10, 1849, 31 Cong., 1 sess., *Sen. Exec. Doc. 1*, 289.

Captain W. B. Johns, C Company, 3rd Infantry, commanding company and post.

1st Lieutenant and Brevet Captain A. W. Bowman, C Company, 3rd Infantry, absent, Regimental Quarter Master.

2nd Lieutenant W. H. Wood, C Company, 3rd Infantry, absent in command of K Company, 3rd Infantry.

Officers in command of ——— military posts.

Captain Johns, the only officer with his company or at the post, is able and assiduous in the performance of the various duties devolved upon him.

Non-Commissioned Officers, &c.

Are well instructed and soldierlike in their appearance.

Company Books.

Are well and regularly kept.

Quarter Masters and Commissary of Subsistence.

These duties are carefully performed. But having been only sixteen days at the post with his company, no accounts have yet been rendered. He has in his hands [in] Quarter Master funds $650.

Medical Department.

A citizen physician is employed to attend the troops. At present there are none on the sick report. A portion of the presideo building is prepared for a hospital, etc.

Repairs to Forts, Barracks, &c.

Portions of the old presideo or fort have been repaired by the troops and occupied as quarters for the men, hospital, storehouses, etc. Further repairs, to no great extent, would give extensive and safe store rooms for large supplies.

This is the only building belonging to [the] government at the post. The cost of quarters for officers (commanding officer and acting surgeon) is $45 per month.[54]

[54] Major Swords mentioned only that quarters were rented for the officers at "about five dollars per room," which he commended as moderate,

Arms.

Are in good order and well preserved.

Clothing and Equipments.

No woolen clothing [is] on hand; a requisition has been made on the Quarter Master at Santafé.

Forage.

Corn sufficient for the demands of the post may be had in the vicinity at $6.50 the fanega.

Hay in large quantities of medium quality may be had at $28 per ton. Grazing lands are extensive within two to four miles.

Subsistence Department.

There is on hand a full supply for twelve months, all of good quality.

Quarters and Barracks.

Are in good order.

Miscellaneous.

One company of Infantry stationed here, or at El Paso, or equally divided between the two (say forty-two men, each) would be, I consider, a sufficient force on this section of the frontier.

If only one of these posts be occupied, this of the two is preferable, for the reason that the old presideo, with little expense, may be made to afford quarters, hospital, and store houses, all well adapted for troops; while the expense of hiring them at El Paso is $350 per month, or $4,200 per annum.

Fuel is abundant at the distance of four or five miles, and building timber (cottonwood) can be got within eight miles.

I am very respectfully [etc.]

George A. McCall, *Inspector General*

*Major General R. Jones, Adjutant General, U.S.A.*
*Washington City, D.C.* [Received December 26, 1850.]

---

considering the costs elsewhere in the department. Swords to Jesup, October 25, 1851, 32 Cong., 1 sess., *House Exec. Doc. 2*, 237.

# VI. McCALL'S REPORT ON THE DEFENSIVE NEEDS OF NEW MEXICO

Inspector General's Office
PHILADELPHIA, December 26th 1850.

GENERAL,

In obedience to instructions from the War Department, embraced in a letter from your office, dated the 24th June 1850, I have the honor to submit a report on the several subjects therein referred to, viz:

"1st. The probable number of lives lost and of persons taken captives by the Indians within the last eighteen months in New Mexico; also the probable value of property stolen or destroyed within the same period."

In pursuing my inquiries on this subject, I found it extremely difficult, although I visited towns or settlements where, or in the neighbourhood of which, depredations had been committed by the Nabajoes, Utahs, or Apaches within twelve or eighteen months previous, to collect from the people information at all explicit or reliable; while the cases reported at the Head Quarters of the Department, or the office of the Secretary of State [of New Mexico], do not cover two-thirds, perhaps one-half, of all that occurred. However, on the northern frontier, from Abiquiu to Las Vegas, there were enumerated to me about fifty-three persons who have been killed on that line within twelve months, from September 1, 1849, to September 1, 1850. In the six months preceding, there were some shepherds killed at different points along that line, probably ten or twelve, though I could not arrive at the number with any precision. These murders were committed by the Nabajoes, Utahs, and Jicarilla Apaches, but principally by the latter. In the lower country, and along the Rio Grande from Santa Fé to El Paso, about twenty persons have been killed within eighteen months. These were by the Nabajoes and White Mountain and Sacramento Mountain Apaches. The number of captives carried off from New Mexico within the same period amount in all to thirteen that are known and enumerated. The probability, however, is that many obscure persons have been killed, and children carried off besides those named.

If we assume the total ascertained of killed to be eighty-three and of captives to be thirteen, I incline to the belief that from 15 to 30 per cent might be safely added to these figures without exceeding the truth.

As far as I could ascertain positively, by summing up individual cases, the number of animals driven off by these Indians within eighteen months prior to the 1st September 1850 is as follows:

| | |
|---|---|
| Horses,—181, which at $40 each is | $7,240 |
| Mules,—402, which at $50 each is | 20,100 |
| Horned cattle (many of them work oxen),—788, at $20 | 15,760 |
| Sheep,—47,300, at $1.50 | 70,950 |
| Total | 114,050 |

To this amount 50 per cent may be added. And when it is taken into consideration that for twenty years past the flocks and herds of this people have been yearly diminishing under the constant ravages of the wild tribes, and that districts which were formerly covered with "stock" are now almost bare, the above amounts must be set down as heavy losses. For further information on this point, I beg leave to refer to my report of the 15th July last, now on file in the department.[1]

[1] Beyond question, the number of stock killed or driven off by the In-

"2nd. The capacity of the people of New Mexico to resist the incursions of the Indians; and the necessary military force to secure protection."

With regard to the first clause of the inquiry, the history of the country during the period of two hundred years past illustrates the fact which impresses itself on every one who visits New Mexico, that the people within themselves are altogether incapable of resisting the inroads of the Indians into the very heart of their territory. They have been from generation to generation so deeply imbued with the fear of their savage neighbours that it is only necessary to raise the cry of "los Indios," and a dozen of them will run from a couple of Apaches armed with lance and bow. On several expeditions against

dians in New Mexico was high, though impossible to determine with accuracy. It appears that the most serious and consistent losses were sustained following the renewal of hostilities with the Navahos in the 1770's. Many incidents are recorded, but the number of animals involved is often uncertain. United States occupation and subsequent acquisition of New Mexico brought no immediate improvement. In fact, James S. Calhoun reported in 1849, "The wild Indians of this country have been so much more successful in their robberies since Genl Kearney took possession of the country, they do not believe we have the power to chastise them." Calhoun to Medill, October 1, 1849, Abel (ed.), *Official Correspondence*, 32. Indians stole livestock from emigrants, settlers, freighters, and even the army with apparent impunity. There are a surprising number of reports of horses and mules taken within sight of military posts and not recovered. Sheep, however, formed the largest portion of the stock taken. For the years 1846–50, inclusive, Bartlett recorded that 12,887 mules, 7,050 horses, 31,581 cattle, and 453,293 sheep had been lost to the Indians in New Mexico. *Personal Narrative*, II, 386. See also Calhoun to Lea, February 2, 1851, Abel (ed.), *Official Correspondence*, 289. These figures take on added significance when compared to the probably inexact census of 1850, which gave the following number of animals in New Mexico: asses and mules, 8,654; horses, 5,079; cattle, 32,977; swine, 7,314; and sheep, 377,271. *Seventh Census of the United States*, 1007. Not until the decade of the 1860's was any real progress made toward curbing Indian depredations.

these Indians, they have been organized into companies and have marched with the regular troops; but their chief exploits have been to secure the booty, after the enemy had been attacked and routed by the regulars. In most of these instances they have been allowed, as an encouragement, to possess themselves of the entire spoil; but while this continues to be their sole object, as it does now seem to be, they will not greatly expose their persons in the conflict. And I should, therefore, rate their capacity for Indian warfare at very little above zero.

Better auxiliaries may be found in the Pueblo (or civilized) Indians of the territory; and I would here respectfully repeat what I had the honor to present to the notice of the department in my report of the 15th July, viz: that advantages may accrue from extending to these people a marked kindness, and securing their confidence in the friendship and justice of our government.

In replying to the latter clause of the second query, I would in the first place beg leave to invite attention to the facts stated in a preceding paragraph, i.e., the known losses sustained yearly and monthly by the inhabitants of this territory from the inroads of large tribes of wild Indians, whose country envelopes the territory, without interval, on the north, south, east, and west. From the facts to which I refer it must appear either that the military force at present in New Mexico is idle and inefficient, or that the extent of frontier intrusted to its protection is out of proportion to its strength and the character of its organization. A single glance at the map, and a reference to the total number of troops for duty, as stated in the last report from the 9th Department Head Quarters,[2] will clearly demonstrate the truth of the last position.

The question is, what, at the lowest calculation, is "the necessary military force to secure protection?" In stationing a military force here there are, apparently, two objects in view requiring separate fields of action. The first is to afford protection to the lives and

[2] The total number of officers and men present in the department, according to the annual report of the Secretary of War, was 1,019. 31 Cong., 2 sess., *Sen. Exec. Doc. 1*, part II, 116d.

property of the inhabitants; the second, to effectually check the marauding spirit of the Indians, and at a subsequent period to induce them to dwell in fixed habitations, to cultivate the soil to some extent, and to raise their own stock. The first must be effected as far as practicable by stationing small bodies of troops in the principal settlements. The second can only be accomplished by the permanent establishment of a strong force within the Indian country. To do this, I should answer that, for present service, the lowest figure at which this force can be put is 2,200 (two thousand two hundred) effective men, of whom at least 1,400 (fourteen hundred) should be mounted.

The question may, perhaps, be more satisfactorily answered by an illustration of the mode of warfare and pillage pursued by the Indians against whom the troops are to act, and a description of the country in which they are to operate, presuming that the tribes above named (independently of the Comanches) count from forty-five hundred to five thousand warriors. If we take Santa Fé, the seat of government and principal depôt of munitions, as the central point, then the northern line of posts for defense or protection may be drawn through Abiquiu, on the northwest; Taos, Rayado, and Mora, on the north; to Las Vegas, on the northeast. These are all important and thriving settlements, but each one is separated from the next by rugged mountain regions of from twenty to forty-five miles in width, running back into the Indian country, and thus affording from the latter easy and concealed approaches on the flanks of all of them. For the protection of life, of the crops, of the working animals, and all property immediately around the homesteads of these people, a small force at each of the points named is considered to be sufficient. But the principal wealth of the people is in their flocks and herds; and these must be sent, particularly in winter, into narrow mountain glades affording fine pasturage, at the distance of from five to twenty miles from the settlements, where they are left for months at a time under charge of a few simple and unarmed shepherds. Here they are an easy prey to the Utahs and Jicarilla Apaches, who, crawling upon the listless shepherds, shoot them with arrows to prevent their carrying information and then drive off the stock with impunity; or, if a shepherd escaping brings intelligence to the nearest military post, experience has shown that the pursuit is almost always fruitless.

The other line of settlements that should be occupied is from Santafé southward, along the valley of the Rio Grande to El Paso. Here, small garrisons at Albuquerque (or Bernallio), Cibolletta, Socorro (or twenty-seven miles below, opposite Valberde), Don' Aña, and El Paso (or San Elizario) would in the same way give security to the homesteads, but nothing more. The only way in which a military force can be advantageously and effectively employed to put an end to Indian spoliations in New Mexico is to post them, not in our settlements or on our borders but in the heart of the Indian country. And here, they must be in sufficient strength to awe the Indians, to punish them in their strongholds for the offences they commit beyond their own boundaries. Three stations of this kind are deemed requisite, viz: one in the Nabajo country near the Cañon of Chi [Chelly]; one in the Apache country east, somewhere on the eastern slope of the Sacramento Mountains, where water, grass, and timber of excellent quality may be found; and one in the south, on the Gila River or near the old copper mines. The latter is a very eligible position. It is a high country with a pure air, and possessing all the requisites for the establishment of a military post, together with abundance of game. At the first two posts there should be from four hundred and fifty to five hundred men each. At the last, three hundred and fifty. At most of the other points named above a single company would be sufficient.[3]

[3] These recommendations were carried out, in part, within the next few years. All of the posts located at settlements, except Santa Fe, were abandoned. Fort Defiance was established in the Navaho country in 1851. The old private defensive post near the Santa Rita copper mines was occupied by the escort for the United States–Mexican Boundary Commission in April, 1851. When the commission moved on in October, the army occupied the post, which was then designated Fort Webster. In 1852 the post was moved to the Mimbres River. It was abandoned in 1853. Fort Bayard, which was located about five miles west of the copper mines, was established in 1866. Fort Stanton was established in 1855, not in the

On completing the tour of the military posts in this territory it appears to me that the following would be a proper disposition of the troops at this time.

| | | *Organ-ization total.* | *Probable effective strength total.* |
|---|---|---|---|
| Abiquiu | 1 Company of Infantry | 84 | 75 |
| Taos | 1 Company of Infantry | 84 | 75 |
| *Rayado | 2 Companies of Dragoons | 170 | 150 |
| Las Vegas | 1 Company of Infantry | 84 | 75 |
| Santa Fé | 1 Company of Infantry | 84 | 75 |
| Albuquerque | 1 Company of Infantry | 84 | 75 |
| *Cibolletta | 1 Company of Dragoons and 1 Company of Infantry | 169 | 150 |
| Socorro | 1 Company of Dragoons | 85 | 75 |
| Don' Aña | 1 Company of Dragoons and 1 Company of Infantry | 169 | 150 |
| El Paso | 1 Company of Infantry | 84 | 75 |
| Nabajo country | 4 Companies of Dragoons and 1 Company of Artillery with a battery of Mountain Howitzers, and 1 Company of Infantry | 508 | 450 |
| Apache Country | 5 Companies of Dragoons and 1 Company of Artillery with a battery of Mountain Howitzers | 509 | 450 |
| Gila River | 3 Companies of Dragoons and 1 Company of Infantry | 339 | 300 |
| | Grand Total | 2,453 | 2,175 |

[*Rayado and Cibolletta are positions from which operations may

Sacramento Mountains but on the eastern slope of the Sierra Blanca (White Mountains). The idea of establishing posts in the Indian country did not originate with McCall. See Brent to Jesup, January 31, 1850, *ibid.*, 294; and Bowman to Brent, April 21, 1850, *ibid.*, 295.

be successfully carried into the Indian country. (See inspection reports numbers 5 and 7.)—McCall's footnote.]

Owing to the usual casualties of service I do not consider that the average effective strength of companies can be safely estimated at more than seventy-five total.

The following troops are at present in New Mexico:

| | *Organization* | | *Total present, September 30, 1850* |
|---|---|---|---|
| 7 Companies of Dragoons | 595 | | 334 |
| 2 Companies of Artillery | 168 | | 99 |
| 10 Companies of Infantry | 840 | | 554 |
| Total | 1,603 | | 987 |
| Add to the above one full Regiment of Dragoons or Mounted Riflemen, | | | |
| 10 Companies of Riflemen | 840 | probable strength | 750 |
| | 2,443 | | 1,737 |

The above total present in New Mexico on the 30th of September last, viz: 987, would give only an average of fifty-two total to a company; say, then, that each company is filled to seventy-five total, there will be:

| | |
|---|---|
| 19 Companies at 75 each | 1,425 |
| add 10 Companies of Rifles at 75 each | 750 |
| This will give a total of | 2,175 |

Thus, one Regiment of Mounted Riflemen, in addition to the force now in New Mexico, may be considered a sufficient, or necessary military force to secure protection, but this is placing it at the very lowest figure at which it can safely be put.

The nature of the service in this country requires mounted troops almost exclusively; the distribution of supplies and munitions from the general depôts to the frontier posts, the frequent visits of staff officers (Pay Masters, Quarter Masters, etc.) from post to post in the necessary discharge of their duties, the transmittal of orders and reports of constant occurrance in the usual course of service, all require mounted escorts or express riders. The law authorizing the mounting of a portion of the Infantry regiments would in some measure supply the deficiency of cavalry in the organization of the army; but there are many objections to this, one alone, it is sufficient to cite, viz: the increased expense. This, my own observation satisfies me, will be the result in a few years of the adoption of this system. A better one, I believe, would be to change the organization of one or two of the foot regiments and convert them into Mounted Riflemen. Among the advantages of adopting this course in preference to raising new regiments the following may be named. The officers of the Infantry in general, particularly from the rank of Captain descending, are fine horsemen. Their lives are passed almost entirely on the frontiers. Hunting is a favorite recreation with them, and a majority of them keep their own horses. They are, consequently, good judges of horses, and well skilled in every respect in their management and treatment. They would, therefore, become at once capable and efficient cavalry officers, for they are already well grounded in the tactics. Again, the experience of twenty-five years has shown me that on an average about one-half the Infantry soldiers are more or less accustomed to horses, and would be *at least* on an equality with Dragoon *recruits* in all that regards the horse. The remainder, with some exceptions( who might be transferred to other foot regiments) would in a few months manage their horses sufficiently well for all service on this frontier; whereas they would possess, over any newly organized regiments, all the important qualifications of discipline and a knowledge of the use of their arms.

I advance, General, for the consideration of the department, the proposition to change the organization of one or two of the foot regiments, not as an expedient to remove the necessity so loudly calling for an addition to the army of one or more new regiments of Dragoons or Mounted Riflemen, but because I am persuaded that the nature of the service to be required of the army for the next ten years will be such as to require that the cavalry arm shall greatly predominate in its organization.

"3rd. The best means of supplying the troops in New Mexico with recruits, horses, and subsistence."

In order to keep the companies in New Mexico full at the present standard, recruiting in the Atlantic and Middle States must be chiefly depended upon; re-enlistment will do but little towards it.

While in this territory my attention was requested by an officer of the medical department to the subject of the enlistment of hospital stewards especially for that office; and I have pleasure in submitting his views, viz: that they should be enlisted or employed especially for that duty [and] that their pay should be increased to that of Pay Master's clerk. The advantages would be that they would only be removed from the hospital at the expiration of their service, that the hazzard incurred in putting men whose previous education has not fitted them for the duty into the hospital is very great, and that by the course recommended the government would save largely in men as well as in medicines and hospital stores, that the increased pay proposed would bring into the service graduates of the Schools of Pharmacy, of good character.

With respect to horses, they cannot be procured of sufficient size and strength in the territory. It will therefore be necessary to purchase them in the Middle States. But the horses from Missouri and Illinois, from which states most of the horses now in the territory have been brought, are not found to stand the change of climate as well as those from a lower and more temperate latitude, as Tennessee and Kentucky. All horses, however, even from the last named states, experience more or less ill effects of the change, and many drop and fall away although not in active service, so that, as a general rule, a twelve month elapses after horses are brought into this country before they are acclimated or have recovered their natural vigour and endurance. The average duration of horses, here, I have learned from Dragoon officers, has but little exceeded three years. This may be owing in some measure to their having been put upon hard service too soon after their arrival.

In view of this, I would recommend that grazing farms be established, which, I believe, in ten years would save the government a large outlay in horses. Let three and four year old colts, bought in Tennessee, be kept on these farms for twelve or eighteen months before they are put in service, and they will last at least twice as long as those above referred to. Whilst in England in 1848, I conversed much with Cavalry officers on the subject of horses, and their treatment in that service. I was informed that colts purchased at three years of age and placed on duty with the recruiting or depôt squadrons, where they were lightly exercised for three years before being put into the service squadrons, served after joining the service squadrons on an average ten years, or to the age of sixteen. This fact was established by a careful examination of the records of the service during a long period.

There is every possibility that the service in New Mexico will, for many years to come, require the maintenance on the part of the United States of a large mounted force. As there is little doubt that to make this force efficient a provision of the kind recommended is advisable. On more than one occasion, the Apaches have escaped from Dragoons, when almost within their grasp, where the fleetness of their horses was put to test by the troops on their broken down animals.[4]

[4] The relative merits of horses for dragoon service were a matter of natural concern to the army. The native stock found in the area newly acquired from Mexico were considered inferior, but the animals imported from the East also created a variety of problems. Colonel Mansfield, when he inspected the department in 1853, condemned 82 out of 465 dragoon mounts as unserviceable. Frazer (ed.), *Mansfield*, 224. Where, then, did the Apaches secure their superior, or, at least, fleeter animals? Actually, they came from a variety of sources. Some were native New Mexican and California stock. Even more came from Old Mexico, acquired in the frequent Indian raids. Others were American horses, stolen from emigrants, freighters, settlers, and the army. Part of the problem facing the dragoons was the fact that, in addition to their clothing, they carried with them arms and equipment weighing seventy-eight pounds. "Weight of dragoon armament and equipment," 32 Cong., 1 sess., *House Exec. Doc. 2*, 253. Compared with the Apache, the dragoon was greatly overbur-

On the subject of supplying the troops in New Mexico with subsistence, I had the honor to report on the 14th instant. I would only further add that it was remarked to me by Captain Bowman, Regimental Quarter Master of the 3rd Infantry and Assistant Commissary of Subsistence at El Paso, that much expense in transporting subsistence across the plains was incurred by packing bacon, hard bread, etc., in barrels, the bacon sides being cut into square pieces (the bones were *not* removed) left large interstices in the barrels, and these again leave interals [*sic*] in the wagon bodies, by which much space is lost. He recommended that square boxes of convenient size and made to fit in the wagon bodies be used instead of barrels; also that hard bread be baked in square cakes and be packed in similar boxes. I examined the weight of some of the barrels (whiskey barrels) used for bread and found they ranged from forty-five to fifty-six pounds, while the hard bread contained did not exceed from ninety to one hundred and twelve pounds. Boxes would be lighter than these barrels, but it is questionable whether the bread would be as well preserved.[5]

---

dened; moreover, the soldier was usually more considerate of his mount, if only to avoid walking home.

John Greiner, writing in 1852, when he was Indian agent in New Mexico, summed up the situation succinctly, if not grammatically: "There are 92,000 Indians (estimated) in this Territory. Many of them are at war. We have not 1,000 troops here under Colonel Sumner to manage them. Our troops are of no earthly account. They cannot catch a single Indian. A dragoon mounted will weigh 225 pounds. Their horses are all as poor as carrion. The Indians have nothing but their bows and arrows and their ponies are as fleet as deer. Cipher it up. Heavy dragoons on poor horses, who know nothing of the country, sent after Indians who are at home anywhere and who always have some hours start, how long will it take to catch them? So far, although several expeditions have started after them, not a single Indian has been caught!"—Greiner to ———, March 31, 1852, in Galloway (ed.), "Private Letters of a Government Official in the Southwest," *The Journal of American History*, Vol. III (No. 4, 1909), 549.

There is, however, no reason why all the hard bread required for use in New Mexico should not be made there, and fcr this purpose it would be well to send out one or two competent bakers.

"4th. The probable number of inhabitants of New Mexico, Americans, Mexicans, and Pueblo Indians; also the number of each class within its limits whilst a territory of Mexico."

I have answered this query in my report of the 15th July last, as fully, I believe, as I could possibly now by going over the same ground again.

I am, very respectfully [etc.]

GEORGE A. MCCALL, *Inspector General.*

*Major General Roger Jones, Adjutant General, U.S.A.*
*Washington City, D.C.*

[5] By 1853 a change had been effected in the method of packing bacon for shipment across the plains. The individual sides of bacon were encased in canvas and packed without other protection. Colonel Mansfield pointed out, "When put up in large piles, the understrata are subjected to a heavy pressure, which no canvas can relieve, and which in a warm climate forces out the grease to waste; and here where butter and lard are scarce [this] is a great disadvantage to the consumer." Frazer (ed.), *Mansfield*, 61. By this date the production of flour in the department was adequate to meet the needs of the military, and no mention was made of the shipment of bread.

# APPENDIX A: MILITARY PERSONNEL MENTIONED IN THE McCALL REPORTS

In the list of military personnel the following information is provided. Rank, both regular and brevet, at the time of McCall's inspection is given. U.S.M.A. indicates that the officer attended the United States Military Academy. The number in parentheses is his rank in the class, and the date is that of graduation. C.S.A. indicates that the officer served in the Confederate States Army with the rank given. Otherwise, the highest rank attained in the United States Army is given. The date of death is given, if known. The information is taken from Heitman, *Historical Register*; and Robert M. Danford (ed.), *Register of Graduates and Former Cadets, United States Military Academy* (1953 ed.).

Adams, John. Second Lieutenant, Second Dragoons, and Brevet First Lieutenant. U.S.M.A. (25) 1846. Resigned May 31, 1861. Brigadier General, C.S.A. Killed November 30, 1864, at Franklin, Tennessee.

Alexander, Edmund B. Captain, Third Infantry, and Brevet Lieutenant Colonel. U.S.M.A. (33) 1823. Colonel and Brevet Brigadier General. Retired February 22, 1869. d. January 3, 1888.

Allen, Harvey A. First Lieutenant, Second Artillery, and Brevet Captain. U.S.M.A. (15) 1841. Lieutenant Colonel. Retired April 10, 1879. d. September 20, 1882.

Barton, Seth M. Second Lieutenant, First Infantry. U.S.M.A. (28) 1849. Resigned June 11, 1861. Brigadier General, C.S.A. d. April 11, 1900.

Beall, Lloyd. Second Lieutenant, Second Artillery. Dismissed September 12, 1862. Private, Artillery, C.S.A.

Bee, Barnard E. Second Lieutenant, Third Infantry, and Brevet Captain. U.S.M.A. (33) 1845. Resigned March 3, 1861. Brigadier General, C.S.A. Killed July 21, 1861, in the Battle of Bull Run.

Blair, William B. First Lieutenant, Second Artillery, and Brevet Captain. U.S.M.A. (11) 1838. Resigned May 14, 1861. Major, C.S.A. d. March 23, 1883.

Bowman, Andrew W. First Lieutenant, Third Infantry, and Brevet Captain. U.S.M.A. (40) 1841. Lieutenant Colonel. d. July 17, 1869.

Brooks, Horace. Captain, Second Artillery, and Brevet Lieutenant Colonel. U.S.M.A. (9) 1835. Colonel and Brevet Brigadier General. Retired January 10, 1877. d. January 13, 1894.

Brooks, William T. H. First Lieutenant, Third Infantry, and Brevet Major. U.S.M.A. (46) 1841. Major General (Vols.). Resigned July 14, 1864. d. July 19, 1870.

Brower, Charles B. Second Lieutenant, Third Infantry. Dismissed July 24, 1851.

Buell, Don Carlos. First Lieutenant, Third Infantry, and Brevet Captain. U.S.M.A. (32) 1841. Major General (Vols.). Resigned June 1, 1864. d. November 19, 1898.

Buford, Abraham. First Lieutenant, First Dragoons, and Brevet Captain. U.S.M.A. (51) 1841. Resigned October 22, 1854. Brigadier General, C.S.A. d. June 9, 1884.

Buford, John. Second Lieutenant, Second Dragoons. U.S.M.A. (16) 1848. Major General (Vols.). d. December 16, 1863.

Byrne, John. Assistant Surgeon. Resigned October 11, 1857.

Campbell, Reuben P. First Lieutenant, Second Dragoons, and Brevet Captain. U.S.M.A. (27) 1840. Resigned May 11, 1861. Colonel, C.S.A. Killed June 27, 1862, in the Battle of Gaines Mill, Virginia.

Chandler, Daniel T. Captain, Third Infantry, and Brevet Lieutenant Colonel. Resigned December 24, 1862. Lieutenant Colonel, C.S.A. d. October 14, 1877.

Clitz, Henry B. Second Lieutenant, Third Infantry, and Brevet First Lieutenant. U.S.M.A. (36) 1845. Colonel and Brevet Brigadier General. Retired July 1, 1885. Drowned October 30, 1888.

Craig, Louis S. Captain, Third Infantry, and Brevet Lieutenant Colonel. Killed by deserters, June 6, 1852.

Cunningham, Francis A. Major Paymaster. Retired August 27, 1863. d. August 16, 1864.

Easton, Langdon C. Captain, Assistant Quartermaster. U.S.M.A. (22) 1838. Colonel and Brevet Major General. Retired January 24, 1881. d. April 29, 1884.

Eaton, Joseph H. Captain, Third Infantry, and Brevet Lieutenant Colonel. U.S.M.A. (43) 1835. Major and Brevet Brigadier General. Retired January 24, 1881. d. January 20, 1896.

Ewell, Richard S. Captain, First Dragoons. U.S.M.A. (13) 1840. Resigned May 7, 1861. Lieutenant General C.S.A. d. January 25, 1872.

Field, Charles W. Brevet Second Lieutenant, Second Dragoons. U.S.M.A. (27) 1849. Resigned May 30, 1861. Major General, C.S.A. d. April 9, 1892.

Freeman, William G. Captain, Fourth Infantry, and Brevet Lieutenant Colonel. U.S.M.A. (15) 1843. Resigned March 31, 1856. d. November 12, 1866.

Givens, Newton C. First Lieutenant, Second Dragoons. U.S.M.A. (30) 1845. Captain. d. March 9, 1859.

Gordon, William H. Captain, Third Infantry, and Brevet Major. Major. Retired March 15, 1862. d. December 7, 1865.

Graham, Lawrence P. Captain, Second Dragoons, and Brevet Major. Brigadier General (Vols.). Retired December 15, 1870.

Grier, William N. Captain, First Dragoons, and Brevet Major. U.S.M.A. (54) 1835. Colonel and Brevet Brigadier General. Retired December 15, 1870. d. July 8, 1885.

Griffin, Charles. First Lieutenant, Second Artillery. U.S.M.A. (23) 1847. Major General (Vols.). d. December 15, 1867.

Hagner, John R. Major Paymaster. d. December 6, 1856.

Hammond, John Fox. Assistant Surgeon. Colonel. Retired December 7, 1884. d. September 29, 1886.

Hammond, William A. Assistant Surgeon. Brigadier General. d. January 5, 1900.

Henry, William S. Captain, Third Infantry, and Brevet Major. U.S.M.A. (40) 1835. d. March 5, 1851.

Hitchcock, Ethan Allen. Lieutenant Colonel, Third Infantry, and Brevet Brigadier General. U.S.M.A. 1817. Major General (Vols.). Mustered out, October 1, 1867. d. August 5, 1870. Prior to 1818 the classes graduating from the Military Academy were not ranked.

Howe, Marshall S. Major, Second Dragoons. Colonel. Retired August 31, 1866. d. December 8, 1878.

Jackson, Andrew. Second Lieutenant, Third Infantry. Dismissed June 6, 1861. Lieutenant Colonel, C.S.A.

Johns, William B. Captain, Third Infantry. U.S.M.A. (39) 1840. Dropped April 11, 1861. d. October 18, 1894.

Jones, Roger. Colonel and Adjutant General, Brevet Major General. d. July 15, 1852.

Jordan, Thomas. Captain, Assistant Quartermaster. U.S.M.A. (41) 1840. Resigned May 21, 1861. Brigadier General, C.S.A. d. November 27, 1895.

Jouett, William R. Lieutenant Colonel, Second Infantry. d. May 1, 1852.

Judd, Henry B. Captain, Third Artillery. U.S.M.A. (14) 1839. Major and Brevet Colonel. Retired November 21, 1861. d. July 27, 1892.

Kane, Elias K. Captain, Assistant Quartermaster. U.S.M.A. (47) 1841. d. July 9, 1853.

Kendrick, Henry L. Captain, Second Artillery, and Brevet Major. U.S.M.A. (16) 1835. Retired December 13, 1880. d. May 24, 1891.

Ker, Croghan. Captain, Second Dragoons. Resigned November 10, 1851.

McCormick, Charles. Assistant Surgeon. Lieutenant Colonel. d. April 28, 1877.

McDougall, Charles. Major Surgeon. Lieutenant Colonel and Brevet Brigadier General. Retired February 22, 1869. d. July 25, 1885.

McFerran, John C. First Lieutenant, Third Infantry. U.S.M.A. (34) 1843. Colonel and Brevet Brigadier General. d. April 25, 1872.

McLaws, Lafayette. First Lieutenant, Seventh Infantry. U.S.M.A. (48) 1842. Resigned March 23, 1861. Major General, C.S.A. d. July 24, 1897.

McParlin, Thomas A. Assistant Surgeon. Colonel and Brevet Brigadier General. Retired July 10, 1889. d. January 29, 1897.

Macrae, Nathaniel C. Captain, Third Infantry. U.S.M.A. (33) 1826. Major and Brevet Colonel. Retired September 25, 1861. d. February 5, 1878.

Magruder, David L. Assistant Surgeon. Colonel. Retired April 23, 1889.

Many, James B. Colonel, Third Infantry. d. February 23, 1852.

Marshall, Louis H. Brevet Second Lieutenant, Third Infantry. U.S.M.A. (41) 1849. Colonel. Resigned November 23, 1868. d. October 8, 1891.

Mason, Thomas J. Second Lieutenant, Third Infantry. Drowned May 22, 1850.

May, Charles A. Captain, Second Dragoons, and Brevet Colonel. Major. Resigned April 20, 1861. d. December 24, 1864.

Morris, Gouverneur. Major, Third Infantry. U.S.M.A. (did not graduate). Lieutenant Colonel. Retired September 9, 1861. d. October 18, 1868.

Munroe, John. Major, Second Artillery, and Brevet Colonel. U.S.M.A., 1814. Lieutenant Colonel. d. April 28, 1861.

Nones, Jefferson H. Second Lieutenant, Second Artillery. Resigned March 12, 1856. d. March 24, 1903.

O'Bannon, Laurence W. Second Lieutenant, Third Infantry. Resigned March 31, 1861. Lieutenant Colonel, C.S.A. d. June 2, 1882.

Parke, John G. Brevet Second Lieutenant, Topographical Engineers. U.S.M.A. (2) 1849. Major General (Vols.). Retired July 2, 1889. d. December 16, 1900.

Peck, John J. First Lieutenant, Second Artillery, and Brevet Captain. U.S.M.A. (8) 1843. Major General (Vols.). Mustered out August 24, 1865. d. August 21, 1878.

Pleasonton, Alfred. First Lieutenant, Second Dragoons. U.S.M.A. (7) 1844. Major General (Vols.). Resigned January 1, 1868. d. February 17, 1897.

Read, Hiram W. Chaplain, Fort Marcy, July 16, 1849, to March 15, 1852.

Reynolds, Alexander W. Captain, Assistant Quartermaster. U.S.M.A. (35) 1838. Dismissed October 4, 1861. Brigadier General, C.S.A. d. May 26, 1876.

Richardson, Israel B. First Lieutenant, Third Infantry, and Brevet Major. U.S.M.A. (38) 1841. Major General (Vols.). d. November 3, 1862, of wounds received in the Battle of Antietam.

Robertson, Beverly H. Second Lieutenant, Second Dragoons. U.S.M.A. (25) 1849. Dismissed August 8, 1861. Brigadier General, C.S.A. d. November 10, 1912.

Saunders, William H. Captain, Second Dragoons. Resigned June 30, 1851. d. July 6, 1857.

Schroeder, Henry B. First Lieutenant, Third Infantry. U.S.M.A. (22) 1844. Captain. Resigned May 30, 1861. d. December 21, 1904.

Shepherd, Oliver L. Captain, Third Infantry, and Brevet Major. U.S.M.A. (33) 1840. Colonel and Brevet Brigadier General. Retired December 15, 1870. d. April 15, 1894.

Shoemaker, William R. Military Store Keeper, Ordnance. Captain. Retired June 30, 1882. d. September 16, 1886.

Simpson, James H. First Lieutenant, Topographical Engineers. U.S.M.A. (18) 1832. Colonel and Brevet Brigadier General. Retired March 31, 1880. d. March 2, 1883.

Smith, William D. Second Lieutenant, Second Dragoons. U.S.M.A. (35) 1846. Resigned January 28, 1861. Brigadier General, C.S.A. d. October 4, 1862.

Steen, Enoch. Captain, First Dragoons, and Brevet Major. Lieutenant Colonel. Retired September 23, 1863. d. January 22, 1880.

Stone, Lyman H. Assistant Surgeon. Major. Dismissed September 16, 1862.

Sturgis, Samuel D. Second Lieutenant, First Dragoons. U.S.M.A. (32) 1846. Brigadier General (Vols.), and Brevet Major General. Retired June 11, 1886. d. September 28, 1889.

Sykes, George. First Lieutenant, Third Infantry, and Brevet Captain. U.S.M.A. (39) 1842. Brigadier General (Vols.), and Brevet Major General. d. February 8, 1880.

Taylor, Oliver H. P. Second Lieutenant, First Dragoons, and Brevet Captain. U.S.M.A. (31) 1846. First Lieutenant. Killed by Spokane Indians, Washington Territory, May 17, 1858.

Ten Broeck, Peter G. S. Assistant Surgeon. Major and Brevet Lieutenant Colonel. d. December 19, 1867.

Thomas, Francis J. First Lieutenant, Third Artillery. U.S.M.A. (6) 1844. Resigned June 30, 1852. Colonel, Ordnance, C.S.A. Killed July 21, 1861, in the Battle of Bull Run.

Tree, Arthur D. Second Lieutenant, Second Dragoons, and Brevet First Lieutenant. First Lieutenant. d. February 2, 1857.

Trevitt, John. First Lieutenant, Third Infantry. U.S.M.A. (12) 1844. Captain. Resigned April 17, 1861. d. March 24, 1893.

Twiggs, David E. Brigadier General and Brevet Major General. Dismissed March 1, 1861. Major General, C.S.A. d. July 15, 1862.

Van Horne, Jefferson. Captain, Third Infantry, and Brevet Major. U.S.M.A. (30) 1827. d. September 28, 1857.

Ward, James N. Second Lieutenant, Third Infantry, and Brevet First Lieutenant. U.S.M.A. (28) 1845. Captain. d. December 6, 1858.

Whistler, Joseph N. G. Second Lieutenant, Third Infantry, and Brevet First Lieutenant. U.S.M.A. (47) 1846. Colonel and

Brevet Brigadier General. Retired October 19, 1886. d. April 20, 1898.

Whittlesey, Joseph H. First Lieutenant, First Dragoons. U.S.M.A. (2) 1844. Major. Retired November 30, 1863. d. August 2, 1886.

Wilkins, John D. Second Lieutenant, Third Infantry, and Brevet First Lieutenant. U.S.M.A. (46) 1846. Colonel. Retired August 2, 1886. d. February 20, 1900.

Williamson, Andrew J. First Lieutenant, Third Infantry. U.S.M.A. (46) 1842. Resigned September 9, 1851.

Winship, Oscar F. First Lieutenant, Second Dragoons, and Brevet Major. U.S.M.A. (22) 1840. Captain. d. December 13, 1855.

Wirtz, Horace R. Assistant Surgeon. Major and Brevet Lieutenant Colonel. d. January 24, 1874.

Wood, William H. Second Lieutenant, Third Infantry. U.S.M.A. (37) 1845. Colonel. Retired June 26, 1882. d. January 1, 1887.

# APPENDIX B: LETTER FROM SURGEON GENERAL THOMAS LAWSON TO ADJUTANT GENERAL ROGER JONES

Surgeon General's Office,
December 5th 1850.

SIR:

I have to acknowledge the receipt of the following extract from the report of Inspector General G. A. McCall, dated Santa Fé, New Mexico, August 31st, 1850. "Surgeon McDougall reports the supply of Medicines recently received here for distribution in the Department to be by no means adequate to the demand. In some particulars his requisitions have not been filled."

In reply I have to state, that the Medical supplies required by the Senior Medical Officer in New Mexico for distribution in that Department during the current year have all been furnished with the single exception of "Fluid Extract of Sarsaparilla," which is not on the Medical Supply Table, and of course is not issued by the Medical Purveyors.

A small portion of the supplies called for, contained in eighteen packages, were forwarded from the depôt at Fort Leavenworth in May, and were received by Surgeon McDougall at Santa Fé in August last. These are the supplies of medicine "recently received" and which were reported to be "by no means adequate to the demand." The bulk of the medical supplies intended for the troops in

New Mexico were originally furnished from New York, and were forwarded from Fort Leavenworth, in one hundred and five packages, on the 17th of June, reaching Santa Fé perhaps in September last, and subsequent to the date of the Inspector General's report. In addition to the foregoing, a further supply of medical stores were ordered from Fort Leavenworth on the 2nd of July last, to meet the demand consequent upon the accession made to the military force in New Mexico.

The medical stores, etc., already ordered from New York and Fort Leavenworth are deemed an ample supply for all the troops stationed in New Mexico for the period of one year; but should it be otherwise, the Medical Director and other officers are fully authorized to draw upon the depôt at Fort Leavenworth for whatever articles of supply are immediately required, and which may be forwarded by the return train of waggons [*sic*].

It is difficult to conceive how Surgeon McDougall could have brought himself to believe that the small supply he received from Fort Leavenworth was all that was intended to be furnished for the service in New Mexico, and the more especially as the invoices of the supplies forwarded from New York had been received at Santa Fé by Assistant Surgeon [Lewis A.] Edwards, and by him turned over to Surgeon McDougall.

Again, I am at a loss to know what is meant by the expression, "In some particulars his (McDougall's) requisitions have not been filled." Surgeon McDougall did not reach Santa Fé until the 11th of July last, and he has not before nor since made any requisition for medical supplies, the requisition for the annual supply of medicines, etc., for the troops in New Mexico having been previously prepared and forwarded on to this office by the preceding Medical Director of that military department.

As Surgeon McDougall's statement, or the report of it by Inspector General McCall, conveys the idea that there has been neglect of duty somewhere, it is proper that this counter statement should accompany the Inspector General's report whithersoever it goes; and with this view, it is respectfully submitted to the Adjutant General of the Army.

I have the honor to be [etc.]

THOMAS LAWSON, *Surgeon General.*

*General R. Jones, Adjutant General*

# BIBLIOGRAPHY


## I. Unpublished Materials

### *1. The National Archives, Washington, D.C.*

Commission Branch, File M752 of 1863, Relating to George A. McCall, Records of the Office of the Adjutant General, Record Group 94.

McCall's Inspection Report, Department of New Mexico, 1850, Records of the Office of the Adjutant General, Record Group 94.

McCall's Inspection Report, Department of the Pacific, 1852, Records of the Office of the Adjutant General, Record Group 94.

Post Returns of Fort Marcy, New Mexico, 1849–94, Records of the Office of the Adjutant General, Record Group 94.

United States Military Academy, Application Papers for George A. McCall, File 30 of 1818, Records of the Office of the Adjutant General, Record Group 94.

### *2. State of New Mexico, Records Center and Archives, Santa Fe*

Alvarez Papers

Executive Record, 1851–67

Governors' Papers

Historical Society of New Mexico, Miscellaneous Collection

Journal of the House of Representatives of the Territory of New

Mexico being the second session of the first legislative Assembly, 1851–52
Miscellaneous Territorial Records
Read Collection
Vigil Papers

*3. Library of the Museum of New Mexico, Santa Fe*

Reuter, B. A. "Flour Mill Erected by Gov. Vigil and Other Mills of Pecos District." Typescript, July 28, 1939.

Sena, Bernardino de. "Will and Testament," July 17, 1758, Archivo 860, Public Survey Office (translation).

II. Government Documents

Abel, Annie Heloise, ed. *The Official Correspondence of James S. Calhoun while Indian Agent at Santa Fé and Superintendent of Indian Affairs in New Mexico.* Washington, D.C., 1915.

Abert, James W. *Report and Map of the Examination of New Mexico.* 30 Cong., 1 sess., *Sen. Exec. Doc. 23.* Washington, D.C., 1848.

Conrad, Charles M. *Report of the Secretary of War Communicating . . . Colonel McCall's Reports in Relation to New Mexico.* 31 Cong., 2 sess., *Sen. Exec. Doc. 26.* Washington, D.C., 1851.

*Constitución del Estado de Nuevo Méjico* [Santa Fe, 1850].

Crawford, George W. *Peace Establishment—Number of Indians in Oregon, California, and New Mexico, &c.* 30 Cong., 1 sess., *House Exec. Doc. 76.* Washington, D.C., 1848.

———. *Report from the Secretary of War, Communicating . . . a Copy of the Official Journal of Lieutenant Colonel Philip St. George Cooke, from Santa Fé to San Diego &c.* 31 Cong., Special sess., *Sen. Doc. 2.* Washington, D.C., 1849.

Emory, William H. *Notes of a Military Reconnoissance, from Fort Leavenworth in Missouri, to San Diego, in California, Including Part of the Arkansas, del Norte, and Gila Rivers.* 30 Cong., 1 sess., *House Exec. Doc. 41.* Washington, D.C., 1848.

Fillmore, Millard. *Message from the President of the United States.* 31 Cong., 2 sess., *Sen. Exec. Doc. 1.* Washington, D.C., 1850. Part II contains the report of Secretary of War Conrad for 1850.

———. *Message from the President of the United States.* 32 Cong., 1 sess., *House Exec. Doc. 2.* Washington, D.C., 1851. Contains the report of Secretary of War Conrad for 1851.

———. *Message from the President of the United States.* 32 Cong., 2 sess., *House Exec. Doc. 1.* Washington, D.C., 1852. Part II contains the report of Secretary of War Conrad for 1852.

———. *Message from the President of the United States, Transmitting a Copy of the Constitution Adopted by the Inhabitants of New Mexico* . . . . 31 Cong., 1 sess., *Sen. Exec. Doc. 74.* Washington, D.C., 1850.

———. *Texas Boundary.* 31 Cong., 2 sess., *House Exec. Doc. 8.* Washington, D.C., 1850.

*General Regulations for the Army of the United States, The.* Washington, D.C., 1847.

Heitman, Francis B. *Historical Register and Dictionary of the United States Army.* 2 vols. Washington, D.C., 1903.

Hodge, Frederick Webb, ed. *Handbook of American Indians North of Mexico.* 2 vols. Washington, D.C., 1912.

Lane, William Carr. *Message of . . . Governor of the Territory of New Mexico, to the Legislative Assembly of the Territory, at Santa Fé, Dec. 7, 1852.* Santa Fe, 1852.

Lewis, Berkeley R. *Small Arms and Ammunition in the United States Service.* Washington, D.C., 1956.

Pierce, Franklin. *Boundary Between Texas and the Territories.* 33 Cong., 2 sess., *House Exec. Doc. 89.* Washington, D.C., 1855.

Polk, James K. *Messages of the President of the United States, with the Correspondence, Therewith Communicated, Between the Secretary of War and Other Officers of the Government, on the Subject of the Mexican War.* 30 Cong., 1 sess., *House Exec. Doc. 60.* Washington, D.C., 1848.

———. *New Mexico and California.* 30 Cong., 1 sess., *House Exec. Doc. 70.* Washington, D.C., 1848.

Romero, Matías. *Memoria de Hacienda y Crédito Público, Correspondiente al Cuadragésimoquinto Año Económico.* Mexico, D.F., 1870.

*Seventh Census of the United States: 1850.* Washington, D.C., 1853.

Taylor, Zachary. *California and New Mexico.* 31 Cong., 1 sess., *House Exec. Doc. 17.* Washington, D.C., 1850.

———. *Information in Relation to the Formation of a State Government in New Mexico.* 31 Cong., 1 sess., *Sen. Exec. Doc. 60*, Washington, D.C., 1850.

———. *Message from the President of the United States*, 30 Cong., 2 sess., *Sen. Exec. Doc. 1.* Washington, D.C., 1848. Contains the report of Secretary of War Marcy for 1848.

———. *Message from the President of the United States.* 31 Cong., 1 sess., *Sen. Exec. Doc. 1*, Washington, D.C., 1849. Contains the report of Secretary of War Crawford for 1849.

———. *Message from the President of the United States with Copies of the Correspondence in Relation to the Boundary of Texas.* 31 Cong., 1 sess., *Sen. Exec. Doc. 24*, Washington, D.C., 1850.

Thian, Raphael P. *Notes Illustrating the Military Geography of the United States.* Washington, D.C., 1881.

United States House of Representatives. *Hugh N. Smith, Delegate from New Mexico.* 31 Cong., 1 sess., *House Report 220*, Washington, D.C., 1850.

———. *New Mexico—Convention of Delegates.* 31 Cong., 1 sess., *House Misc. Doc. 39*, Washington, D.C., 1850.

*War of the Rebellion: A Compilation of the Official Records of the Union and Confederate Armies.* 128 vols. Washington, D.C., 1880–1901.

Weightman, Richard H. *Communication of . . . and Accompanying Memorial of the Legislature of New Mexico, Setting Forth Sundry Grievances, and Calling upon Congress for Their Correction.* 31 Cong., 1 sess., *Sen. Exec. Doc. 76.* Washington, D.C., 1850.

## III. Newspapers

*Santa Fe Republican*, September 10, 1847–October 16, 1847.

*Santa Fe Weekly Gazette*, March 26, 1853; April 30, 1867.

## IV. Books

Abert, James W. *Abert's New Mexico Report, 1846–'47*. Albuquerque, 1962.

Arrowsmith, Rex. *Mines of the Old Southwest*. Santa Fe, 1963.

Bancroft, Hubert Howe. *History of Arizona and New Mexico*. (Vol. XVII of *Works*). San Francisco, 1889.

Bailey, L. R. *Indian Slave Trade in the Southwest*. Los Angeles, 1966.

Bandelier, Adolph F. *Final Report of Investigations Among the Indians of the Southwestern United States, Carried on Mainly in the Years from 1880 to 1885*. 2 vols. Cambridge, 1890–92.

Barreiro, Antonio. See Carroll and Haggard, eds.

Bartlett, John Russell. *Personal Narrative of Explorations and Incidents in Texas, New Mexico, California, Sonora, and Chihuahua, Connected with the United States and Mexican Boundary Commission During the Years 1850, '51, '52, and '53*. 2 vols. New York, 1854.

Beck, Warren A. *New Mexico: A History of Four Centuries*. Norman, 1962.

Bender, Averam B. *The March of Empire: Frontier Defense in the Southwest, 1848–1860*. Lawrence, Kansas, 1952.

Bieber, Ralph P., and Averam B. Bender, eds. *Exploring Southwestern Trails, 1846–1854*. Glendale, 1938.

Bolton, Herbert E., ed. *Spanish Exploration in the Southwest, 1542–1706*. New York, 1959.

Bourke, John G. *An Apache Campaign in the Sierra Madre*. New York, 1958.

Brayer, Herbert O. *Pueblo Indian Land Grants of the "Rio Abajo," New Mexico*. Albuquerque, 1939.

Calderón, Francisco R. *La República Restaurada, La Vida Económica* (Vol. 2 of *Historia Moderna de México*). Ed. by Daniel Cosío Villegas. Mexico, D.F., 1955.

Callahan, James Morton. *American Foreign Policy in Mexican Relations*. New York, 1932.

Carroll, H. Bailey, and J. Villasana Haggard, trans. and eds. *Three New Mexico Chronicles.* Albuquerque, 1942.

Chapel, Charles E. *Guns of the Old West.* New York, 1961.

Chávez, Angélico. *Archives of the Archdiocese of Santa Fe, 1678–1900.* Washington, D.C., 1957.

———. *Origins of New Mexico Families.* Santa Fe, 1954.

Clarke, Dwight L. *Stephen Watts Kearny, Soldier of the West.* Norman, 1961.

Conkling, Roscoe P., and Margaret B. *The Butterfield Overland Mail, 1857–1869.* 3 vols. Glendale, 1947.

Copeland, Fayette. *Kendall of the Picayune.* Norman, 1943.

Danford, Robert W., ed. *Register of Graduates and Former Cadets of the United States Military Academy.* New York, 1953.

Davis, William W. H. *El Gringo; or, New Mexico and Her People.* New York, 1857.

Field, Matthew. *Matt Field on the Santa Fe Trail.* Ed. by John E. Sunder. Norman, 1960.

Frazer, Robert W., ed. *Mansfield on the Condition of the Western Forts, 1853–54.* Norman, 1963.

Gregg, Josiah. *Commerce of the Prairies.* Ed. by Max Moorhead. Norman, 1954.

Goetzmann, William H. *Army Exploration in the American West, 1803–1863.* New Haven, 1959.

Hafen, LeRoy R., ed. *Ruxton of the Rockies.* Norman, 1950.

———, and Ann W. *Old Spanish Trail, Santa Fé to Los Angeles.* Glendale, 1954.

Hodge, Frederick Webb, George P. Hammond, and Agapito Rey, trans. and eds. *Fray Alonso de Benavides' Revised Memorial of 1634.* Albuquerque, 1945.

Horn, Calvin. *New Mexico's Troubled Years.* Albuquerque, 1963.

Hughes, John T. *Doniphan's Expedition.* Cincinnati, 1848.

Humboldt, Alexander von. *Ensayo Político sobre el Reino de la Nueva España.* 4 vols. and atlas. Mexico, 1941.

James, Thomas. *Three Years Among the Indians and Mexicans.* Philadelphia, 1962.

Keleher, William A. *Turmoil in New Mexico, 1846–1868*. Santa Fe, 1952.

La Farge, Oliver. *Santa Fe*. Norman, 1959.

Lavender, David. *Bent's Fort*. New York, 1954.

McCall, George A. *Letters from the Frontier, Written During a Period of Thirty Years' Service in the Army of the United States*. Philadelphia, 1868.

McCarty, John. *Maverick Town, the Story of Old Tascosa*. Norman, 1946.

Mansfield, Col. Joseph K. F. See Frazer, ed.

Martin, Douglas D. *Yuma Crossing*. Albuquerque, 1954.

Moorhead, Max. *New Mexico's Royal Road*. Norman, 1958.

Navarro y Noriega, Fernando. *Memoria sobre la Población del Reino de Nueva España*. Llanes, Spain, 1954.

Northrop, Stuart A. *Minerals of New Mexico*. Albuquerque, 1959.

Pattie, James Ohio. *Personal Narrative*. Philadelphia, 1962.

Pearson, Jim Berry. *The Maxwell Land Grant*. Norman, 1961.

Pino, Pedro Bautista. See Carroll and Haggard, eds.

Prince, L. Bradford. *Historical Sketches of New Mexico from the Earliest Records to the American Occupation*. Kansas City, 1883.

Reeve, Frank D. *History of New Mexico*. 2 vols. New York, 1961.

Richardson, Rupert N. *The Comanche Barrier to South Plains Settlement*. Glendale, 1933.

Rouaix, Pastor. *Diccionario Geográfico, Histórico y Biográfico del Estado de Durango*. Mexico, 1946.

Russell, Carl P. *Guns on the Early Frontiers*. Berkeley and Los Angeles, 1957.

Saunders, Lyle. *A Guide to Materials Bearing on Cultural Relations in New Mexico*. Albuquerque, 1944.

Spicer, Edward H. *Cycles of Conquest*. Tucson, 1963.

Thomas, Alfred B., trans. and ed. *Forgotten Frontiers: A Study of the Spanish Indian Policy of Don Juan Bautista de Anza, Governor of New Mexico, 1777–1787*. Norman, 1932.

———. *The Plains Indians and New Mexico, 1751–1778*. Albuquerque, 1940.

Thomlinson, M. H. *The Garrison of Fort Bliss, 1849–1916.* El Paso, 1945.

Twitchell, Ralph Emerson. *The Leading Facts of New Mexican History.* 5 vols., Cedar Rapids, Iowa, 1911–17.

———. *Old Santa Fe.* Chicago, 1962.

———. *The Spanish Archives of New Mexico.* 2 vols. Cedar Rapids, Iowa, 1914.

Underhill, Ruth M. *The Navajos.* Norman, 1956.

Wagner, Henry R., and Charles L. Camp. *The Plains and the Rockies.* Columbus, Ohio, 1953.

Wagner, Henry R. *The Spanish Southwest, 1542–1794.* 2 vols. Albuquerque, 1937.

Wallace, Ernest, and E. A. Hoebel. *The Comanches.* Norman, 1952.

Webb, James Josiah. *Adventures in the Santa Fé Trade, 1844–1847.* Ed. by Ralph P. Bieber. Glendale, 1931.

Whipple, Amiel W. *The Whipple Report.* Ed. by E. I. Edwards. Los Angeles, 1961.

Woodward, Arthur. *Feud on the Colorado.* Los Angeles, 1955.

## V. Articles and Pamphlets

Bender, Averam B. "Frontier Defense in New Mexico, 1846–1853," *New Mexico Historical Review*, Vol. IX (July, 1934), 249–72.

———. "Military Posts in the Southwest, 1848–1860," *New Mexico Historical Review*, Vol. XVI (April, 1941), 125–47.

Binkley, William C. "Reports from a Texan Agent in New Mexico, 1849," in *New Spain and the West*, Vol. II, Los Angeles, 1932, 157–83.

Bloom, John P. "New Mexico Viewed by Anglo-Americans, 1846–1849," *New Mexico Historical Review*, Vol. XXXIV (July, 1959), 165–98.

Bloom, Lansing B., ed. "Bourke on the Southwest," *New Mexico Historical Review*, Vol. X, part VI (January, 1935), 1–35; part VII (October, 1935), 271–322.

———. "Historical Society Minutes, 1859–1863," *New Mexico Historical Review*, Vol. XVIII (October, 1943), 394–428.

———. "New Mexico under Mexican Administration, 1821–1846," part I, *Old Santa Fe*, Vol. I (July, 1913), 3–49.

———. "The Rev. Hiram Walter Read, Baptist Missionary to New Mexico," *New Mexico Historical Review*, Vol. XVII (April, 1942), 113–47.

Espinosa, José Manuel. "The Legend of Sierra Azul," *New Mexico Historical Review*, Vol. IX (April, 1934), 113–58.

Frazer, Robert W. "Governor Mendinueta's Post on the Cerro de San Antonio," *University of Wichita Studies* (No. 49, 1961).

Galloway, Tod B., ed. "Private Letters of a Government Official in the Southwest," *The Journal of American History*, Vol. III (No. 4, 1909), 541–54. Letters of John Greiner.

Haley, J. Evetts. "The Comanchero Trade," *Southwestern Historical Quarterly*, Vol. XXXVIII (January, 1935), 157–76.

Lacy, James M. "New Mexican Women in Early American Writings," *New Mexico Historical Review*, Vol. XXXIV (January, 1959), 41–51.

"Note on the Population of New Mexico, 1846–1849," *New Mexico Historical Review*, Vol. XXXIV (July, 1959), 200–202.

Ortega, Melquiades Antonio, to the Editors of the *Registro Oficial*, January 31, 1831. In "Notes and Documents," *New Mexico Historical Review*, Vol. XXIV (October, 1949), 332–40.

Reeve, Frank D. "Navaho-Spanish Diplomacy, 1770–1790," *New Mexico Historical Review*, Vol. XXXV (July, 1960), 200–35.

———. "The Navaho-Spanish Peace: 1720's–1770's," *New Mexico Historical Review*, Vol. XXXIV (January, 1959), 9–40.

Rodríguez, Arnold L. "New Mexico in Transition," *New Mexico Historical Review*, Vol. XXIV (July, 1949), 184–221; (October, 1949), 267–99.

Scholes, France V. "Civil Government and Society in New Mexico in the Seventeenth Century," *New Mexico Historical Review*, Vol. X (April, 1935), 71–111.

Socorro, N.M. Newspaper description of the area, 1855. In "Notes and Documents," *New Mexico Historical Review*, Vol. XXVII (April, 1932), 170–73.

Thomas, Chauncey. "The Spanish Fort in Colorado, 1819," *Colorado Magazine*, Vol. XIV (May, 1937), 81–85.

Twitchell, Ralph Emerson. "The Story of the Conquest of Santa Fe, New Mexico, and the Building of Old Fort Marcy, A. D. 1846," *Publications of the Historical Society of New Mexico* (No. 24, n.d.).

Walter, Paul A. F. "New Mexico's Pioneer Bank and Bankers," *New Mexico Historical Review*, Vol. XXI (July, 1946), 209–25.

## VI. Maps

Disturnell, J. "*Mapa de los Estados Unidos de Méjico.*" New York, 1847 (facsimile edition, Department of State, Map Series, No. 5, Washington, D.C., 1935).

Parke, John G. "A Map of the Territory of New Mexico," Washington, D.C., 1851.

Strickland, Rex W. "Six Who Came to El Paso, Pioneers of the 1840's," *Southwestern Studies*, Vol. I (Fall, 1963).

United States Geological Survey Maps. Washington, D.C., latest editions.

# INDEX

Abel, Annie Heloise, on McCall's instructions: 66
Abert, James W.: 11; biographical sketch of, 11n.; map by, 15; quoted, 41n.; on gold production, 49; on education, 57n.
Abert, John J.: 11n., 12n.
Abiquiu, N. M.: 30, 53, 94, 97, 102, 151n., 177, 181; facilities rented at, 126; military importance of, 128; roads to, 128–30 & n.
Abiquiu, Post of: 37; freight costs to, 61n.; report on, 123–30; recommended garrison at, 183
Academy of Our Lady of Light, established: 57
Adams, John: 137, 145, 157, 190
Adams-Onís Treaty: 18
Adjutant General's Office, McCall's report to: 73
Adobes, as building material: 151–52
Agriculture: 27, 90ff.; discussed, 39–40; military, 62
Albuquerque, N. M.: 35, 47, 56, 88n., 158, 161, 182; freight costs to, 60; post established at, 153n.; facilities rented at, 155 & n.; military importance of, 156
Albuquerque, Post of: 142; report on, 153–56; recommended garrison at, 183
Alexander, Edmund B.: 136, 137, 190
Algodones, N. M.: 93
Allen, Harvey A.: 114, 190
Alvarez, Manuel: elected lieutenant governor, 69; biographical sketch of, 69n.; acting governor, 70; dispute with Munroe, 71; vote for, 109
Angney, William Z.: takes sheep to California, 53; biographical sketch of, 53n.
Ankrim, Joel L.: 174n.
Anton Chico, N. M.: 95, 96, 97, 142
Anza, Juan Bautista de: defeats Comanches, 28–29; governor of New Mexico, 28n.
Apache Indians: 17, 26n., 28, 31, 48, 49, 88, 99, 149, 150, 167, 169, 173, 177, 179n.; sheep stealing by, 89; discussed, 103–108; killed by Glanton, 106n.; numbers of, 110; post recommended among, 182, 183; horses of, 187n; *see also under band names*
Arable land, discussed: 91–98 & n.
Arapaho Indians: 102

Arizpe, Sonora: 159n.
Arkansas River: 102, 104, 143, 150, 151; agricultural potential, 96
Armijo, Antonio, opens California trade: 52
Armijo, Manuel: 10; census by, 38
Arms, at posts: 120–21, 126, 133, 139–40, 148, 155, 160, 164, 168, 172, 176
Arroyo Hondo, N. M.: 44n.
Artillery pieces, at posts: 117, 139, 147, 154, 172
Atrisco, N. M.: 88n.
Aubrey, Francis Xavier: and Marco's Apaches, 107–108; biographical sketch of, 107n.
Azunia, identified: 159n.; *see also* Zuñi Pueblo

Bacon, packing of: 188, 189n.
Bandelier, Adolph F. A., on mining: 51n.
Barcelo, María Gertrudes (La Tules): 120n.
Barclay, Alexander: 95n.
Barclay's Fort: 95, 97, 152; established, 95n.; discussed, 143–44
Barreiro, Antonio: 7; biographical sketch of, 7n.; on sheep, 40–41; on New Mexico's exports, 52; on education, 56
Bartlett, John Russell: 18; quoted, 159n.; on stolen livestock, 179n.
Barton, Seth M.: 137, 138, 191
Beall, Lloyd: 114, 191
Beans: 46, 173; cost, 169
Beaubien, Charles: 148n.
Beaubien, Luz: 148n.
Bee, Barnard E.: 114, 171, 191
Beef: cost and availability of, 46, 161, 165, 169, 173; lack of market for, 128
Belen, N. M.: 56, 88n.
Benavides, Alonso de: 5
Bent, Charles: 20, 21n., 35, 44n., 110n., 130n.; biographical sketch of, 20n.; on numbers of Indians, 26
Bent, St. Vrain and Company: 44n., 54n., 147n.
Bent, William: 54n.
Bent's Fort: 3n., 54n., 132n., 151
Bernalillo, N. M.: 45, 156, 182
Big Timbers (on Arkansas River): 150
Blair, William B.: 114, 191
Bliss, William W. S.: 73
Bosque Grande (on Pecos River): 54; extent of, 95
Bosque Redondo (on Pecos River), extent of: 95
Boundaries of New Mexico, described: 17–19
Bourke, John G.: describes flour mill, 43; biographical sketch of, 43n.
Bowman, Andrew W.: 114, 118, 171, 175, 191; quotes an Indian, 33; on packing supplies, 188
Brent, Thomas L.: describes arable land, 97–98n.; estimates corn production, 121n.
Brooks, Horace: 114, 116, 120, 191
Brooks, William T. H.: 136, 191
Brower, Charles B.: 153, 154, 191
Buchanan, James, on maps of New Mexico: 14
Buell, Don Carlos: 171, 191
Buford, Abraham: 167, 191
Buford, John: 137, 138, 139, 157, 191
Burgwin, John H. K.: 130n.
Byrne, John: 153, 191

Cabeza de Baca, Francisco Tomás, defeated for governor: 109
Calhoun, James S.: 63n., 68, 120n.; maps Indian tribes, 16; biographical sketch of, 16n.; instructions to, 22–23, 66; on Pueblo Indians, 23–24; on Indian hostilities, 26–27; on mineral wealth, 50–51; on school land, 58; on population of New Mexico, 82n.;

on Pueblo Indian citizenship, 83n.; on Indian depredations, 179n.
California: 3n., 14n., 18, 19, 20, 35n., 39, 46, 51, 70, 102, 113n.; commerce with, 41, 42, 52; as sheep market, 53–54; statehood recommended for, 65–66; influence on New Mexico, 68
Campbell, Reuben P.: 162, 163, 191
Camp Independence, Calif.: 47n.
Cañada: *see* Santa Cruz de la Cañada
Canadian (Red) River: 12n., 54, 104, 150
Cañon de Chelly: 182
Cantonment Burgwin, N. M.: 130n.
Cantonment Loring, Idaho: 47n.
Carleton, James H.: 101n.
Carson, Kit: 148n., 150; Navaho campaign, 101n.
Cattle: 40; discussed, 88–89; stolen by Indians, 178, 179n.
Cebolleta, N. M.: 89n., 155, 182; post established at, 157; military importance of, 161
Cebolleta, Post of: 37, 77, 137, 142, 154; freight costs to, 61n.; report on, 157–62; recommended garrison at, 183
Cerro de San Antonio, N. M., post on: 30n.
Chama (Chamas) River: 96, 128, 129n.; arable land on, 94, 97
Chandler, Daniel T.: 157, 158, 159, 192
Charleston, W. Va.: 20n.
Chávez, José Mariano, widow of: 69n.
Chávez family: 88n.
Cheyenne Indians: 102
Chihuahua (city): 10n., 40, 51, 69n., 88, 173; mining district, 41; funds obtained in, 118 & n., 171–72
Chihuahua (state): 17, 46, 103, 104, 106n., 107; encourages New Mexican migration, 80–81n.; flour from, 173
Cieneguilla (Pilar), N. M.: 128n.
Cimarron, N. M.: 148n.
Cimarron River, forage sent to: 141
Civil War, McCall's service in: 75–76
Clitz, Henry B.: 114–15 & n., 192
Collier, James, escorted to California: 152–53n.
Colorado River: 4n., 8, 18n, 54, 152n.
Comanche Indians: 7, 26n., 142–43, 150, 181; Anza treaty with, 28–29; trade with, 54–55; discussed, 102–103; traditional route of, 151n.
Comanchero trade: 54–55, 103
Commerce, discussed: 38–39, 51–55
Commissary Department: *see* Subsistence Department
Compromise of 1850: 18–19
Connelly, Henry: 142; elected governor, 69; biographical sketch of, 69n.; vote for, 109; losses to Jicarillas, 142n.
Conrad, Charles M.: on wild Indians, 28n.; instructions to Munroe, 71
Cooke, Philip St. George: 4, 11n.; biographical sketch of, 4n.
Coons, Benjamin Franklin: 35; biographical sketch of, 35–36n.; facilities rented from, 172n.
Copper mines: *see* Santa Rita copper mines
Corn: *see* forage
Coronado, Francisco de: 5
Costilla, N. M., established: 28
Craig, Louis S.: 162, 192
Crawford, George W.: 65, 73, 77; instructions to McCall, 66–67; report to, 79–110
Creuzbaur, Robert: 8
Croix, Teodoro de: 29–30n.
Cunningham, Francis A.: 113, 118, 192; elected senator, 70; biographical sketch of, 70n.

*Daily Picayune* (New Orleans, La.): 9
Davis, William W. H.: 21; on metal smithing, 42; offices held by, 42n.

Department of the Interior (United States): 16
Disturnell map: 14, 15n.
Division of the Pacific, McCall inspects: 73–74
Doña Ana, N. M.: 4n., 29n., 35, 36, 92, 96, 97n., 105, 107, 182; established, 17–18; post established at, 167; facilities rented at, 168 & n.; military importance of, 170
Doña Ana, Post of: 36, 46, 77, 162; freight costs to, 61 n.; report on, 166–70; recommended garrison at, 183
Don Fernandez de Taos: *see* Taos, N. M.
Doniphan, Alexander: 10n.
Doyle, Joseph B.: 95n.
Durán y Chávez, Pedro: 88n.
Durango, Bishop of, visits New Mexico: 159 & n.
Durango, Mexico, trade with: 88–89n.
Durango (state): 103

Easton, Langdon C.: 113, 120n., 192
Eaton, Joseph H.: 153, 192
Education: 27; discussed, 56–58
Edwards, Lewis A.: 199
*El Crepúsculo* (Taos, N. M.): 9n.
El Paso, Post of: 37, 46, 77, 168; established, 35, 36n.; freight costs to, 60, 61 n.; depot at, 169; report on, 170–74; facilities rented at, 172 & n., 176; military importance of, 173–74n.; recommended garrison at, 183
El Paso del Norte, Chihuahua: 12ff., 27 & n., 34, 37, 45n., 46n., 67, 81 & n., 92ff., 106, 108, 178, 182; presidio at, 29; post established opposite, 35–37 & n., 170n.
El Paso district: 47, 50n., 173n.; transferred to Chihuahua, 17; wines of, 45; fertility of, 174n.
Embudo Plaza (Dixon), N. M.: 129n.
Emory, William H.: 11 n., 34n.
Ensenada Choctaw (Choctaw Creek): 34
Espejo, Antonio de: 5; discovers silver, 48
Ewell, Richard S.: 145, 192

Field, Charles W.: 123, 192
Field, Mathew C.: 9
Florida: 18; McCall in, 64, 65
Flour, New Mexican: 165; availability and quality of, 46, 122, 127, 134, 141, 150; effect on price of corn, 46, 134; cost, 169; from Chihuahua, 173; *see also* grist mills
Forage: 46, 163; cost and availability, 97n., 121 & n., 127, 130, 133–34 & n., 140–41, 148, 155, 160, 164–65, 166n., 169, 172, 176; unusual consumption of, 140–41 & n.; depot of, recommended, 156; green wheat as, 166n.
Fort Adobe, Texas: 54n.
Fort Armstrong, Ill.: 64–65
Fort Bayard, N. M., established: 182n.
Fort Bliss, Texas, established: 170n.
Fort Conrad, N. M., established: 166n.
Fort Defiance, Ariz., established: 182n.
Fort Hall, Idaho.: 10n.
Fort Leavenworth, Kans.: 3n., 11 n., 59, 60, 77, 136, 145, 152, 153, 167, 199
Fort McRae, N. M., established: 92n.
Fort Marcy, N. M.: 47, 57; established, 34–35; described, 116n.; *see also* Santa Fe, Post of
Fort Massachusetts, Colo., established: 151n.
Fort Scott, Kans.: 65
Fort Selden, N. M.: 29n.
Fort Smith, Ark.: 12
Fort Stanton, N. M., established: 182–83n.
Fort Thorne, N. M., established: 152n.
Fort Union, N. M.: 148n.; supply depot at, 142n.
Fort Webster, N. M., established: 182n.

Fort Yuma, Calif.: 47n.
Franklin, Texas: 36n.
Fray Cristóbal, N. M.: 93 & n., 96
Freeman, William G.: 192
Frémont, John C.: 18n., 147n.
French, Samuel G.: on El Paso wines, 45; biographical sketch of, 45n.
Fuel: 47; cost and availability of, 122, 130, 136, 144, 151, 161, 166, 176
Funds, availability of: from St. Louis, 118; from Chihuahua, 118 & n., 171–72; at Taos, 119; at Santa Fe, 125, 139, 147, 154, 159; at El Paso, 168; from New Orleans, 171

Gadsden Purchase: 4n., 15, 18n., 32n.
Gaines, Edmund P.: 64
Gallatin, Albert: 6n.
Gallinas River: 105, 143
Garland, John: 74
Garrard, Hector Lewis: 8–9
*Gazette* (Santa Fe): 9n.
General Regulations, Article LVI quoted: 115–16n.
Gila Apaches: 101; discussed, 106–107; numbers of, 110
Gila River: 3, 4n., 35n., 99, 104, 107, 167, 181; post recommended near, 182; garrison recommended at, 183
Givens, Newton C.: 123, 192
Glanton, John: attacks Gomez' band, 106; biographical sketch of, 106n.
Gomez (Mescalero Apache), band of: 105–106
Gordon, William H.: 130, 131, 192
Gorman, Samuel, maintains school: 57
Government documents on New Mexico: 10–12
Graham, Lawrence P.: 123, 124, 192
Grazing: extent and quality of, 88, 127, 170; camp for department, 165
Gregg, Josiah: 7, 51; on metal smithing, 42; on gold production, 49, 50; on Comanchero trade, 54
Greiner, John: on mineral wealth, 50; biographical sketch of, 50n.; on inability to control Indians, 188n.
Grier, William N.: 131, 145, 146, 147, 150, 192
Griffin, Charles: 114, 124, 192
Grist mills: 134; described, 43–44; at Mora, 44, 140, 150, 165, 169; at El Paso, 169n.
Guadalupe, Chihuahua: 81 & n.
Guadalupe Hidalgo, Treaty of: 20, 25, 28n., 35, 39, 81n.; obligations to protect New Mexico in, 32
Guadalupe Mountains: 105, 173; location of, 173n.
Guadalupe Pass: 173n.

Hagner, John B.: 113, 125, 132, 147, 193
Hakluyt, Richard: 5
Hammond, John Fox: 162, 193
Hammond, William A.: 157, 193
Hardy, R. W. H.: 7
Hart, Simeon, as flour contractor: 46n., 169n.
Hay: *see* forage
Henry, William S.: 170, 193
Henry E. Huntington Library: 5
Hitchcock, Ethan Allen: 113, 193; commands Pacific Division, 113n.
Hopi (Moqui) Indians: 24, 28; discussed, 101–102; location of, 101n.; resist Apaches, 104
Horses: 40, 41n., 156; shortage of, 77, 116; at posts, 115, 123, 126, 137, 145, 157, 162; condition of, 126, 140, 148–49, 164, 168, 188n.; expense of keeping, 143; stolen by Indians, 178, 179n.; recommendations regarding, 186–87; Apache, source of, 187n.
Houghton, Joab: 23, 24; biographical sketch of, 23–24n.
Howe, Marshall S.: 153, 154, 157, 193
Huerfano River: 151n.
Hughes, John T.: 10

Humboldt, Alexander von: 6, 14, 38n.

Illinois (state): 164
Independence, Mo.: 60
Indian Affairs, Office of: 3, 23, 25
Indian Intercourse Act (1834): 23, 25
Indianola, Texas: 67
Indians (wild): depredations of, 22, 26–27, 28, 39, 98, 177–78 & n.; lack of knowledge of, 23; numbers of, 26, 80n.; effect on economy of, 33, 39–40, 87–90; described, 98–110; need of United States to impress, 108; Spanish-American fear of, 179n.; number of warriors, 181; mode of warfare, 181–82
Iron works: 87
Isleta, N. M.: 88n.
Isleta, Texas: 34, 174n.

Jackson, Andrew: 131, 137, 193
James, Thomas: 8
Jefferson Barracks, Mo.: 36, 64, 65
Jemez River, 96
Jesup, Thomas S.: on Indian depredations, 32–33; on quartermaster expenses, 60; on military sites, 63
Jicarilla Apaches: 50n., 84n., 101, 135, 142, 144, 178, 181; unites with Utes, 102; discussed, 104–105; atrocities, 104–105n.; numbers of, 110; attack Connelly's train, 142n.
Johns, William B.: 175, 193
Johnston, Abraham R.: 11n.
Johnston, Joseph E.: 45n.
Jones, Roger: 77, 193
Jordan, Thomas: 162, 193
Jornada del Muerto: 91, 93 & n., 105, 142; described, 92
Jouett, William R.: 113, 193; transferred to California, 113n.
Judd, Henry B.: 137, 193

Kane, Elias K.: 157, 193
Kaskaskia, Ill.: 147n.
Kearny, Stephen Watts: 3, 4n., 11n., 20n., 21n., 24n., 33, 53, 70n., 179n.; route of, during Mexican War, 3n.; instructions to, 19; provides government for New Mexico, 20; promises protection, 31
Kearny Code: 20 & n.
Kendall, George W.: 9–10
Kendrick, Henry L.: 114, 116, 193
Ker, Croghan: 136, 137, 157, 194
Kiowa (Kayugua) Indians: 103, 110
Kirker, James: 48n.

Laguna Pueblo: 57
La Joya (Velarde), N. M.: 94, 97, 109, 129n.; commissary depot at, 134 & n.
Lamy, Jean B.: 57
Lane, William Carr: quoted, 4; biographical sketch of, 4n.; on Mesilla question, 15n.; on conditions in New Mexico, 27; on gold production, 49n.
Las Ruedas, N. M.: 57
Las Vegas, N. M.: 31, 89, 95, 97, 132, 143n., 150, 152, 177, 181; post established at, 136n.; facilities rented in, 139 & n.; wheat raised near, 140; as depot, 142, 144
Las Vegas, Post of: 37, 156, 163; freight costs to, 61n.; report on, 136–44; recommended garrison at, 183
Lawson, Thomas, letter from: 198–200
Lentis, N. M.: 24
Limpia River: 108 & n.
López de Zubiría y Escalante, José Antonio Laureano, visits New Mexico: 159 & n.
Los Angeles, Calif.: 53
Los Chávez, N. M.: 88n.
Los Padillas, N. M.: 88n., 109
Luis Lopez, N. M.: 93 & n.

McCall, George Archibald: 63, 69, 113n., 116n., 117, 131n., 198, 199; early career of, 64–65; instructions to, 65–67, 79; arrives in Santa Fe,

67; promotes statehood, 68; opinion of Santa Fe, 72; commissioned inspector general, 73; inspection tours of, 73–74; resigns commission, 74, 76; in Civil War, 74–75; writes book, 76; death of, 76; critical of New Mexico, 85–86; recommendations of, 180–82, 188
McClellan, George B., recommends McCall's promotion: 75
McCormick, Charles: 169, 194
McDougall, Charles: 113, 119, 120n., 133, 194, 198, 199
McFerran, John C.: 157, 194
McKnight, Robert: 48n.
McLaws, Lafayette: 113, 120n., 194
McParlin, Thomas A.: 136, 194
Macrae, Nathaniel C.: 114, 194
Magruder, David L.: 145, 147, 194
Mansfield, Joseph K. F.: 74; on schools, 57; biographical sketch of, 74n.; criticizes musketoon, 120n.; condemns dragoon horses, 187n.; on bacon, 189n.
Manufacturing: in Mexican period, 41–42; discussed, 86–87
Many, James B.: 113, 194
Manzano, N. M.: 44
Maps of New Mexico, discussed: 13–16
Marco (Mescalero Apache): band of, 105–106, 110; on need for food, 108
Marcy, Randolph B.: 12 & n.
Marcy, William L.: promises protection, plans for New Mexico, 35
Marshall, Louis H.: 115, 194
Martínez, Antonio José: 9n.
Martínez de Lejanza, Mariano, census by: 38, 79–80 & n.
Martínez de Montoya, Juan: 5
Mason, Thomas J.: 163, 194
Maxwell, Lucien B.: 147, 150; biographical sketch of, 147–48n.
Maxwell Land Grant: 37, 148n.
May, Charles A.: 162, 163, 194
Medical Department: of department, 119; of posts, 125, 132, 139, 147, 155, 159, 164, 168, 172, 175
Medill, William, on location of Indian tribes: 26n.
Memphis, Tenn.: 65
Mendinueta, Pedro Fermín de, military post of: 30n.
Mescalero Apaches: 103; numbers of, 110
Mesilla, N. M.: 81n.
Metal smithing: 42
Mexicans (Spanish-Americans): American attitude toward, 55–56, 70n.; described by McCall, 85–86
Mexican War: 20, 35, 59; accounts of, 10
Mexico, Republic of: 19n., 33; military defense for New Mexico, 31; New Mexicans loyal to, 80–82
Mexico City, D. F.: 7, 88
Military Department No. 9: 59; described, 34; headquarters, 111–13
Military expenses: discussed, 46–47; increase in, 59; for transportation, 59–60; considered excessive, 62
Military policy: 33, 35–37
Militia, New Mexican: 27, 30, 32 & n.; ineffectiveness of, 180
Mimbres River, post on: 182n.
Mining: 27, 87–88; in Spanish period, 47–48; in Mexican period, 49; American impressions of, 50–51
Miranda, Guadalupe: 148n.
Missouri (state): 41, 51, 52, 90, 164
Mitchell, Robert B., proclamation abolishing peonage: 86
Mojave Desert: 54
Moqui Indians: *see* Hopi Indians
Mora, N. M.: 132n, 181; mill at, 44n., 140, 141, 150, 169; arable land near, 95, 97, 102
Mora River: 44, 95n.
Mormon Battalion: 4n.
Morris, Gouverneur: 114 & n., 117, 194
Mount Blanca, post near: 151n.

Mules: 41n., 89; source of, 51; among Comanches, 103; cost of keeping, 143n.; as dragoon mounts, 149; stolen by Indians, 178, 179n.
Mule trails: *see* roads
Munroe, John: 63n., 112, 119, 120n., 156, 194; calls statehood convention, 68; commands department, 68n., 116; calls election, 69; attitude toward state government, 70; on Mexican character, 70n.; dispute with Alvarez, 71
Musketoon, discussed: 120–21 & n.
Mutton: *see* sheep

Narbona, Antonio, census by: 38n.
Navaho (Nabajoe) Indians: 24, 28, 31, 32n., 84n., 88, 104, 109, 128, 161, 177, 178, 179n.; sheep-stealing by, 89–90; discussed, 99–101; relations with Utes, 101n.; post recommended among, 182–83
Navarro y Noriega, Fernando, census by: 37–38
Negroes: population (1850), 38n.; denied suffrage, 83n.
*New Mexican* (Santa Fe): 9n.
New Orleans, La.: 67; funds obtained in, 171
New Placer mining district: 49
Newspaper accounts of New Mexico: 9 & n.
New York, N. Y.: 199
*Niles Weekly Register*: 9
Niza, Marcos de: 5
Nones, Jefferson H.: 114, 194
Nueces River: 19n.
Nueva Vizcaya: 17
Nuevo León: 17

Oak Creek, post on: 31n.
O'Bannon, Laurence W.: 167, 195
Ocaté Creek: 132n.
Ojo Caliente, N. M.: 151n.
Ojo del Muerto: 92 & n.
Old Placer mining district: 49
Old Spanish Trail: 52
Ordnance Department: of department, 119; of posts, 139, 147, 172
Organ Mountains: 50
Ortiz, Ramón, encourages New Mexican migration: 80–81n.
Ortiz Mountains: 49

Palace of the Governors: 63, 72n., 120n.; repairs to, 119
Parke, John G.: 113, 195; map by, 15 & n.
Pattie, James Ohio: 7, 48n.
Paymaster Department: 118–19, 125, 132
Peck, John J.: 114, 195
Peck, William G.: 11n.; map by, 15
Pecos, N.M.: 95, 97; school at, 57
Pecos Pueblo: 29
Pecos River: 44, 54, 91, 102, 103, 104, 105, 143; arable lands on, 95
Peña Blanca, N. M.: 91, 93, 95, 96
Peonage: 85–86n.
Peralta, N. M.: 69n.
Perea, Estevan de: 5
Philadelphia, Pa.: 64, 65, 67, 73
Picuris, N. M.: 129n.
Pike, Zebulon Montgomery: 6
Pino, Pedro Bautista: 6; deputy to Spanish Cortes, 6–7n.; on mineral wealth, 48
Plains Indians: 37, 51, 54, 80n.; *see also under tribe names*
Pleasonton, Alfred: 136, 195
Point of Rocks, N. M.: 104 & n., 143, 152
Polk, James K.: 14; on Texas claims, 18–19n.; on New Mexico's government, 20
Ponce de León, Juan María: 35n.
Pope Pius IX: 159n.
Population: Pueblo Indian, 23–24, 38n., 80n., 84n., 110; wild Indian, 26, 38n.; New Mexico, 37–38 & n., 79–

82; Negro, 38n.; Navaho, 99, 110; Hopi, 102, 110; Ute, 102, 110; Cheyenne and Arapahoe, 102, 110; Comanche, 103, 110; Kiowa, 103, 110; Apache, 105–107, 110
Portales Valley: 54
Prescott, Ariz.: 48n.
Presidio del Norte, Chihuahua: 105
Price, Sterling: 21n.
Prices in Santa Fe: 62n.
Prince, L. Bradford, estimates population: 80n.
Pueblo Indians: 16, 29, 30, 55, 99; location and numbers of, 23–24, 38n., 80n., 84n.; land grants to, 24–25, 84–85; political status of, 25; as military auxiliaries, 30 & n., 32n., 180; agriculture of, 39–40; described by McCall, 82–85; citizenship for, 82, 83n.; and wild Indians, 84n.; and Navahos, 101; ignorance of United States regarding, 108
Pueblo Land Act (1924): 25
Pueblo Revolt (1680): 30, 48, 93n.

Quartermaster's Department: 63, 171; expenses in, 59–60; facilities erected by, 63; of department, 117; of posts, 117–18, 125, 132, 138, 147, 154, 159, 163, 168, 171, 175; repairs by, 119, 126, 160, 175

Ramusio, Gian Battista: 5
Ranchos de Taos, N. M.: 129n.
Ration, army, components available in New Mexico: 46, 122, 165, 169
Raton Mountains: 150, 151
Raton Pass: 3n
Rayado, Post of: 37, 131, 132, 134, 135, 142, 143, 144, 151n., 157, 181; arable land near, 95, 97; roads to Taos from, 132n.; report on, 145–53; description of rented quarters, 148n.; garrison recommended for, 183
Rayado Creek: 148n., 150
Read, Hiram W.: 115, 195; maintains school, 57
Red (Colorado) River: 34
*Registro Oficial* (Mexico City): 9
Rented facilities: attempt to curtail, 63; at posts, 119 & n., 126 & n., 133 & n., 147–48 & n., 155 & n., 165n., 168 & n., 172 & n.
Reynolds, Alexander W.: 113, 117, 120n., 195
Richardson, Israel B.: 171, 195
Richmond, Va.: 75
Riley, Bennett: 70
Río Abajo Country: 45, 142, 161
Río Arriba Country: 46
Río Grande: 3, 4n., 15, 34, 47, 51, 81, 89, 128n., 129n., 163, 178, 182; claimed as Texas boundary, 12, 18–19 & n.; pueblos on, 23–24; navigability of, 91; arable land on, 91–97, 97–98n.; Apaches on, 105, 107; high waters on, 127, 130; "La Isla" in, 174n.
Río Puerco: 89, 91, 96
Río San José: 96
Roads: 27; along Río Grande, 3; Cooke's wagon, 4n.; Fort Smith–Santa Fe, 12; Santa Fe–Abiquiu, 128 & n.; Abiquiu-Taos, 128–29 & n.; Santa Fe–Taos, 129n., 135; east of Taos, 132n.; Taos–La Joya, 134; projected, 150–51; Santa Fe–El Paso, 173 & n.
Robertson, Beverly H.: 162, 195
Robledo, N. M.: 29n.
Rubí, Marqués de: 29n.
Ruxton, George F. A.: 8; describes Turley's mill, 44n.

Sacramento Mountain Apaches: 167, 178, 182; discussed, 105; numbers of, 110
Sage, Rufus B.: 8
St. Louis, Mo.: 10n., 20n., 36, 69n., 118

St. Vrain, Ceran: 20n., 54n.; flour mill of, 44, 140; biographical sketch of, 44n.; defeated for lieutenant governor, 109
San Antonio, Texas: 12, 67, 106n., 107
San Diego, Calif.: 4n.
San Diego crossing, of Río Grande: 4n.
Sandoval, N. M.: 105
San Elizario, Presidio (Post) of: 34, 36, 37, 46, 47, 77, 171; established, 29; freight costs to, 61n.; military importance of, 173–74, 176; history of, 174n.; report on, 174–76
San Elizario, Texas: 3, 27, 34, 174n., 182; presidio established at, 29; military facilities in, 63, 175; facilities rented in, 175 & n.
San Francisco, Calif.: 53, 152n.
San Gabriel Mission, Calif.: 52
Sangre de Cristo Grant: 148n.
Sangre de Cristo Pass: 151n.
San José, N. M.: 95, 97; school at, 57–58
San Juan, N. M.: 128, 130
San Juan Pueblo, N. M.: 129n.
San Juan River: 99, 102
San Luis Valley, Colo.: 151n.
San Miguel del Bado, N. M.: 30, 56, 95, 97, 103, 143; former importance of, 143n.
San Pedro Mountains: 49
Santa Clara Spring: 104 & n.
Santa Cruz de la Cañada: 43, 56, 94, 95, 97, 130, 133
Santa Fe, N. M.: 3n., 10n., 12, 22, 39, 47, 50n., 51, 70n., 73, 92, 109, 133, 143n., 152, 155, 161, 178, 181, 182, 198, 199; United States consul in, 11n., 69n.; Calhoun arrives at, 16n., 66; conventions in, 20, 21, 68; Spanish military force in, 30 & n.; Mexican military force in, 31; Fort Marcy established at, 34–35, 116n.; schools in, 56–57; freight costs to, 60, 61n.; prices in, 62n.; military facilities in, 63, 119–20 & n.; McCall arrives at, 67; state legislature in, 70; McCall's opinion of, 72; American impact on, 85; garrison in, 111; roads from, 128 & n., 129n., 130, 132, 135, 142, 151; recommended garrison at, 183
Santa Fe, Post of: 76, 77; report on, 111–22; depot at, 122, 127, 150, 152, 155, 181
Santa Fe–Chihuahua trade: 29, 37, 50n., 51
*Santa Fe Republican*: 9
Santa Fe River, arable land on: 95
Santa Fe trade: 37–38, 42, 51, 69n., 143n.; writings on, 7–9
Santa Fe Trail: 3, 47, 104 & n., 142n., 143n., 152
Santa Rita copper mines: 48, 49, 182; output of, 48n.; post established near, 182n.
Saunders, William H.: 157, 158, 195
Sawmills, lack of: 41
Schools: *see* education
Schroeder, Henry B.: 153, 195
Scott, Winfield, on army strength: 61–62n.
Sena, Bernardino de, property of: 72n.
Sena, Juan, McCall rents quarters from: 72 & n.
Seven Cities of Cíbola: 48
Sheep: as source of wealth, 40–41; Indian depredations on, 41n., 88–90, 178, 179n.; mutton in ration, 46, 128, 161; California as market for, 53–54
Shepherd, Oliver L.: 167, 195
Shoemaker, William R.: 115, 119, 195
Sigüenza y Góngora, Carlos: 5
Simpson, James H.: 12 & n., 113, 195
Sinaloa (state): 17
Slidell, John: 14 & n.
Smith, Hugh N.: 71; instructions to, 21–22; in Washington, D.C., 21n.
Smith, William: 36n.
Smith, William D.: 157, 158, 196

Socorro, N. M.: 17, 18, 27n., 30, 35, 43, 89, 97n., 182; post established at, 162n.; quarters rented at, 165
Socorro, Post of: 46, 131n., 142; freight costs to, 61n.; report on, 162–66; forage costs at, 166n.; recommended garrison at, 183
Socorro, Texas: 34, 174n.
Sonora (state): 103, 104
South Park, Colo.: 96n.
Spain, military defense for New Mexico: 29–30
Squier, Ephraim G.: 6n.
Statehood, New Mexican: efforts to achieve, 65–71; constitution quoted, 83n.; vote on constitution, 109
Steen, Enoch: 162, 166, 167, 196
Stephenson, Archibald: 50n.
Stephenson, Hugh: operates lead mine, 49; biographical sketch of, 50n.
Stock raising: 27, 44n.; discussed, 40–41; 88–90
Stone, Lyman H.: 170, 196
Storrs, Augustus: 11 & n.
Sturgis, Samuel D.: 167, 196
Subsistence Department: meat supply for, 46; of department, 122; of posts, 127, 132, 134, 139, 141, 150, 155, 161, 165, 169, 172–73, 176
Sumner, Edwin Vose: 74, 188n.; commands department, 74n.; critical of New Mexico, 85n.
Supreme Court, United States, and Pueblo Indians: 25
Swords, Thomas: on corn as forage, 141n.; on Socorro, 166n.
Sykes, George: 114, 196

Taos, N. M.: 3, 8, 20n., 27, 28n., 30, 39, 47, 50n., 51, 56, 94, 97n., 102, 119, 130, 134n., 141, 147, 148n., 150, 151n., 181; roads to, 128–30, 132n., 134, 135; post established at, 130n.; facilities rented in, 133; military importance of, 135
Taos, Post of: 77, 94n., 137, 145, 146, 147; freight costs to, 61n.; report on, 130–36; recommended garrison at, 183
Taos lightning (whiskey): 45, 134–35n.
Taos Mountains: 129, 134, 135; identified, 129n.
Taos Pueblo, N. M.: 135
Taos River: 94, 128n.
Taos uprising: 9, 130n.
Taos Valley: arable land in, 94, 97, 150; described, 94n.; forage produced in, 133–34; turbulence of inhabitants, 135
Taylor, Benjamin F.: 8
Taylor, Oliver H. P.: 145, 196
Taylor, Zachary: 65, 71, 73; recommends statehood, 65–66
Tecolote, N. M.: 95, 97
Ten Broeck, Peter G. S.: 167, 196
Ternaux-Compans, Henri: 6n.
Texan–Santa Fe expedition: 9
Texas, Republic of: 174n.; claims to New Mexico, 18–19
Texas (state): 33, 46, 47, 55, 65, 106n.; boundary of, 18–19; claims to New Mexico, 19n.; freight costs in, 61n.
Texas Boundary Act: 19
Texas–New Mexico boundary: documents on, 12; settlement of, 18–19
Thomas, Francis J.: 113, 196
Thorne, Herman: 152n.
Tome, N. M.: 35, 36
Trampas, N. M.: 129n.
Transportation, army, in New Mexico: 122, 130, 135–36, 150, 161, 165; cost of, 59–60, 61n., 152
Tree, Arthur D.: 137, 196
Trevitt, John: 167, 196
Trias, Angel, report to: 80–81n.
Truth or Consequences, N. M.: 3–4n.
Tucson, Ariz.: 4n.
Turley, Simeon, mill of: 44n.
Twiggs, David E.: 136, 196

United States Army: strength in New Mexico of, 33–34, 36–37, 61, 184; military departments of, 59; legal strength of, 61; garrisons at posts, 77, 113–15, 123, 130–31, 136–37, 145, 153, 157, 162, 167–68, 170–71, 174–75; shortage of officers, 77; suffrage of in New Mexico, 83n.; use of Indian auxiliaries, 84n., 180; proficiency of troops, 116–17, 124–25, 131–32, 138, 146, 154, 158–59, 163, 167, 171; strength recommended by McCall, 180–84; mounted troops recommended, 184–85; recruiting for, 186; hospital stewards recommended for, 186
United States–Mexican boundary: 14–15, 18; survey of, 15n.; commission, 182n.
Ute Indians: 28, 50n., 84n., 101, 104, 128, 135, 177, 178, 181; relations with Navahos, 101 & n.; discussed, 102

Valverde, N. M.: 17, 93 & n., 182
Van Horne, Jefferson: 36n., 45n., 170, 171, 196
Vargas, Diego de: 5
Vetancurt, Agustín de: 5
Vigil, Donaciano: calls convention, 20; biographical sketch of, 20–21n; on New Mexican economy, 39; flour mill of, 44; restricts Ortiz, 81
Villagrá, Gaspar de: 5
Volunteers, New Mexican: *see* militia, New Mexican
Volunteers, United States Army, during Mexican War: 33

Wagon Mound, tragedies near: 104–105n.
Ward, James N.: 131, 138, 162, 163, 196
War Department: 3, 16, 37; concern about costs of, 61
Washington, D.C.: 65, 71, 73; ignorance of New Mexico in, 23
Washington, John Macrae: 12, 21, 80; as military governor, 12n.; urges permanent government, 21n.; authorizes volunteers, 32 & n.
Weaving: 42, 87, 99, 102
Weightman, Richard: elected senator, 70; biographical sketch of, 70n; on opposition to statehood, 71; in Washington, D.C., 71–72; kills F. X. Aubrey, 107n.
Whistler, Joseph N. G.: 157, 196
White, John M., and party killed by Jicarillas: 104n.
White Mountain Apaches: 142, 178; discussed, 105; numbers of, 110
White Mountains, post established in: 183n.
Whiting, William H. C.: on El Paso wines, 45; biographical sketch of, 45n.; on El Paso district, 174n.
Whittlesey, Joseph H.: 145, 197; describes Taos Valley, 94n.; describes roads, 128n., 129n., 132n.; on flour shortage, 134–35n.
Wilkins, John D.: 171, 172, 197
Williamson, Andrew J.: 131, 197
Wine making: 44–46
Winship, Oscar F.: 123, 197
Wirtz, Horace R.: 123, 125, 197
Wislizenus, Frederick A.: 10; biographical sketch of, 10n.
Wood, William H.: 171, 175, 197
Wool: value of, 41 & n., 87; manufactured, 42, 87, 99, 102; as article of commerce, 51, 52, 87, 90

Yuma crossing, Colorado River: 4n., 106n.
Yuma Indians: 106n.

Zacatecas, Mexico, trade with: 88–89n.
Zuñi Pueblo: 23, 28, 161; corn purchased from, 160–61

*New Mexico in 1850* has been set on the Linotype in 11½-point Caslon, a faithful rendering of an original type designed by William Caslon. The paper on which the book is printed bears the watermark of the University of Oklahoma Press and has an effective life of at least three hundred years.